MARCH 1939:
THE BRITISH GUARANTEE
TO POLAND

MARCH 1939:
THE BRITISH GUARANTEE
TO POLAND

*A Study in the Continuity of
British Foreign Policy*

SIMON NEWMAN

OXFORD
AT THE CLARENDON PRESS
1976

Oxford University Press, Ely House, London W. 1
GLASGOW NEW YORK TORONTO MELBOURNE WELLINGTON
CAPE TOWN IBADAN NAIROBI DAR ES SALAAM LUSAKA ADDIS ABABA
DELHI BOMBAY CALCUTTA MADRAS KARACHI DACCA
KUALA LUMPUR SINGAPORE HONG KONG TOKYO

ISBN 0 19 822532 6

© Oxford University Press 1976

All rights reserved. No part of this publication may be reproduced, stored in a retrieval system, or transmitted, in any form or by any means, electronic, mechanical, photocopying, recording, or otherwise, without the prior permission of Oxford University Press

Printed in Great Britain
at the University Press, Oxford
by Vivian Ridler
Printer to the University

TO
THE MEMORY OF
MY MOTHER

PREFACE

ON 1 September 1939 Germany began the invasion of Poland. On 3 September Britain and France entered the conflict in fulfilment of the guarantee to Poland announced by Neville Chamberlain in the House of Commons on 31 March 1939. The purpose of this book is to examine the origins of that guarantee. Most historians would probably agree that 'few foreign policy decisions are more obscure in their formulation and consequently more difficult for the historian to explain with satisfactory precision'.[1] In attempting to explain it I have drawn extensively on the British documentary evidence made available since the Public Records Act of 1967 reduced from fifty to thirty years the period that must elapse before State archives are opened to public scrutiny. Needless to say the new documents do not provide all the answers. But they do provide valuable insight into the way in which decisions were made, and allow us to paint a much more sophisticated picture of policy and its formulation than could be done on the basis of the published documents. The argument of the sceptics that the new documents merely provide ammunition for one side or the other in the historical controversy over Neville Chamberlain's foreign policy underrates their value.

This study was originally intended to be a decision-making analysis on lines pioneered by Richard Snyder and his colleagues, and used by Glenn Paige in his analysis of the Truman administration's decision to go to war in Korea.[2] But I found the need to classify all the variables into such rather artificial categories as 'spheres of competence' and 'decisional units' more constraining than helpful. Perhaps I am a slave to my European upbringing, but in any case the value of a 'single-case' study seems to be very questionable if one is serious about building a theory of decision-making. Above all the restricted time frame which a decision-making analysis entails militates against the study of long-term causes, which in this case

[1] William R. Rock, 'The British Guarantee to Poland, March, 1939: A Problem in Diplomatic Decision-Making', *South Atlantic Quarterly*, 65, no. 2 (Spring 1966), 230.
[2] Richard Snyder, H. W. Bruck, and Burton Sapin, *Decision-Making as an Approach to the Study of International Politics* (Princeton, 1954); Glenn Paige, *The Korean Decision: June 24–30, 1950* (New York, 1968).

are particularly interesting. This seems to me to be the greatest disadvantage of such studies. Their conceptual framework discourages the fullest answer to the question 'why?' Nevertheless I have retained the basic outlook of decision-making analysis in that this is a study of how the British Government and their advisers saw things in 1938–9.

For their encouragement and substantive comments on all or parts of this study, which originated as a doctoral thesis for the Johns Hopkins University School of Advanced International Studies in Washington, D.C., I am immensely grateful to David P. Calleo (dissertation director), John A. Lukacs (who suggested the topic), Kendall Myers, Ben Rowland, and Robert Skidelsky (whose clear thinking, stimulating ideas, and infectious enthusiasm have been a constant source of inspiration). Naturally any mistakes are my own.

For responding to various inquiries I would like to thank the late Virgil Tilea, the late Princess Bibesco, Lord Avon, Lord Strang, Lord Butler, Lord Gladwyn, Lord Sherfield, Sir Frank Roberts, Sir Anthony Rumbold, Sidney Aster, Mrs. Jan Ciechanowski, Major T. L. Ingram, and the staff of the Public Record Office.

I am grateful to the following for permission to consult, and where necessary to quote from, various collections of papers: Lady Vansittart; Lord Halifax; Lord Caldecote; Mr. Nigel Nicolson, Wm. Collins and Co. Ltd., and Balliol College, Oxford; Cambridge University Library; and Churchill College, Cambridge. All Crown Copyright material is reproduced by permission of the Controller, Her Majesty's Stationery Office, London.

For financial support I am indebted to the Johns Hopkins University School of Advanced International Studies; the Ford Foundation; the Woodrow Wilson National Fellowship Foundation; and to my father-in-law, Mr. William M. Harrison, who has been extraordinarily kind to me and has given me a degree of moral and material support that would have far surpassed the tolerance of any less exceptional and understanding man.

I would also like to thank Susan W. Gray and Nicholas Hampson for their help and Mrs. Glenn Anglin for typing the final draft.

Finally, it is impossible to find words which adequately express my loving gratitude to my wife Cecile, who bore my neglect of family duty with extraordinary patience, typed the first drafts, and challenged both my grammar and my logic.

S. K. N.

CONTENTS

Preface	vii
1. Introduction	1
2. The British Dilemma	8
3. 'Silver Bullets'	33
4. New Approaches to Germany	54
5. The Ides of March	88
6. A Tentative Initiative	107
7. A Conditional Commitment	130
8. Britain, Germany, and Poland	157
9. The Unconditional Guarantee	174
10. Aftermath	205
11. Conclusion	217
Appendix: The Doubling of the Territorial Army on 29 March 1939	223
Bibliography	226
Index	239

1

INTRODUCTION

HISTORIANS have long wondered why the British, having acquiesced in the German reoccupation of the Rhineland in March 1936, the *Anschluss* with Austria in March 1938, and the annexation of the Sudetenland in September of that year, should have chosen six months later to make their stand in defence of Polish rights in Danzig—a decision which they knew would almost certainly plunge them into war with Germany. The purpose of this study is to examine in detail the events leading up to this apparent shift in policy.

Most explanations of British policy towards Germany in this period postulate a dichotomy between the 'appeasement' pursued until March 1939 and the policy of 'resistance' that followed. The first of these interpretations, commonly referred to as 'orthodox', has completely dominated the historiography of the period until recently. Its proponents believe that British inaction resulted from guilt derived from the Versailles settlement, or personal gullibility, or predisposition towards the Nazi dictatorship. 'Peace' was bought at the expense of British security, interests, and honour. Neville Chamberlain and the 'appeasers' were led by the nose and lulled into complacency with continual promises of good behaviour by Hitler, whose real aim, of course, was to dominate not only Europe but also the world.

According to this view the 'appeasers' suddenly 'awoke' to the reality of Hitler's aggressive design for world domination following the German invasion of Bohemia and Moravia on 15 March 1939. Where before Chamberlain had been prepared to allow Germany a free hand in eastern Europe (provided of course that Hitler would abide by the rules of common decency and morality in his expansion), popular outrage now forced him to resist any further extension of German power. Thus the British guarantee to Poland was a diplomatic revolution not only in the sense that it was the first peacetime guarantee of an eastern-European state but above all because it demonstrated that Chamberlain had abandoned his old policy of 'appeasement'. Instead of 'throwing another baby to the wolves', he had now 'beaten his furled umbrella into a flaming sword'.¹

The second interpretation of British policy, which was originally advanced by the policy-makers themselves and has returned to the fore as a 'revisionist' view, is that British inaction before March 1939 was the inevitable result of various decisive constraints. These included military and economic weakness, the isolationist attitude of the Dominions and of public opinion, and the global 'responsibilities' which dictated the avoidance of war with Germany for fear that Japan, Italy, and even the United States would also benefit at the expense of the Empire. Chamberlain was thus far from gullible or idealistic in his view of Anglo-German relations, he was merely realistic. In this interpretation the guarantee to Poland is easy to explain. Britain was now strong enough to challenge Germany openly. Where before the 'realists' had had no choice but to abandon eastern Europe, they were now able to reverse the process. The guarantee is still seen as a revolution of sorts, for where before Britain had done nothing, she was now able to venture forth with military guarantees.²

The dichotomy on which both these interpretations rest has come under attack by British historians since the early 1960s. For the most part these have concentrated on refuting the assumption that British policy after March 1939 was resistance to Germany. Rather it was more 'appeasement'.³ It is only much more recently that historians have begun to challenge the assumption behind the first half of the dichotomy, i.e. that resistance began only in March 1939. Professor W. N. Medlicott's examination of the Cabinet documents for the period 1933 to 1937 convinced him that the British were not prepared to allow any real changes in the *status quo* in eastern

---

¹ John W. Wheeler-Bennett, *Munich, Prologue to Tragedy* (London, 1948), pp. 364 and 376. See also R. W. Seton-Watson, *From Munich to Danzig* (London, 1939); Lewis B. Namier, *Diplomatic Prelude 1938–1939* (London, 1948) and *Europe in Decay 1936–1940* (London, 1950); Martin Richard and Gilbert Gott, *The Appeasers* (London, 1963). This is only a sample. The orthodox view is deeply entrenched on both sides of the Atlantic.

² See in particular W. N. Medlicott, *The Coming of War in 1939* (London, 1963); also Keith Feiling, *The Life of Neville Chamberlain* (London, 1946); Viscount Templewood (Sir Samuel Hoare), *Nine Troubled Years* (London, 1954); Lord Halifax, *Fullness of Days* (London, 1957); David Dilks, 'Appeasement Revisited', *University of Leeds Review*, 15, no. 1 (May 1972), 28–56.

³ A. J. P. Taylor, *The Origins of the Second World War* (London, 1961). This is also the view of Gilbert and Gott, *The Appeasers*, in all other respects a purely orthodox statement of the case.

Europe.¹ The implication of this finding is that after March 1939 resistance to Germany was pursued even at the cost of war whereas before it had been pursued short of war. Keith Middlemas's study of British policy up to the Munich Agreement reinforces this implication by showing that the attempt to maintain the *status quo* in eastern Europe was also a characteristic of Neville Chamberlain's administration.² But Middlemas does not draw out the implications of this, and his conclusions are in some respects contrary to the evidence he presents. It was left to Robert Skidelsky to point out that 'there was much more continuity between 1938 and 1939, and of a different kind, than either orthodox or revisionist historians have allowed: only on this assumption do the extraordinary British actions of March 1939 become comprehensible'.³

All this enables us to take a far more sophisticated view of British foreign policy in the late 1930s. Until now the assumption has always been that Britain faced two mutually exclusive policy alternatives: either concessions or an anti-German coalition. In fact there was a third, which she adopted: a policy of limited resistance to German expansion within the limits of British power, i.e. by all means short of war. In practical terms this translated into using Britain's financial and economic power as a means of attaining her foreign-policy aims. Of course even this form of power was rapidly waning, a fact which brought the Foreign Office into frequent conflict with the Treasury. Nevertheless these 'invisible' means were used not only to resist German expansion in central and south-eastern Europe but also to resist Japanese expansion in China.

Obviously this also has implications for our understanding of

[1] W. N. Medlicott, *Britain and Germany: The Search for Agreement 1933-1937* (London, 1969). This view was foreshadowed in D. C. Watt, 'Appeasement. The Rise of a Revisionist School?', *Political Quarterly*, 36 (1965), 191-213. It has of course always been the thesis favoured by the Right in Germany. See the works published under the auspices of the Institut für deutsche Nachkriegsgeschichte in Tübingen, which include David L. Hoggan, *Der erzwungene Krieg. Die Ursachen und Urheber des 2. Weltkriegs* (Tübingen: Verlag der Deutschen Hochschullehrer-Zeitung, 1964), and Peter H. Nicoll, *Englands Krieg gegen Deutschland. Die Ursachen, Methoden und Folgen des zweiten Weltkriegs* (Tübingen, 1963). The latter work is polemical in nature. For a discussion of the former see Kurt Glaser, *Der zweite Weltkrieg und die Kriegsschuldfrage (die Hoggan Kontroverse)* (Würzburg, 1965). Their arguments deserve more consideration than they have been given.
[2] Keith Middlemas, *Diplomacy of Illusion. The British Government and Germany, 1937-39* (London, 1972).
[3] Robert Skidelsky, 'Going to War with Germany. Between Revisionism and Orthodoxy', *Encounter*, 39, no. 1 (July 1972), 60.

what Neville Chamberlain was trying to do. In the autumn of 1934 he wrote that

at this moment . . . there is no immediate threat to our safety. But there is a universal feeling of apprehension about the future, whether it be a matter of 2, 3, 5, or 10 years, that such a threat may materialise, and that the quarter from which it will come is Germany.[1]

Britain might survive a war with Germany if it were confined to Europe. But

if we had to contemplate the division of our forces so as to protect our Far Eastern interests, while prosecuting a war in Europe, then it must be evident that not only India, Hong-Kong, and Australasia would be in dire peril, but that we ourselves would stand in far greater danger of destruction by a fully armed and organised Germany.[2]

In July 1937, after Italy had been added to the list of potential enemies, Chamberlain told the Committee of Imperial Defence that the ideal for Britain was to be in a position to fight Germany, Italy, and Japan simultaneously. 'That, however, was a counsel of perfection which it was impossible to follow. There were limits to our resources, both physical and financial, and it was vain to contemplate fighting singlehanded the three strongest Powers in combination.'[3] This prompted the attempt to reach agreement with Italy and Germany, the underlying assumption being that both powers threatened British interests and must be contained. But these agreements were sought on British terms.

The Anglo-Italian Agreement, signed in April 1938, though not ratified until November, was clearly meant to safeguard the *status quo* in the Mediterranean, and specifically included that requirement. Negotiations with Germany on similar principles were interrupted by the *Anschluss* and the problem of the Sudetenland. Thereafter Chamberlain tried again to get an agreement with Germany on the basis of the *status quo*. This was the idea behind the Anglo-German Declaration, misconceived as it was as an instrument, which was signed on the morrow of Munich. Chamberlain wanted Germany to disarm; to abandon the attempt to transform central Europe and the Balkans into an exclusive economic bloc under German political leadership; and to cease her cut-price competition with British exports in world markets. All the time the German threat to Britain,

---

[1] Quoted in Feiling, *Chamberlain*, p. 253.   [2] Quoted ibid., pp. 253-4.
[3] Quoted in Dilks, 'Appeasement Revisited', pp. 39-40.

both political-strategic and economic, was in the back of his mind. His illusion was that an agreement with Germany was possible on these terms, an illusion fully shared at first by Halifax and by his closest advisers in the Foreign Office. Chamberlain cherished this illusion far longer than they did, however, because he misinterpreted Germany's desire to enter into trade negotiations. The Germans needed convertible currency and, in order to acquire it, were reluctantly prepared to soften their competition with British exports in return for easier access to United Kingdom and Empire markets. Chamberlain mistakenly took this as evidence that the Germans were impressed with the difficulties of autarky and were anxious to re-enter the liberal economic fold. Once again, the Foreign Office also believed this for a while.

What has led to the belief, so long held, that Chamberlain was stupidly trying to buy peace for Britain by offering Germany concessions in Europe and allowing her a free hand in the east? Much of the trouble derives from the continued use of the term 'appeasement' to describe what Chamberlain was trying to do. The dictionary defines it as an attempt 'to conciliate or bribe (a potential aggressor) by making concessions, frequently with implication of sacrifice of principles'.[1] As long as this definition prevails, there is little hope for rational understanding or discussion of the ends and means of Chamberlain's policy, for they are already assumed. It is the task of historians to challenge such assumptions. Instead they have all too readily accepted this rigid and misleading analytical framework, which derives from the polemics of the post-Munich era. This has led them down some notoriously false trails, and to ignore completely, for instance, the efforts that were being made in Britain to resist German expansion. The misunderstanding emerges particularly clearly, of course, in the orthodox interpretation of the events of March 1939.

If earlier attempts to preserve the European *status quo* are taken into account, the events of March 1939 appear in a different light. The aim of this study is to provide solid evidence for the view that Britain never intended Germany to have a free hand in eastern Europe at all. Thus the guarantee to Poland should not be interpreted as a revolution in British foreign policy, as has so often been argued, but should be seen as the culmination, or rather the explicit

[1] *Concise Oxford Dictionary* (5th edn., Oxford, 1964). I have put the word in quotation marks where I could not avoid using it altogether.

manifestation, of a strand of British policy going back to before September 1938 which has until recently been overlooked or ignored—the attempt to stem German expansion in eastern Europe by any means short of war but in the last resort by war itself.

Why has this aspect of British policy been so neglected? After all, those who conducted British policy at the time later justified their actions in terms very similar to those subsequently used by the 'revisionists'. The reason is that the 'appeasers' never mentioned, let alone emphasized, the efforts that were being made by Britain to maintain the territorial and economic *status quo* in Europe. Wishing to give the appearance of British goodwill and sweet reasonableness, of a Britain forced reluctantly into war, they stressed Britain's efforts to view Germany's grievances sympathetically, and thus, paradoxically, reinforced the orthodox interpretation of their policy. It is only with the opening of the British archives that we are beginning to understand that they were not in fact so sympathetic towards Germany's revisionist aims in Europe, and that they sought to prevent their fulfilment by offering Germany colonial territory and by the use of Britain's economic weight. This omission on the part of the apologists is understandable. For the implication of these facts is that Hitler's unique responsibility for the Second World War is undermined. Instead of a German war of aggrandizement, the war becomes one of Anglo-German rivalry for power and influence, the culmination of the struggle for the right to determine the future configuration of Europe.

Britain in the 1930s was in the classic situation of a declining power trying to fight off the challenge of a stronger one. Great powers rarely surrender their inherited positions without a struggle, and it is a profound mistake to imagine that the 'appeasers' were any more prepared than their die-hard opponents to accept a major redistribution of power in Europe. Their illusion, before March 1939, was that they could maintain the existing 'balance' without going to war, an illusion itself based on a compelling recognition of Britain's weakness. They were aware that Britain and France alone could not stop Germany. In order to do so they would have to bring in the United States and the Soviet Union. But this would destroy the European balance by other means, since Britain and France could not be co-equal partners in such a combination.

This only half-conscious recognition of Europe's dwarfing added impetus to the search for agreement with Germany. For such an agreement might encompass even more than a guarantee of British security and the maintenance of the *status quo* in Europe. Indeed, behind Chamberlain's desire for economic negotiations in 1938-9 may be seen the idea of a European Four-Power Directorate, serving to assure the continued prosperity and power of Europe in the face of the emerging superpowers. This model of European order had already been suggested by the French Foreign Minister Briand at Locarno in 1925, and more concretely by Mussolini's proposal, never ratified, for a Four-Power Pact in 1933. But this vision foundered on the impossible nature of Hitler's demands. Chamberlain was never prepared to allow Germany to dictate the terms, and, faced with Hitler's continued determination to do so, the 'appeasers' chose the lesser evil—going to war. But it would be unfair to say that they did so without recognizing the implications this involved for Britain and Europe.

2

THE BRITISH DILEMMA

In November 1937 the Chiefs of Staff concluded that

> we cannot foresee the time when our defence forces will be strong enough to safeguard our territory, trade and vital interests against Germany, Italy, and Japan simultaneously. We cannot therefore exaggerate the importance, from the point of view of Imperial Defence, of any political or international action that can be taken to reduce the numbers of our potential enemies and to gain the support of great allies.[1]

It was this assessment of Britain's weakness rather than guilt derived from the Versailles settlement or personal gullibility or predisposition towards the rulers of Germany or Italy that was primarily responsible for the policy of 'appeasement' with which Neville Chamberlain's name is, without justification, almost exclusively associated. The purpose of this chapter is to discuss how the situation described by the Chiefs of Staff came about.

Britain emerged from the First World War with vast defence forces, so that in the interest of economy, defence spending was kept to a minimum. In August 1919 the Government ruled that future defence estimates should be based on the assumption that Britain would not be engaged in any great war during the next ten years. This 'ten year rule' was repeated annually from 1925 until in 1928 it became a self-perpetuating, though alterable, dictum, whose strictures would hold good for ten years at any point in time. But Britain's formal obligations expanded in 1925, under the Locarno Treaties, to include a guarantee of the inviolability of the Franco-German and Belgo-German frontiers and the demilitarized zone of the Rhineland. In 1928 the British Chiefs of Staff began to warn the Government that Britain's defence forces were insufficient to fulfil her obligations, let alone to defend her vast Empire. This warning was disregarded, not because of blind acceptance of Treasury

---

[1] Quoted in Ian Colvin, *The Chamberlain Cabinet* (New York, 1971), p. 64.

doctrine, but because of real financial constraints, strongly pacifist sentiment in public opinion, and, in the final analysis, because the Government thought it unlikely that Britain's obligations would in fact have to be met in the foreseeable future. The odds revived with the Japanese conquest of Manchuria in March 1932. The 'ten year rule' was then abandoned on the advice of the Chiefs of Staff, fearful of the implications for British Empire security. The Cabinet warned, however, that this was not to be taken as a signal for large-scale rearmament, and although work was resumed on the naval base at Singapore in June 1932, little else was done.

There were two main reasons for this slow start. First, Britain had been forced off the gold standard in September 1931, and the National Government under Ramsay MacDonald saw its prime duty in retrenchment. As Baldwin, then Lord President of the Council, later explained, 'the financial risks were so grave that, until we were in a position where we felt that they no longer existed everything must give way, and must wait'.[1] The 1932 Defence Budget was the lowest in the inter-war period, reflecting the Treasury view that not strategic, but 'financial and economic risks are far the most serious and urgent that the country has to face'.[2] Secondly, the Government hoped to avoid the need for large-scale rearmament by finding a formula acceptable to both France and Germany at the League of Nations Disarmament Conference held at Geneva from February 1932 to April 1934.

The chief aim of British diplomacy was to reconcile the French need for security with the German demand for equality of status without extending the British commitment to France further than that undertaken at Locarno. Even when this task seemed hopeless, the Government could not abandon its efforts without attracting the wrath of public and parliamentary opinion. The Conference raised great hopes fed by pacifist sentiment, and when Germany withdrew from the Conference (as well as from the League of Nations) in October 1933, the British public rather irrationally blamed their own Government for the failure. This fact was reflected in by-elections held in 1933–4, which showed a 22 per cent swing against the Government. Baldwin was particularly affected by the resounding

[1] Quoted in R. K. Middlemas and A. J. L. Barnes, *Baldwin* (London, 1969), p. 742.
[2] Quoted in Michael Howard, *The Continental Commitment. The dilemma of British defence policy in the era of the two world wars* (London, 1972), p. 98.

Government defeat at East Fulham, where the election was fought mainly on the disarmament issue.[1]

Meanwhile the British Chiefs of Staff heightened the urgency of their warnings, constantly repeated since 1928, that Britain could not meet her commitments at existing force levels. In November 1933 they reminded the Cabinet that Britain was in no position to intervene in a European war and that the situation would worsen as German rearmament, already under way, gathered momentum.[2]

Thus the Government faced the dilemma of striking a balance between conflicting demands on the resources of the nation, so as to satisfy the requirements of British security without jeopardizing other aspects of Government policy. To this was added the complicating but all-important factor of public opinion, which at this time appeared to be strongly in favour of disarmament, and strongly against any drastic reorientation of peacetime economic priorities. The Government therefore had to proceed warily.

From November 1933 to July 1934 Britain's defence requirements were reviewed by the specially appointed Defence Requirements Sub-Committee (D.R.C.) of the Committee of Imperial Defence (C.I.D.), by the Cabinet Committee on Preparations for the Disarmament Conference, and by the Cabinet itself. The first report of the D.R.C., submitted in February 1934, covered not only concrete measures of rearmament but also strategy and diplomacy. The political assumption was that although Japan represented the most immediate threat to the Empire, Germany must be viewed as the object of Britain's long-term war plans. The stress was therefore on remedying army and especially air-force deficiencies. The D.R.C. recommended that the strength of the continental expeditionary force should be increased to five from the existing two divisions and that a further forty squadrons should be completed to bring the air force up to a peacetime strength of fifty-two, approved as long ago as 1923. As for the navy, the report confirmed the importance of modernizing bases in the Far East and the fleet itself, but allied this to the exhortation that Anglo-Japanese relations should be improved, whatever the likelihood of offending the United States.

Neville Chamberlain, the Chancellor of the Exchequer, deemed the estimated cost of £76 million over the next five years excessive.

[1] Middlemas and Barnes, *Baldwin*, p. 746.
[2] Correlli Barnett, *The Collapse of British Power* (New York, 1972), p. 411.

THE BRITISH DILEMMA

He proposed, on the assumption that Britain could bring about a *rapprochement* with Japan, that the navy take second place to the air force, whose main strength should be devoted to home defence. Furthermore, and in defiance of the strategic calculations of the Chiefs of Staff, he advocated a doctrine of 'limited liability' which would cut back the size of the continental expeditionary force. In this way about a third of the cost could be saved.[1]

Chamberlain's priorities were, in their broad essentials, allowed to predominate, and a further twenty-five squadrons were promised for the air force. Although the Cabinet agreed that the defence of the Low Countries constituted a vital interest, necessitating an expeditionary field force, no decision was taken to provide the army with its requirements for the job. Likewise decision on the navy was postponed.[2] Thus during the course of policy-making financial considerations were allowed to determine the pattern of rearmament, itself the determinant of strategy. Chamberlain, as Chancellor of the Exchequer, began to feel the measure of his power, tempered only by that of Baldwin, who throughout exercised his influence to blunt the Treasury axe.

Henceforth, the expansion of the air force took priority in defence planning. The importance attached to air power derived partly from the assumption, long held by the Air Ministry and uncritically accepted by politicians and the public alike during the 1930s, that a German bombing force could cripple Britain with a 'knock-out blow'. Although the rate of air-force expansion authorized in the successive schemes outlined in Table 1 constantly fell short of British estimates of the German rate of production and of the Air Ministry's requirements, the British ideal was always to build superior bombing strength for a counter-offensive. In practice this aim was achieved only from 1933 to 1935. From 1935 to early 1938 the practical aim became parity, and until the September crisis of that year British production plans were determined not in relation to estimated German strength but in relation to British productive capacity. Thereafter, with the building of heavy bombers, the practical aim again became superiority.

It should be pointed out here that there is scant evidence for the belief that during the spring and summer of 1934, Baldwin's 'view of ultimate defensive strategy had now become that of a balance of

[1] Howard, *The Continental Commitment*, pp. 105-9.
[2] Barnett, *The Collapse of British Power*, p. 412.

power based on mutual and equal deterrents'.[1] First, Baldwin's understanding of air-force strategy was informed by the principle adopted by the Air Staff as a result of experience during the First World War, 'that only an offensive force capable of throwing on Germany a greater weight of bombs than Germany could throw on

TABLE I

Scheme	Sanctioned	For completion	Bombers	Fighters	Other	Total*
A	July 1934	1938/9	500	336	124	960
C	April 1935	Spring 1937	840	420	252	1,512
F	February 1936	March 1939	990	420	326	1,736
J	October 1937†	—	1,442	563	326	2,331
K	February 1938†	—	1,320	544	326	2,190
L	April 1938	Spring 1940	1,352	608	413	2,373
M	November 1938	1942	1,360	800	389	2,549

* Front line aircraft, excluding Fleet Air Arm and overseas strength.
† Proposed.
Source: Basil Collier, *The Defence of the United Kingdom* (London, 1957), passim.

Britain would enable the war to be won'.[2] The Air Staff did not believe ideally in 'parity', but in superiority. It was only the belief in Germany's capacity to outbuild Britain and the British Government's reluctance to provide sufficient funds that forced the Air Staff to cling desperately to the notion of parity and then to that of minimum requirements. The ideal was deterrence based on superior strength, which was the idea behind Scheme A. Baldwin defended it against Churchill's attacks in November 1934 by assuring the House of Commons that Britain would enjoy a 50 per cent margin of superiority for at least a year, although he refused to look further ahead.[3]

Secondly, not even the specialists in aerial warfare were able at that time to produce a definition of 'parity' or 'equality'. Not only was agreement internationally impossible, as was shown by the interminable discussions preliminary to the Disarmament Conference, but it eluded the Air Staff itself. As the official historians have written:

'Parity' came to be defined first as the number of aircraft, then as the

[1] Middlemas and Barnes, *Baldwin*, p. 757.
[2] C. K. Webster and N. Frankland, *The Strategic Air Offensive Against Germany* (London, 1961), i. 74.
[3] Middlemas and Barnes, *Baldwin*, p. 788.

number of bombers, then as the number of long-range bombers and finally as the weight of bombs that could be dropped on Germany and Britain by the opposing air forces. Even then everything would depend not only on the first line of operational aircraft but on the reserves of aircraft and men behind it.[1]

Thirdly, although British intelligence was able, at a later date, to provide fairly accurate information about German front-line strength, the Air Ministry admitted in October 1938 that they were unable to produce exact details of bomb loads or reserves.[2]

Thus there was no idea in Baldwin's mind, reading from modern nuclear strategy, that equal force at a certain level on each side would provide sufficient capacity to inflict unacceptable destruction in a counter-strike. Superiority, not parity, was thought to be necessary for deterrence. This conception underlay Chamberlain's rationalization of 'limited liability': only if deterrence failed would Britain have to resort to a continental expeditionary force.[3] Although Chamberlain later stressed the defensive aspect of British air power, he could not free himself from the shackles of professional opinion: in the two new air programmes sanctioned during his peacetime administration, the ratio of fighters to bombers remained substantially the same at 1:2, with special emphasis on the heavy bomber. This was hardly a defensive strategy.[4] The British margin of superiority was intended at first to deter Germany not only from aggression, but also from pursuing an arms race.[5] This latter, rather incredible, delusion was soon belied. Alarming reports were received about German capacity and intentions, not least Hitler's own declaration in March 1935 to Simon and Eden, the two Ministers jointly responsible for foreign affairs, that the German air force was equal to Britain's. This produced panic in the Cabinet, but a sceptical response from the Air Ministry. Nevertheless collation of evidence revealed an estimate of approximately 1,500 first-line aircraft by the spring of 1937.[6] To this the Government responded in May 1935 with Scheme C, providing for the same number of aircraft by the same date. Numerical parity with Germany was now the aim,

---

[1] Webster and Frankland, *The Strategic Air Offensive*, i. 66.
[2] 'Relative Air Strengths and Proposals for the Improvement of this Country's Position', Oct. 1938, CP 218 (38) in CAB 24/279.
[3] Howard, *The Continental Commitment*, p. 109.
[4] See below, pp. 59–61.
[5] Middlemas, *Diplomacy of Illusion*, p. 34 n.
[6] Collier, *The Defence of the United Kingdom*, p. 30.

defined specifically as such by the Air Parity Sub-Committee of the C.I.D.[1] This is not to say that superiority did not remain the ideal. Schemes A and C were designed for front-line visibility rather than strength in depth. This was due less to financial stringency than to reluctance on the part of the Air Ministry to order reserves that would, because of new models on the drawing boards, prove immediately obsolescent.[2]

The year 1935 was a watershed in British rearmament. The D.R.C. and the Defence Policy and Requirements Committee (D.P.R.C.) undertook a major review working on the assumption that by 1939 'each service should have advanced its state of readiness to the widest necessary extent in relation to the military needs of national defence'.[3] As a result, a quantitative and qualitative leap was made in February 1936 with the introduction of Scheme F for the air force, which provided not only for 225 per cent reserves but also for the new models, including faster fighters and heavier bombers.

Furthermore, the Committee advised that the navy be brought up to the ideal two-power standard.[4] The Washington Naval Treaty of 1922 prohibited capital ship-building for ten years and established a 5:5:3 ratio in capital ships between the United States, Britain, and Japan. The London Naval Treaty of 1930, which expired in 1936, extended both the 'naval holiday' and the coverage of the ratio to destroyers and submarines. More significantly, it limited British cruiser strength to fifty, well short of the minimum seventy considered necessary for the protection of trade-routes. There is little doubt, however, that the Government, if not the Admiralty, regarded these agreements as satisfactory in view of the financial restrictions which would anyway have limited naval strength to a one-power standard.[5]

Threatened by the Japanese renunciation of the London Treaty in 1934, the British Government could only provide sufficient strength in the Far East by tying down the size of the German navy. The Anglo-German Naval Agreement of June 1935 achieved this aim,

[1] Middlemas, *Diplomacy of Illusion*, p. 34.
[2] M. M. Postan, *British War Production* (London, 1952), p. 15.
[3] Quoted in Barnett, *The Collapse of British Power*, p. 414.
[4] The contemporary idea of a two-power naval standard was not the traditional equality with the two strongest world navies combined, which would have included the United States navy. Instead a sufficient force was required to protect British interests simultaneously against Germany and Japan (Postan, *British War Production*, p. 23 n.).
[5] S. W. Roskill, *Naval Policy Between the Wars* (London, 1968), p. 330.

albeit at a higher ratio (3·5:10) than thought desirable. Germany was allowed, subject to prior warning, to build submarines up to 100 per cent of British Empire tonnage. The crisis over the Italian invasion of Abyssinia, by emphasizing the threat to British communications in the Mediterranean, underlined the significance of the agreement, which the naval staff judged to be 'of incalculable value'.[1]

In 1936, free from international treaty restrictions, the Cabinet authorized a naval programme which allowed for capital ship replacement and the minimum requirement of seventy cruisers. But it was not the two-power standard recommended by the D.R.C., which was continually rejected until the summer of 1939.

The army fared worse. The D.R.C. recommended a continental expeditionary force of five Regular divisions reinforced with twelve Territorial divisions. But Neville Chamberlain's views, foreshadowed in 1934, were now allowed to predominate: 'I believe our resources will be more profitably employed in the air and on the sea than in building up great armies.'[2] Thus although the five-division expeditionary force was approved in 1936, its twelve-division reinforcement was not.[3]

In 1936 the international situation took several turns for the worse. Germany reoccupied the Rhineland and signed the Anti-Comintern Pact with Japan. The Spanish Civil War, which was to sap so much of Britain's energy and attention over the next three years, revealed a community of German and Italian interests, and the German-Italian Axis was proclaimed. Trouble broke out again in Palestine to harass the British Government as much as it delighted Dr. Goebbels at the German Propaganda Ministry.

In spite of these developments, and although British rearmament had now entered its second, expansive phase, the need for economy remained uppermost in Ministers' minds and the public failed to respond to the Government's, and especially Baldwin's, attempts to educate it. The Labour Opposition voted against the 1936 Service Estimates where previously they had abstained. By 1937 the five-year defence estimates for the armed services had increased from £1,047 million to £1,500 million, with demands for more. Chamberlain, who succeeded Baldwin as Prime Minister in May, had already

[1] Middlemas, *Diplomacy of Illusion*, p. 222 n.
[2] Quoted in Feiling, *Chamberlain*, pp. 314–15.
[3] Howard, *The Continental Commitment*, p. 114.

concluded that a defence loan was required. In April the Government was granted power to borrow £400 million over five years for defence, the first peacetime defence loan since 1889.[1] At the same time, Chamberlain and Sir John Simon, the new Chancellor of the Exchequer, tightened the Treasury grip even further, by imposing a 'global total' on defence spending.

It has been argued that this system of rationing wrested from the Service advisers a large part of their traditional functions. Until then, whatever the financial exigencies, they had been able to argue that since the Cabinet laid down their obligations the Cabinet must provide the resources which they, as experts, declared to be necessary. If these could not be provided, then the Cabinet must modify the commitments. Now the resources were to be laid down from above by the politicians . . . without benefit of expert advice, and the Services were to be left to make what response they could.[2]

But in the first place, it has always been the Cabinet's function to decide on budget totals and priorities. The sum allocated to defence would depend on the strategic situation as assessed by the Service Ministers and the financial and economic situation as assessed by the Chancellor of the Exchequer. Secondly, the Service advisers were not deprived of the opportunity to emphasize the disparity between Britain's commitments and the resources available to meet them. They had long done so and long continued to do so. Thirdly, the fixed ceiling envisaged by Chamberlain was never in practice adopted. The net result of the new Prime Minister's intentions was that in December 1937 the Minister for Co-ordination of Defence, Sir Thomas Inskip, produced a memorandum, with the benefit of advice from the Chiefs of Staff and Treasury officials, entitled 'Defence Expenditure in Future Years'.[3] This merely repeated the views long since advocated by Chamberlain: that economic and financial stability were as vital a component of British war potential as the strength of the defences. Therefore 'every effort must be made to bring the total defence expenditure within the five years 1937–1941 within a total of £1,500 millions'. But less than two months later the Chancellor of the Exchequer, 'though he did so with a heavy heart',

[1] A new and expensive programme was introduced in 1889 to strengthen the British navy not against the embryonic German fleet but against a Franco-Russian combination. Alarm over plans for the German navy arose only ten years later.
[2] Middlemas, *Diplomacy of Illusion*, p. 120.
[3] 15 Dec. 1937, CP 316 (37).

abandoned this figure in favour of new service estimates amounting to £1,650 millions.¹

Nevertheless, Chamberlain's determination to economize confirmed the decline of the army. In defining British strategic priorities, Inskip assumed in his memorandum that 'the greatest danger against which we have to provide protection is attack from the air on the United Kingdom, designed to inflict a knock-out blow at the initial stage of the war', and that for ultimate victory 'we must contemplate a long war, in course of which we should have to mobilize all our resources and those of the Dominions and other countries overseas'. Britain's strategic objectives were therefore to protect first the home base, second the trade-routes, third the Empire, and fourth allied territories. The army's role would have to change from continental intervention to imperial commitments, anti-aircraft defence, and internal security at home. With an irresponsible disregard for the consequences, the Cabinet now reversed the decision taken in 1936 to provide for a five-division expeditionary force and reduced it to two divisions, in spite of Inskip's own warning that 'if France were again to be in danger of being over-run by land armies, the situation might arise when, as in the last war, we had to improvise an army to assist her'.²

The doctrine of 'limited liability' now reached its ultimate expression. Michael Howard has pointed out that 'if that doctrine had been the product of strategic rather than simply financial calculation, it must have been based on the assumption that the French Army and its allies in Eastern Europe were capable on their own of holding the German land forces in check'.³ So it was. But it was also based on the assumption that the British would back up the French effort with air power, one of Chamberlain's favourite rationalizations.⁴ This was why the ratio of bombers to fighters in the air force, despite Chamberlain's emphasis in public on its defensive role, was always about two to one.

¹ Colvin, *The Chamberlain Cabinet*, p. 96.
² Quoted in Middlemas, *Diplomacy of Illusion*, p. 124.
³ Howard, *The Continental Commitment*, p. 125. The British always overestimated French land strength, particularly on the assumption that it would be used defensively. The collapse of France in 1940 came as a complete shock.
⁴ Cf. Record of Anglo-French Conversations, 25 Nov. 1938, Great Britain, *Documents on British Foreign Policy, 1919–1945*, ed. E. L. Woodward and Rohan Butler, 3rd series, 1938–9, 9 vols. (London, 1949–55), iii, no. 325. This collection is cited hereafter as *DBFP*. References are to the 3rd series unless otherwise indicated.

In the spring of 1938, after the German *Anschluss* with Austria, a further landmark was reached in British rearmament. From the beginning the programme had been hampered by the doctrine of 'no interference with normal trade', which meant simply that firms filling Government orders had to compete for resources on the same terms as, for example, firms filling orders for export. Rearmament production therefore proceeded only as fast as the free-enterprise system would allow it. Already in September 1937 the Secretary of State for Air, Lord Swinton, had argued that the rule would cause a two-year delay in the air programme. In February 1938 the Chiefs of Staff wrote that

> We are attempting to carry out an armaments programme on a scale never yet attempted except in war, in peace conditions, and subject to a policy of non-interference with normal trade, which cannot fail to be a serious handicap with potential enemies whose whole financial, social and industrial system has, in effect, been mobilized on a war footing for at least three years.[1]

Although the rule was rescinded in March 1938, bottle-necks continued to impede rapid progress. The worst of these limitations were shortages of skilled labour and machine tools, inadequate plant, management inexperience, and restrictive practices on the part of trade unions.[2] This was particularly true of the air expansion programme, which with the adoption of Scheme L in April 1938 was virtually freed from financial restrictions. The Cabinet authorized the Air Ministry to order all the aircraft that could be produced in the next two years, estimated to be 12,000. Priority was to be given to fighter production, in response to Chamberlain's desire 'to strengthen our *defensive* strength so that we should not be at the mercy of a foreign power'.[3] The existing ratio of bombers to fighters was nevertheless maintained at about 10:4, leaving Air Staff doctrine unchallenged. Neither superiority nor parity were henceforth the practical criteria underlying British aircraft production until after Munich. As Kingsley Wood, the new Secretary of State for Air, wrote in October 1938, Scheme L was dictated by 'what were . . . considered to be the limitations of aircraft production and

---

[1] Quoted in W. K. Hancock and M. M. Gowing, *British War Economy* (London, 1949), p. 70.
[2] For a detailed description see Barnett, *The Collapse of British Power*, pp. 476–94.
[3] Quoted in Middlemas, *Diplomacy of Illusion*, p. 220.

THE BRITISH DILEMMA 19

was not related to the possible German air strength by the date (i.e. March 1940) when it was due for completion'.[1]

In March 1938 the British Government decided on the policy that led to the Munich Agreement in September. All too conscious of Britain's inability to risk a war against Germany, Italy, and Japan simultaneously, the Cabinet agreed to put pressure on the Czechoslovak Government to meet the Sudeten German demands as a preferable alternative to an alliance with France and Russia or a guarantee to Czechoslovakia. The state of British rearmament at that point was one of the main factors in that decision. As Chamberlain wrote on 20 March 1938, Czechoslovakia 'would simply be a pretext for going to war with Germany. That we could not think of, unless we had a reasonable prospect of being able to beat her to her knees in reasonable time and of that I see no sign.'[2]

Chamberlain's assessment was supported by the Chiefs of Staff, who unlike Churchill thought little of Czechoslovakia's powers of resistance and did not think of Czechoslovakia as a strategic asset. They concluded that

no military pressure we can exert by sea, or land or in the air can prevent Germany either from invading and overrunning Bohemia or inflicting a decisive defeat on the Czechoslovakian Army. If politically it is deemed necessary to restore Czechoslovakia's lost integrity, this aim will entail war with Germany, and her defeat may mean a prolonged struggle.[3]

The main criticism of Britain's rearmament programme has been that the Government failed to tap the huge reserves of unemployed

[1] 'Relative Air Strengths and Proposals for the Improvement of this Country's Position', Oct. 1938, CP 218 (38), CAB 24/279. The British, especially the politicians, but also the intelligence services, constantly over-estimated German aircraft-production figures. According to M. M. Postan, who based his account on the United States Strategic Bombing Survey and other sources, 'the best estimates of German and British aircraft production available at the time gave a terrifying picture of British inferiority. The real figures, had they been known, would have revealed an inferiority in first-line strength up to sixty per cent, and a slight inferiority in monthly output figures until 1939; and this was bad enough. But the estimates current in 1938 with their slight exaggeration of German strength and slight under-estimate of British potentialities gave the impression that Germany was twice as strong numerically and was expected to retain that lead' (Postan, *British War Production*, p. 56). According to Burton Klein, actual German production at the outbreak of war was only 60 per cent of the production credited by British Intelligence (Burton Klein, *Germany's Economic Preparations for War* (Cambridge, Mass., 1959), p. 19).
[2] Quoted in Middlemas, *Diplomacy of Illusion*, p. 188.
[3] Memorandum by the Chiefs of Staff: 'Military Implications of German Aggression Against Czechoslovakia', 28 Mar. 1938, DP(P)22, CAB 16/183A.

labour and productive capacity which were then available as a result of the Depression. These could have been mobilized by the simple expedient of deficit financing, thereby releasing rearmament from financial constraint and the country from unemployment. The orthodox view is that Chamberlain was unwilling to do this because of a doctrinaire obsession with balanced budgets. Even if we overlook the fact that this argument rests on Keynesian hindsight, the economic aspects of rearmament went deeper than this. The programme depended to a large extent on highly skilled labour. Most of the unemployed were casualties of the old staple export industries such as coal, textiles, and ship-building, where idle plant was also to be found. Thus a major constraint was seen in terms of industrial adaptation to the requirements of technologically advanced production. This problem was overcome to some extent, particularly in the early years, by relying on imports and diverting the resources of the export industry. The Economic Advisory Council, established in 1930 to keep Britain's over-all economic position under review, recognized that reliance on this method to rearm would eventually be self-defeating. They reported in December 1938 that 'a series of adverse balances of payments which led to a substantial loss of gold might set in motion a withdrawal of short-term funds from London which would quickly exhaust the resources available to meet it'. This would result in exchange control and

it would be necessary to confine British purchases abroad strictly within the limits set by our current receipts from abroad. This would be a serious handicap to the rearmament programme, for, in so far as we can import armament goods, we can escape from some of the most difficult problems of industrial readjustment.

They concluded that 'the balance of payments is in a sense the key to the whole position'.[1]

It may be argued that reliance on imports and export diversion, in reducing the need for industrial adaptation, slowed the latter process more than would otherwise have been. This requires further examination in the light of statistical research. But it is clear that the strain imposed by the rearmament programme on the balance of payments and the sterling balances, rather than the doctrinaire view that the budget must be balanced, was the main constraint on rearmament spending.

[1] 'Problems of Rearmament', 16 Dec. 1938, CP 296 (38), CAB 24/281.

This constraint was exacerbated by current conceptions of the nature of a future war against Germany. In its larger perspective such a war was viewed not in terms of a struggle between armed forces but in terms of economic staying power. A great war was defined as one which required the nation's total resources.[1] Britain's reliance on imported raw materials and foodstuffs placed her in a particularly vulnerable position, since these could only be paid for with receipts from visible and invisible exports, from the amortization of overseas assets, and in the last resort from borrowing abroad. Britain was already living on repatriated capital,[2] a fact which emphasized that her dilemma, as Sir Thomas Inskip defined it in December 1937, was 'to determine the size and character of the forces which will suffice to ward off defeat in the early days of war ... without making demands on our resources which would impair our stability, and our staying power in peace and war'.[3]

As the Chiefs of Staff pointed out in November 1937, Britain's weakness dictated a policy of trying to reduce the number of her potential enemies. But by 1937 Britain had little room for manœuvre *vis-à-vis* Japan, Italy, and Germany.

Although the Anglo-Japanese Alliance of 1902 had allowed Britain to rely on valuable Japanese assistance in the Far East during the First World War, the British Government decided in 1921 not to extend it. The decision was painful and severely tested the cohesion of the Empire. The Imperial Conference of 1921 debated the question whether the Imperial interest was to renew the alliance with Japan or to maintain the goodwill of the United States, where Anglo-Japanese co-operation in the Far East was feared and resented. The Canadians in particular wished to end the alliance. They argued that one of Britain's main interests was to maintain the 'open door' in China, which coincided with American interests. If the alliance were renewed, the United States might use her undoubted potential to outbuild the combined British and Japanese navies. The very rationale for the alliance, which had been based on the need to prevent further Russian and German intrusion in the Far East, had disappeared. There was a further argument: the

---

[1] Hancock and Gowing, *British War Economy*, p. 46.
[2] W. Arthur Lewis, *Economic Survey 1919–1939* (London, 1949), p. 79.
[3] CP 316 (37) quoted in Colvin, *The Chamberlain Cabinet*, p. 49.

United States might insist upon Britain's repayment of her war debts in full.[1]

Although opinion was divided in Britain, it tended to favour the arguments of the Pacific Dominions, Australia and New Zealand, whose security depended above all on a friendly Japan. That Japan harboured expansionist aims in northern China was well known, and it was argued that Britain would probably have to recognize a Japanese sphere of influence in Shantung, Manchuria, and Mongolia. But renewal of the alliance would allow Britain a degree of control over Japanese ambitions. Above all, abandonment of the alliance carried with it the risk of turning Japan into an enemy, thereby endangering the security not only of British but also of French and Dutch possessions. Britain's one-power naval standard would not suffice to cope with this threat if it were to coincide with trouble in Europe.

When the United States Government proposed a conference to settle Pacific and disarmament questions, the British eagerly took up the idea as a way out of their dilemma. An Anglo-Japanese-American *entente* would allow the opposing views to be reconciled. If on the other hand the Pacific conference failed, then the Anglo-Japanese Alliance could continue.

As we have seen, the Washington Conference of 1921 resulted in agreement on the ratio of naval strength between the United States, Britain, and Japan. It also left Japan in a powerful strategic position in the Far East, since the United States and Britain agreed not to fortify bases within a certain radius in the Pacific. Under its terms the Anglo-Japanese Alliance was allowed to lapse.

Relations between the two countries were further exacerbated by the Manchurian crisis of 1931-2. Although Britain tried to avoid the appearance of hostility towards Japan, she found it hard to reconcile this with loyalty to the principles of the League of Nations Covenant. As the Foreign Secretary, Sir John Simon, told the Cabinet in November 1932,

> We ought to act as a loyal member of the League and avoid, as far as possible, bringing down on ourselves the condemnation which would attach to isolated or prominent individual action. . . . Even if other considerations did not compel this course, we have to remember the serious

[1] W. Roger Louis, *British Strategy in the Far East 1919–1939* (Oxford, 1971), p. 53. See also Ian H. Nish, *Alliance in Decline. A Study of Anglo-Japanese Relations 1908–23* (London, 1972).

THE BRITISH DILEMMA

consequences to our trade of antagonising China. In fact, we must strive to be fair to both sides. But we must not involve ourselves with trouble with Japan.[1]

In March 1933 Japan withdrew from the League of Nations, but not from Manchuria, and from then on the possibility of German-Japanese co-operation haunted the British Government. Neville Chamberlain, for one, regretted that the ending of the Anglo-Japanese Alliance had 'gradually poisoned our relations with Japan'. He was very alarmed by the thought that 'Germany and Japan might come together, and it seemed to him such a situation was conceivable when Germany was sufficiently strong to take a hand against us'.[2]

We have seen that the Defence Requirements Committee's first report in 1934 advised improving relations with Japan, since Germany was viewed as the major long-term threat. Chamberlain, principally because of the financial implications of having to provide simultaneously for hostilities against Germany and Japan, took up the idea of a non-aggression pact. To forestall American objections he suggested that the United States should be included. But Roosevelt would have nothing to do with the proposal, and warned Britain against a separate deal with Japan. The old constraints of 1921-2 came flooding back. Opinion in the Dominions showed how much they now based their security on the United States. 'Any other course', wrote General Smuts, formerly and again subsequently Prime Minister of South Africa, 'would mean building our Commonwealth policy on quicksand.'[3]

Economic interests in China also militated against agreement with Japan. Thus when Sir Frederick Leith-Ross, the British Government's Chief Economic Adviser, returned from a visit to China in 1935, he recommended that Britain should help to strengthen the Chinese economy, and 'should press tirelessly for the abandonment of the Japanese campaign for "autonomy" in North China, which ... threatens both our trading and our financial interests, and ... will undermine both the political and financial stability of China'.[4]

The outbreak of hostilities between Japan and China in July 1937 did not end speculation about an Anglo-Japanese *rapprochement* based on recognition of Japan's special position in North China.

[1] Quoted in Louis, *British Strategy in the Far East*, p. 203.
[2] Quoted ibid., p. 207.   [3] Quoted ibid., p. 214.
[4] Quoted ibid., p. 231.

This policy was advocated by the British Ambassador in Tokyo, Sir Robert Craigie. But in the final analysis Britain was unwilling to sacrifice either her Chinese interests or American friendship. As Lord Halifax, the Foreign Secretary, wrote to Craigie in January 1939, 'any attempt to compromise with Japan would . . . alienate the sympathy of the United States, weakening our chances of collaboration not only in the Far East, but everywhere else. I consider that our aim must be active Anglo-American co-operation wherever possible.'[1] British Far Eastern policy from 1937 to the outbreak of war consisted in giving China as much financial and moral support as possible without intensifying Japanese hostility. In this way Britain hoped to prevent Japanese attacks on British possessions, to prevent a military alliance between Japan and Germany, and to prevent a Sino-Japanese agreement at Britain's expense.[2]

The continuing thread running through Britain's Far Eastern policy between the wars was thus the subordination of all other considerations to the necessity of working for American goodwill, co-operation, and support. British policy-makers, ever conscious of Britain's weakness, felt perhaps instinctively that they would rather entrust the security of the Empire to the United States than leave it hostage to Japan.[3] British and American interests largely coincided in wanting to maintain Chinese independence and integrity as a precondition of increased trade. Furthermore, the United States was not only a Pacific, but also an Atlantic power, and in the last resort strong enough to deal with Japan and Germany simul-

---

[1] Halifax to Craigie, 18 Jan. 1939, F13894/21/23 (FO 436/4).

[2] Halifax to Mallet (Washington), 6 Jan. 1939, F184/11/10 (FO 436/4). See Bradford A. Lee, *Britain and the Sino-Japanese War, 1937–1939. A Study in the Dilemmas of British Decline* (Stanford, 1973).

[3] See Max Beloff, *Imperial Sunset, I, Britain's Liberal Empire, 1897–1921* (London, 1969), pp. 330–43. The British also felt this instinctive preference for the aegis of the United States when faced with the prospect of being dictated to by a dominant Germany. The Germans constantly harped on the theme of American hegemony, attempting to strike a chord they knew existed in Britain. Lord Gladwyn, then Counsellor in the Foreign Office and Private Secretary to the Permanent Under-Secretary, Sir Alexander Cadogan, writes that he touched on the subject in a conversation with Theodor Kordt, Counsellor in the German Embassy in London, in May 1939: Kordt 'observed that if there was a war, and if we won it—a possibility that he was polite enough to say could not be excluded —one thing was certain, the Empire would disappear and we should be reduced to the status of an American dominion. To which I retorted that if such a choice had to present itself, I would infinitely prefer my country to become an American dominion than a German *Gau*' (Lord Gladwyn, *The Memoirs of Lord Gladwyn* (London, 1972), p. 90).

taneously. Because the United States refused to undertake specific commitments, however, and because British rearmament was directed at the German, rather than the Japanese threat, British policy was reduced to virtual impotence in the Far East. In short, Britain's Far Eastern possessions became hostages to American goodwill in the interest of maintaining her security in Europe.

The German threat was explicitly recognized in February 1934. From that moment Britain intensified her efforts to reach an agreement with Germany. In November 1934 the Cabinet accepted Foreign Office proposals for negotiating a comprehensive Anglo-German settlement on the basis of German concessions in return for recognition of Germany's right to rearm. But Britain considered it essential to keep in step with France, and the result was that the French were allowed to determine British policy. They insisted that Britain secure 'German agreement to a system of full political security for France, including the Eastern pact, a Danubian pact, an air pact applying to all the Locarno powers, a reasonable limitation of Germany's armed strength and Germany's return to the League'.[1]

The basic French requirement was an Eastern pact. They envisaged a defensive alliance providing for military assistance in the event of aggression, which would include Germany, the Soviet Union, Poland, Czechoslovakia, and the Baltic States, but which would be open to other states such as France herself. But Hitler had already rejected one such proposal in September 1934, with the argument that Germany would not contemplate going to the assistance of the Soviet Union. In February 1935 he was equally unenthusiastic. Sir Eric Phipps, the British Ambassador in Berlin, went to the heart of the matter when he remarked that he could not 'conceive of a plan which would have enough "teeth" to please the French and Russians, and at the same time be sufficiently toothless to be acceptable to the Germans'.[2]

Hitler's announcement of conscription, a thirty-six-division army, and the Luftwaffe in March 1935 removed Britain's bargaining counter, recognition of Germany's right to rearm. Nevertheless during his talks in March with Simon, the Foreign Secretary, and Eden, the Minister for League of Nations Affairs, Hitler declared his

[1] Medlicott, *Britain and Germany*, p. 13.
[2] Quoted ibid., p. 14.

readiness to negotiate an Eastern pact on a non-aggression basis only, and naval and air agreements with Britain. Although the Anglo-German Naval Agreement was signed in June, the Franco-Soviet Mutual Assistance Pact of May 1935 torpedoed the German offer to negotiate an Eastern pact. Neither the British Government nor their advisers abandoned hope, but the next British offer was made only in March 1936.

Meanwhile, the Abyssinian crisis profoundly altered the political and strategic configuration of Europe, causing the British Chiefs of Staff to warn in February 1937 that 'the days are past when we could count automatically on a friendly and submissive Italy. From hence forward we will have to look to a rival . . .'[1]

Britain required Italian friendship for two basic and vital reasons: first, Italian forces lay across the main line of communication between Britain and her eastern Empire; secondly, Italian support was important to Britain in containing German expansion. During the Abyssinian crisis these two vital interests were sacrificed in favour of British organization and support of the League policy of economic sanctions against Italy. The French Government recognized the danger more clearly than the British, and would have preferred to deal with the situation on the basis of the secret Franco-Italian Agreement of January 1935, which allowed Italy a free hand in Abyssinia. However, British support was no less vital to France, and the French Government was forced to pay at least lip-service to British policy.

The Italian invasion of Abyssinia began in October 1935. The League branded Italy the aggressor and recommended economic sanctions. One of the main influences behind the British decision to support the sanctions policy was public opinion. In June 1935 the results of the famous 'Peace Ballot' were published. Although the questions had been framed in such a way as to determine the response, the answers appeared to demonstrate that the electorate supported the League policy by an overwhelming majority. The Government duly stressed its adherence to League principles in the October 1935 General Election. A further reason for the decision was that Britain hoped to make an example of Mussolini to Hitler. By the application of sanctions she 'might force Italy to a halt, which in turn might make Hitler waver'.[2] Certainly British policy

[1] Quoted in Barnett, *The Collapse of British Power*, p. 381.
[2] Feiling, *Chamberlain*, p. 268.

was not based on the need to protect vital interests. As an interdepartmental committee reported in June 1935, 'no vital interests existed in Ethiopia or its neighbourhood that would make it essential that Britain resist an Italian conquest'.[1]

Economic sanctions had no visible effect on Italy, and pressure grew on the British Government to extend the embargo on exports to Italy to include oil. Instead the Cabinet decided in December 1935 to adopt the alternative approach favoured by Pierre Laval, the French Foreign Minister. On the basis of previous negotiations between British, French, and Italian diplomats, the British Foreign Secretary, Sir Samuel Hoare, agreed with Laval to a proposal giving Italy about two-thirds of Abyssinia and a virtual protectorate over the remainder. But the press got hold of the scheme and roundly denounced it. A wave of angry public opinion forced the Cabinet to accept Hoare's resignation, and the Hoare–Laval pact was dropped. The oil embargo was discussed and again rejected on the grounds that it lacked world-wide support. By April 1936 the Italians seemed to have won and in June Neville Chamberlain, on his own initiative, described sanctions as 'the very midsummer of madness'.[2] In the words of Correlli Barnett, Britain,

a weakly-armed and middle-sized state, now faced not one, not two, but three potential enemies; enemies inconveniently placed so as to threaten the entire spread of empire from the home country to the Pacific. And the third and most recent potential enemy, in the Mediterranean and Middle East, was the utterly needless creation of the British themselves, as Eden himself admitted to the House of Commons on 5 November 1936, in recalling that 'the deterioration in our relations with Italy was due to the fulfilment of our obligations under the Covenant; there had never been an Anglo-Italian quarrel so far as our country was concerned'.[3]

Meanwhile, neither the Government nor the Foreign Office had lost sight of the hoped-for agreement with Germany, designed to moderate her revisionist aims in Europe. The Foreign Office supplied the Cabinet with numerous proposals in early 1936. Sir Robert Vansittart, Permanent Under-Secretary at the Foreign Office, favoured colonial concessions to Germany, in return for which she would have to limit her armaments, abandon her European terri-

---

[1] Quoted in James C. Robertson, 'The Origins of British Opposition to Mussolini over Ethiopia', *Journal of British Studies*, 9, no. 1 (Nov. 1969), 135.
[2] Quoted in Feiling, *Chamberlain*, p. 296.
[3] Barnett, *The Collapse of British Power*, p. 381.

torial claims, and rejoin the League.[1] In February the new Foreign Secretary, Anthony Eden, proposed that Germany should be allowed to reoccupy the Rhineland and be given recognition of her special interests in central and south-eastern Europe in return for arms limitation and a guarantee of western Europe to replace the Locarno Treaty. This proposal was perhaps the closest Britain ever came to accepting the only sort of agreement that meant anything to Hitler, who consistently advocated an agreement based on mutual recognition of Germany's right to a middle-European land empire and Britain's Empire overseas. However, even Eden's proposal required the German promise that she would not exploit her interests 'in a manner which will conflict with the principles which we ourselves profess under the Covenant of the League of Nations'.[2] But the Cabinet rejected the proposal, and decided instead to concentrate on replacing the Locarno Treaty by a firm German guarantee of western Europe, together with arms limitation, in return for remilitarization of the Rhineland. Eden invited Hitler to negotiate on this basis on 6 March 1936. On the very next day Hitler once again seized of his own accord the bargaining counter that Britain offered. German troops reoccupied the demilitarized zone.

The British response to this breach of both the Versailles and the Locarno Treaties was determined partly by Hitler's offer of twenty-five-year non-aggression pacts with France and Belgium, non-aggression pacts in eastern Europe, and an air pact. This seemed to the British as good a basis as any for negotiating a settlement. Their inertia was encouraged by the French attitude, passive and defensive, and by the judgement of the Chiefs of Staff that 'any question of war with Germany while we are as at present heavily committed to the possibility of hostilities in the Mediterranean would be thoroughly dangerous'.[3] Therefore, instead of attempting to persuade France that the Germans should be forced out of the Rhineland, the British Government sent Hitler a questionnaire, seeking assurances of his good intentions.

Negotiations continued during 1936 but foundered on French unwillingness to cut her connections with eastern Europe. Nevertheless British efforts to tie Germany down to the *status quo* in Europe in return for colonial concessions continued in 1937, and were

[1] Medlicott, *Britain and Germany*, p. 21.
[2] Quoted ibid., p. 22.
[3] Quoted in Barnett, *The Collapse of British Power*, p. 383.

intensified when Neville Chamberlain succeeded to the premiership in May. Professor W. N. Medlicott has demonstrated the continuity between Chamberlain's initiatives and those of his predecessors. Under examination, he writes,

> the lines of distinction between the popular stereotypes, appeasers (or peacemakers) and war-mongers (or resisters), between the doves and the hawks of the nineteen-thirties, tend to disappear. Neville Chamberlain, like Vansittart, was a Thirty-Niner.[1] He was a little more hopeful than the Foreign Office people that Hitler might still mend his ways. He showed a strange predilection for Treasury advisers. He thought that Eden had missed chances for a settlement. But as to the time schedule of resistance, the need for armaments, the sinister alternatives to agreement, even the basic lines of a settlement—on all these matters they agreed.[2]

The controversy surrounding Chamberlain's policy of 'appeasement' centres on the method by which Britain's principal aim was to be secured. The aim was to undermine the potential threat to Britain inherent in Germany's policy of expansion. Chamberlain believed that this could be done by granting concessions before Hitler took matters into his own hands, while his right-wing critics advocated containment in the form of an alliance or security pact. There is no doubt about Chamberlain's preference for the former alternative, only doubt about what he was prepared to concede. His policy was a direct descendant of previous attempts to reach agreement with Germany on the basis of concessions in return for good behaviour. Germany's good behaviour was vital to Britain because the use of force against Czechoslovakia, for example, would entail French intervention under the Franco-Czechoslovak Treaty of 1925. Britain would then probably have to defend France, and she was not yet ready for that. On the other hand, nor was Britain ready to wash her hands of eastern Europe. Otherwise Chamberlain would have attempted to force France to abandon her alliances in eastern Europe.[3] It is true that Lord Halifax spoke openly to Hitler in November 1937 of 'possible alterations in the European order which might be destined to come about with the passage of time',[4] words

---

[1] An expression coined by Vansittart to denote one who accepted that Britain would be in a position of strength in 1939.

[2] Medlicott, *Britain and Germany*, p. 32.

[3] Skidelsky, 'Going to War with Germany', p. 61.

[4] Record of Halifax–Hitler Conversation, 19 Nov. 1937, German Foreign Ministry, *Documents on German Foreign Policy, 1918–1945* (Series D; 13 vols., Washington, 1949–54), i, no. 31. This collection is cited hereafter as *DGFP*. Series D is referred to throughout this study.

which alarmed the British Foreign Office but disappointed Hitler,[1] who would have been justified in thinking that 'the British were simply trying to string him along with fair promises while they built up their military strength'.[2]

That Chamberlain did not seriously envisage unilateral concessions in Europe is evident from the fact that in January 1938 he proposed a new colonial plan. Germany would share in the administration and exploitation of a central-African belt in return for the usual considerations: air disarmament, non-aggression in Czechoslovakia, maintenance of Austrian independence, and Germany's return to the League of Nations.[3] The Foreign Office was sceptical but raised no substantial objections. The German Government, however, intent on revising the Versailles Treaty, refused to be bound. On 13 March 1938 Germany occupied Austria and proclaimed the *Anschluss*.

British rearmament up to 1938 was constrained essentially by reluctance to transform the British economy in the interests of war production and the resulting dependence on imports and export diversion. The problem was aggravated by the consequent strain on the balance of payments and on the reserves and by the strategic conception of a war of attrition which presupposed a strong international economic position. German air power was allowed to outstrip British air power, although to a lesser extent than was thought at the time, and Britain's armaments never reached a level that the Chiefs of Staff judged sufficient to fight a war against Germany, Italy, and Japan simultaneously. They never could have. Thus the onus fell on diplomacy to reduce the number of potential enemies. Neville Chamberlain's main efforts were directed at Germany and Italy because by the time he became Prime Minister in May 1937 the impracticability of reaching an agreement with Japan had already been demonstrated. Britain's destiny would be decided in Europe.

Chamberlain's policy of 'appeasement' cannot be understood unless it is viewed in conjunction with the constraints on British power and policy during the inter-war years. It makes no sense to

---

[1] P. Schmidt, *Hitler's Interpreter*, ed. R. H. Steed (New York, 1951), p. 76.
[2] Skidelsky, 'Going to War with Germany', p. 61.
[3] Middlemas, *Diplomacy of Illusion*, pp. 142 and 148.

view it in the smaller perspective of Anglo-German relations. Britain in the 1930s no longer enjoyed unlimited resources and was no longer capable of conducting a foreign policy with Olympian detachment. The main criticism must be that she tried to do so. For although the danger of Britain's isolation was constantly brought home by the Chiefs of Staff, the British Governments of the 1930s, including Chamberlain's, were not prepared to pay the price of friendship with Japan, with Italy, or with Germany. Friendship with Japan fell foul of American objections together with a traditional interest in the 'open door' in China. The Italians were antagonized not through any calculation of British interests but because the public were thought to be demanding adherence to the principles of the League of Nations. British opposition to Italy also derived from the hope that a show of firmness would have a deterrent effect on Hitler. But Hitler was surely unlikely to be impressed by half-hearted economic sanctions. On the contrary, he took advantage of the confusion to re-enter the Rhineland. Chamberlain's grasp of the realities of Britain's predicament, emphasized in particular by his involvement as Chancellor of the Exchequer with the rearmament programme, led him first to champion a *rapprochement* with Japan, then to revive hopes of a settlement with Germany and above all to prevent a closer German-Italian alignment. But he was no less bound by the contemporary conception of British interests than were the majority of British policy-makers during the 1930s. This conception prevented his giving Germany, for example, a free hand in central and south-eastern Europe.

Britain's refusal to give Germany a free hand in the area is one of the main themes of this study. The rationale was both political-strategic and economic. The accretion in strength which German control of the area implied seemed to threaten British vital interests not only in the Low Countries but also in the Mediterranean. Undisputed German predominance seemed to ensure that both the area itself and also Italy would respond to German wishes in the event of war. A further result would be the loss to Britain of a potential Eastern front. On the economic plane, Britain sought to maintain her small but not completely insignificant trade and investment interests, though above all as a means of political leverage. Furthermore, German hegemony was thought to entail an exclusive German economic bloc, which meant that Britain and world trade generally would be denied the benefits of the area's economic growth. The assumption behind all this was that Britain must maintain her options. There was no real disagreement about this objective.

Germany was recognized as the central problem, for if Britain could avoid a European war, then it was unlikely that Japan or Italy would launch attacks on the Empire. Italy and Japan were only in a strong position *vis-à-vis* Britain as long as British resources were fully engaged against Germany. War with Germany could be avoided in one of two ways: by containing her with overwhelming and credible strength, or by granting her requirements wholesale. Britain did neither, and as a result was forced to make concessions piecemeal. What she chose was a middle course: opposing the spread of German influence within the limits of her power.

3

'SILVER BULLETS'

AN examination of British policy towards central and south-eastern Europe in 1938 demonstrates particularly clearly that Britain's alternatives were not limited to concessions on the one hand, and an anti-German coalition on the other. A further option was a middle way between the two—maximizing British influence within the limits of her power. British policy operated on two levels. The first involved pressuring Czechoslovakia to concede the demands of her German minority in the Sudetenland and led straight to the Munich Agreement in September 1938; the second involved efforts to counter the expansion of German economic and political influence in central and south-eastern Europe.

Policy on the first level has been exhaustively described elsewhere.[1] Initiated between 18 and 22 March 1938, little more than a week after the *Anschluss*, it was born of the fear that the dispute would precipitate a European, and therefore a world war. German intervention on behalf of the German minority in the Sudetenland would presumably constitute a *casus foederis* under the Franco-Czechoslovak Treaty of 1925, and France showed every intention of supporting her ally. Russia was in that case also bound to assist Czechoslovakia, and Britain stood a good chance of becoming involved in defence of France. Neville Chamberlain believed that Czechoslovakia would merely be a pretext for war with Germany, and he feared the outcome.[2] Sir Alexander Cadogan, Permanent Under-Secretary at the Foreign Office since January 1938, agreed that the Sudeten question was not 'an issue on which we should be on very strong ground for plunging Europe into war'.[3] This judgement reflected the majority of influential Foreign Office, military, and public opinion, and was in keeping with the pragmatic conduct of British foreign policy. The possibility of German hegemony in Europe

---
[1] For a comprehensive account see Middlemas, *Diplomacy of Illusion*.
[2] See above, p. 19.
[3] Quoted in Middlemas, *Diplomacy of Illusion*, p. 184 n.

as a consequence of her controlling both Austria and the Sudetenland was of less immediate and vital concern than the need to avoid a war in which Britain 'might be defeated and lose all'.[1]

Nevertheless it was the fear of German hegemony that precipitated the second line of British policy towards central and south-eastern Europe in 1938, the importance of which has only come to light with the release of the British documents for this period. The Government decided, on the advice of the Foreign Office, to use Britain's commercial and financial strength to counter German expansion in the area. This policy demonstrated Britain's continued interest in maintaining the independence of the central and south-eastern European states, an interest which most historians do not generally concede.[2] It was an obvious policy. Britain's military weakness prevented her from going to war with Germany, not so much because of German strength, but because such a war would require all Britain's resources and leave the Empire undefended. What better compromise than to fight the effects of German policy by economic means? 'Silver bullets', as the Germans called them,[3] were less visible, allowed the struggle to be localized, and allowed Britain to draw on her major source of strength. In order to understand the genesis of this policy, we must examine the circumstances surrounding the collapse of Germany's monetary system in 1931, and the measures adopted to rebuild it.

The weakness of the German economy in 1929 lay in its dependence on short-term borrowing from overseas, particularly from the United States. Most of these funds were withdrawn as a result of the collapse of the American stock market in that year, thereby weakening the German balance of payments. Although the Reichsbank attempted to maintain the value of the mark, confidence in the German economy failed to revive. Devaluation was considered politically impossible for fear of a return to the inflationary conditions of the early 1920s. Speculation against the mark during the panic months of May and June 1931 drained the Reichsbank of over one billion marks in gold and foreign-exchange reserves. Therefore 'the Government declared its monopoly of foreign exchange dealings and discontinued gold payments. Exchange control made its inauspicious

[1] Quoted in Middlemas, *Diplomacy of Illusion*, p. 186.
[2] e.g. M. Gilbert and R. Gott, *The Appeasers* (London, 1963), pp. 138 and 151: 'Chamberlain's policy was to allow Germany a free hand in Eastern Europe.'
[3] Arnold J. Toynbee, *Survey of International Affairs 1938* (London, 1941), i. 54.

beginning with the fundamental objective of protecting Germany's dwindling gold and foreign exchange holdings.'[1] There was nothing sinister about this. As the United States Tariff Commission reported in 1942, 'the intent of the law was to approve the issuance of foreign drafts, to finance imports, to meet the normal service of foreign investments, but to withhold approval if the withdrawal of capital was intended'.[2]

Although the financial crisis was over by May 1932, changed world economic conditions, and particularly the devaluation of sterling in September 1931, left the mark overvalued. To restore equilibrium the German Government could resort to internal deflation, devaluation, or permanent exchange control. Both alternatives to devaluation were chosen.

The deflationary efforts of the Brüning Government and its successors led to serious unemployment which eventually installed Hitler's National Socialist regime in January 1933. The German Government then abandoned deflation and turned exchange control into a device for regulating the direction, composition, volume, and terms of international trade.

The exchange-control system erected between 1931 and 1934 rested on three main instruments: the Standstill Agreements, exchange restrictions, and exchange-clearing agreements. The main purpose of the Standstill Agreements, negotiated with Germany's foreign creditors, was to extend the time period for short-term debt repayment, since Germany was unable to find the foreign exchange required when these debts fell due. The second instrument, exchange restrictions, meant Government control over all foreign-exchange transactions, with the object of rationing available foreign exchange and specifying its use, usually for essential imports and a certain amount of debt repayment. One of the principal features of these restrictions was the system of 'blocked mark accounts'. Money accruing to foreigners accumulated in special bank accounts in Germany rather than being transferred abroad in the form of foreign exchange.

The rapid spread of exchange control throughout eastern Europe led to the third device: bilateral exchange-clearing agreements. The

---

[1] F. C. Child, *The Theory and Practice of Exchange Control in Germany; a study of monopolistic exploitation in international markets* (The Hague, 1958), p. 13.
[2] Quoted ibid., p. 16.

gold and foreign exchange shortage suffered by these countries severely hampered their trade. Exchange-clearing agreements ensured that all payments for German exports were earmarked to cover payments for German imports. For example, Germans importing goods from Rumania paid their debts, in marks, into the German-Rumanian Clearing Account at the Reichsbank. German exporters, in turn, applied to the Reichsbank for payment out of the same account. The Rumanian Central Bank established a similar account, and the rate of exchange at which the clearing operated was fixed by agreement and frequently renegotiated to take account of changing conditions. Exchange-clearing agreements were negotiated by Germany with most of her eastern-European trading partners, beginning in 1932.

These measures formed the basis of the 'New Plan' introduced by Dr. Hjalmar Schacht, President of the Reichsbank, in September 1934. This 'New Plan' was significant because it was designed to extend the purpose of exchange control from the maintenance of external equilibrium to the promotion of Germany's planned economic requirements. Originally intended as a temporary instrument of monetary policy, exchange control became a permanent instrument of commercial and foreign policy. F. C. Child has summarized the new objectives thus:

(1) To obtain, on the best possible terms, the imports most urgently required by the German economy in exchange for goods which could be exported with the least disadvantage;
(2) to increase the degree of German national self-sufficiency;
(3) to obtain more of the essential, minimum imports from easily accessible areas;
(4) to minimize capital exports;
(5) to separate Germany's trade relationships from the international network and to establish a series of independent bilateral relationships.[1]

In exchange-clearing agreements with the primary producing countries of south-eastern Europe, where Germany sought to obtain most of her raw material and food requirements, the exchange rate was fixed with the mark at a premium, with the object of improving Germany's terms of trade. The countries concerned were forced to acquiesce because Germany's bargaining position was strong:

Germany represented the most important single market for exportable

[1] Child, *Exchange Control in Germany*, p. 133.

'SILVER BULLETS' 37

goods of most Eastern European countries. These countries, therefore, depended upon Germany for a substantial portion of their aggregate demand. At a time when other world markets were flagging, Germany represented an outlet for products which would otherwise be considered surplus. Either on their own initiative or because of political pressure, every Eastern European country undertook to support the price of the mark rather than deny their export industries access to the German market.[1]

Mark balances accumulated in Germany to the credit of these countries as a result of a continuing German trade deficit with the area, and this debt increased Germany's bargaining power still further. These clearing marks could be used only to buy German goods, which were of course expensive and in many cases could have been obtained elsewhere on better terms.

The result of Germany's aggressive commercial policy was that German imports from the area increased from 12·2 per cent in 1934 to 16·6 per cent in 1937, and her exports from 11·1 per cent to 15 per cent, whereas British and French trade remained virtually static at about 2·5 per cent and 4 per cent respectively.[2]

The British reaction centred on the following questions: What were the effects of German commercial policy on the area itself, on Germany, on British interests, and on world trade generally? And what policy should Britain adopt towards it? The Foreign Office Economic Relations Section, created in 1934 under Frank Ashton-Gwatkin, and joined in 1936 by Gladwyn Jebb, addressed itself to these problems in a memorandum written in August 1936.

The writer's assessment was that the area had gained economically from German policy, and would probably continue to do so, a view not shared by contemporary polemicists[3] but certainly borne out by economic analysis today.[4] On the other hand, there was the danger

[1] Ibid., pp. 152–3.
[2] FO Memorandum: 'German Economic Penetration in Central and South-East Europe', 6 May 1938, Table I, C3249/772/18 (FO 433/5). The area included Austria, Bulgaria, Czechoslovakia, Greece, Hungary, Rumania, Turkey, and Yugoslavia. The British economic interest was in finance rather than commerce. Private investments loomed particularly large in Greece and Rumania, but by far the greatest proportion of British capital was tied up in Government loans. For details of involvement in south-eastern Europe see Royal Institute of International Affairs, *South-Eastern Europe. A Political and Economic Survey* (London, 1939).
[3] e.g. P. Einzig, *Bloodless Invasion: German Economic Penetration into the Danubian States and the Balkans* (2nd edn., London, 1939).
[4] See Child, *Exchange Control in Germany*.

that German economic hegemony in the area would result in political control:

> It is not only that Germany would wish to make certain of the benevolent neutrality of the Danubian and Balkan countries in case of war; she wants their benevolent neutrality in time of peace also, i.e., she wants to prevent them from coming preponderantly under the influence of the Franco-Russian group or of Italy ... and she wants to be in such a relationship with them that, in the event of any important conflict of opinion between the Great Powers, it would be the German point of view to which these countries would be primarily responsive. The disadvantage and danger of such a situation to Great Britain and to other Powers is obvious.[1]

The memorandum noted that British trade with the area was not substantial, amounting to just over 2 per cent of total trade, but nor was it insignificant. In practical terms this meant that 'we should not begrudge Germany the extension of her trade in the Danubian and Balkan countries', but it 'does not . . . mean that we should resign ourselves to retiring gracefully from the scene and leaving Germany a completely free hand'. The problem of how to counter the political danger of German penetration remained. Britain could either absorb large additional and unwanted quantities of Balkan products or somehow find alternative markets for Germany's surplus exports. The writer favoured the latter solution, which he said could only be achieved by freer trade all round. Without (probably British) concessions to German exports, 'it would be childish to imagine that an economic bloc under the leadership of Germany will not fairly quickly establish itself in "Mitteleuropa".' He granted that from an economic point of view the development of such a middle-European common market could be beneficial:

> It would provide much-needed export markets for German goods; and it would open up the German import market to countries for which that market is the natural market. Any measure, indeed, even though it be on a preferential basis, which reduces the present barriers to trade in Central Europe would lead to more trade and greater prosperity, and would therefore be economically desirable.

The British Government were very much alive to the danger of German political control of central and south-eastern Europe, and at this time pursued the objective of a settlement with Germany

[1] FO Memorandum: 'German Economic Penetration in Central Europe, the Balkans and Turkey', 17 Aug. 1936, R4969/1167/67 (FO 433/3).

designed to satisfy her with colonial rather than European concessions. But when these efforts failed demonstrably with the German occupation of Austria in March 1938, the question of how to counter further German penetration, short of measures that might lead to war, remained. The Foreign Office memorandum of August 1936 was dug up again in May 1938 and assessed in relation to the implications of the *Anschluss*.[1] The Foreign Secretary, Lord Halifax, now launched a comprehensive debate with a Cabinet memorandum entitled 'British Influence in Central and South-Eastern Europe',[2] in which he advocated setting up an Inter-Departmental Committee to examine how best to counter German economic and political penetration in the area by economic means.

The Foreign Office judged that, as a result of the *Anschluss*, German influence in central and south-eastern Europe now seemed likely 'to extend in a manner and to a degree that has not been witnessed since 1917'.[3] The most important consequences were likely to be the spread of German cultural influence; the strengthening of Germany's potential reservoir of raw materials, particularly foodstuffs, minerals, and oils; the extension of markets for German exports of manufactures; German dominance of the area's communications system, particularly the Danube and railroads; and finally a 'general accretion of strength and prestige and the virtual certainty that in the event of war, some, if not all, of these countries will be dragged in Germany's wake'.

Some of these consequences were no doubt inevitable, given geographical and economic realities, but if, in addition, Germany once again acquired colonies, and if her influence in Spain were consolidated by a Fascist victory, then she would be a direct threat to the British Empire. It had traditionally been Britain's policy to prevent any one power from attaining hegemony on the Continent: an effort to contain German expansion in central and south-eastern Europe now seemed highly desirable, indeed 'vital to our interests'.

The Foreign Office nevertheless warned that the object should not be to create an anti-German coalition. This could be done only if Britain and France were ready to extend their military commitments, which clearly they were not.

---

[1] FO Memorandum: 'German Economic Penetration in Central and South-East Europe', 6 May 1938, C3249/772/18 (FO 433/5).
[2] Cab. Memorandum, 24 May 1938, CP 127 (38), CAB 24/277.
[3] Ibid.

Our object should rather be to endeavour to ensure that this area of Europe shall look specifically for leadership to this country, and generally towards the Western Powers, rather than feel obliged in default of any other *point d'appui* to allow itself to be exploited by Berlin.

If military guarantees were ruled out, how should Britain implement a policy of resistance to German penetration? The Foreign Office suggested economic assistance. The trouble was that

While the Foreign Office tend to regard economics and finance as a means to a political end, the other Departments are naturally bound to judge these from a different point of view. A deadlock is apt to be reached by a political 'desideratum' being brought to nothing by a technical 'non possumus'. This may often be right. Nevertheless, we are constantly told that our most powerful weapon in the international sphere resides in economics and finance. In the present critical state of Europe it seems more than ever necessary that effective use should be made of this weapon, particularly in Central and South-Eastern Europe. Yet no special machinery exists whereby the political and economic aspects of the policy of His Majesty's Government in the countries under review can be properly co-ordinated, with a view to ensuring that the maximum political advantage be extracted from the economic weapon.

The Foreign Office proposed that such machinery be set up in the form of an Inter-Departmental Committee, on which would be represented the Foreign Office, Treasury, Board of Trade, Export Credits Guarantee Department, and Department of Overseas Trade.

The Cabinet passed the memorandum for discussion to the Cabinet Foreign Policy Committee, which met on the same day, 1 June 1938. Halifax recapitulated the Foreign Office arguments:

Briefly stated the position was that we were now confronted with the probability that German influence would penetrate throughout the whole of Central and South-Eastern Europe in the economic sphere, leading to the likelihood of Germany dominating this great area in the political sphere. It seemed highly desirable in the interests of the preservation of European peace that an attempt should be made to check this process before it was too late, and that if this could be done our own position would itself be greatly strengthened.[1]

Chamberlain did not allow Halifax's assumption to go unchallenged:

He was doubtful whether it was right to assume that if Germany's economic life was strengthened that would necessarily be a bad thing.

[1] Foreign Policy Committee Minutes, 1 June 1938, CAB 27/623.

Might not a great improvement in Germany's economic situation result in her becoming quieter and less interested in political adventures?[1]

Chamberlain's comment should not be taken as evidence that he opposed the Foreign Office policy. Rather, it revealed his different perspective. His main concern was to achieve a *rapprochement* with Germany. The most influential officials in the Foreign Office shared this concern,[2] but their job was also to prepare for the possibility of failure. Chamberlain recognized this. In March 1936 he had written that

> the way to talk to Hitler was to say that there were only two ways of getting security and peace. One: Regional pacts on Locarno lines. Two: Alliances and a balance of power. We wanted the first but could not get it without him and if he would not play we should be forced into Two.[3]

Chamberlain therefore allowed the Foreign Office to formulate the means of keeping Britain's options open, and rarely objected to their policy.

The only Minister who was truly sceptical was the Chancellor of the Exchequer, Sir John Simon, who pointed out that 'experience showed that the effect of economic assistance in checking or preventing political changes was very small'.[4] Neither Minister objected in principle to the Foreign Office proposal, however, and the majority of the committee were enthusiastic. The Government's Chief Economic Adviser, Sir Frederick Leith-Ross, was chosen to head the Inter-Departmental Committee on Central and South-Eastern Europe.

The Turkish Government had benefited from this policy even before the Foreign Policy Committee agreed to it. Since 1937 Turkey had requested British credits of at least £10 million for industrial purposes and £6 million for warships, to be ordered in Britain. The Export Credits Guarantee Department objected that Turkish financial security was inadequate. But the British Ambassador to Turkey, Sir Percy Loraine, put the case for overlooking this problem:

> It would seem dismally unfortunate if the financial difficulty stops their order [i.e. the Turkish warship order] being placed. Are we really debarred from using our tremendous money resources, one patent and tangible

[1] Ibid. [2] See below, pp. 61–6.
[3] Quoted in Middlemas, *Diplomacy of Illusion*, p. 53.
[4] FPC Minutes, 1 June 1938, CAB 27/623.

superiority that we possess over our European rivals, for helping our friends, for creating employment at home, for building up in this instance a friendly navy in a region which represents for us a particularly high degree of political and strategical importance, for aiding Turkey to reach a military strength which virtually renders her immune from aggression, and strengthens her influence in the direction of peace and lawful behaviour throughout the Balkan Peninsula and eastwards to Iran and Afghanistan?[1]

The Foreign Secretary, Lord Halifax, impressed by these arguments, urged the Cabinet in May 1938 to agree that the Turkish loan was necessary for political purposes, to which financial objections must be subordinated. Turkish friendship was of vital strategic interest to Britain. As a result of the *Anschluss* with Austria, Germany was now a direct neighbour of one of Turkey's allies, Yugoslavia, and was separated from another ally, Rumania, only by a pro-German Hungary. What was to prevent German influence from spreading down through Bulgaria and into Turkey? This endangered the Middle East and the line of British communications with India and the Far East, especially 'now that the implementation of the Balfour Declaration regarding Palestine may inevitably cost us the friendship of the Arab countries'. Halifax concluded that it was 'scarcely too much to say that Turkey has become not the main but the only obstacle to the *Drang nach Osten*'.[2]

The Cabinet were impressed in turn. Chamberlain was enthusiastic. 'The idea', he said, 'was that we should use our financial strength and resources for political purposes.' Even Sir John Simon agreed that 'if we were able to obtain our political desiderata, it would be very cheap at this price, but it must be realised that we were taking a very novel and a very important step'.[3] According to Loraine the effect on the Turks of this decision to help them was 'electric', as was the reaction in Greece 'by anticipation'.[4]

These decisions were the outcome of a line of British thinking which has been largely overlooked. Its significance lies in the assumption behind it: that the principle of the classic British doctrine of the balance of power remained valid. Chamberlain's critics argued that

[1] Quoted in Cab. Memorandum: 'Credits for Turkey', May 1938, CP 112 (38), CAB 24/277.
[2] Cab. Memorandum: 'Credits for Turkey'.
[3] Cab. Minutes, 11 May 1938, CAB 23/93.
[4] Cab. Minutes, 15 June 1938, CAB 23/94.

his foreign policy demonstrated total disregard for this doctrine,[1] which is commonly believed to have reasserted itself only in March 1939, with the guarantee to Poland. It is true that neither Chamberlain nor the Foreign Office was prepared to maintain the balance of power by means of an alliance between Britain, France, and Russia, or a system of military guarantees to the countries of central and south-eastern Europe, but nor were they prepared to give Germany a free hand. They chose the third option, a limited policy of insurance against German monopoly in the area, which the Foreign Office sought to implement by economic means until such time as British resistance could be strengthened.

Of course the British were never solidly united in the belief that resistance to German expansion in central and south-eastern Europe was either feasible or desirable. There was an ambivalence in British thinking at this time that was symptomatic of an underlying uneasiness about Hitler's capabilities and intentions. Thus Sir Alexander Cadogan, Permanent Under-Secretary at the Foreign Office, thought that

> German economic preponderance in certain countries of central and eastern Europe is bound to develop, provided the German economic and financial structure can stand the strain. It will be a fact to be reckoned with, like the rise of Japan, and it is very doubtful whether, with all our other commitments, we shall be strong enough to withstand it . . . I wonder whether we should try to withstand it.[2]

This gave the cue to Halifax, who wrote to Sir Eric Phipps, the British Ambassador in Paris, in a letter which has hitherto provided the only real guide to Foreign Office thinking on future policy, that 'Henceforward we must count on German predominance in Central Europe. Incidentally I have always felt myself that, when Germany recovered her normal strength, this predominance was inevitable for obvious geographical and economic reasons.'[3] Significantly however, Halifax deleted from the draft of this letter a 'phrase recognizing that it would be a mistake ever to prevent such predominance'.[4] Poland, he thought, could 'presumably only fall more and more into the German orbit', on the assumption that France were

---

[1] Neville Thompson, *The Anti-Appeasers. Conservative Opposition to Appeasement in the 1930s* (Oxford, 1971), pp. 46–7.
[2] Memorandum by Cadogan, 14 Oct. 1938, C14461/41/18 (FO 371/21659).
[3] Halifax letter to Phipps, 1 Nov. 1938, *DBFP* iii, no. 285.
[4] Lord Birkenhead, *Halifax: The Life of Lord Halifax* (Boston, 1966), p. 421.

to relax the Franco-Polish Alliance. But Halifax did not advise Phipps to encourage the French to do this, and he took the same attitude towards the Franco-Soviet Pact: 'the future is still far too uncertain!'

Thus British policy was formulated only hesitantly and pragmatically after Munich. But it is not true to say that at this time 'it was generally and publicly conceded that Germany should be allowed an economic free hand in South-East Europe'.[1] In fact this argument was explicitly rejected by the Government in November 1938, on the ground that as long as Germany's economic system remained closed and her trade relations with the area remained exclusive, there were no advantages to be gained for world trade in general and British trade in particular.[2]

At the beginning of October 1938 Dr. Walther Funk, the German Minister of Economics, began a tour of south-eastern Europe. He held out the prospect of the area becoming 'entirely independent of the great world markets' as a result of Germany's willingness to import its goods. Sir Ronald Campbell, the British Minister in Belgrade, reported that the visit 'appears to mark the beginning of a new economic drive on the part of Germany to capture a still larger proportion of the trade of South Eastern European countries'.[3] Halifax informed the Cabinet that demands for British economic assistance for south-eastern Europe 'had poured in from every quarter'.[4] He proposed that the British Government should buy 200,000 tons of Rumania's wheat surplus of about one and a half million tons 'to steady the position' there. He promised to review the whole question of British policy in central and south-eastern Europe in a memorandum for the Cabinet.

The German Minister of Economics did not in fact visit Rumania, but German-Rumanian economic negotiations, conducted by Clodius, the Deputy Director of the Economic Policy Department of the German Foreign Ministry, resulted in an agreement signed on 10 December 1938. Among other things, this agreement increased Rumanian grain supplies to Germany and altered the exchange rate in the latter's favour. Germany's most important concession was her purchase of 400,000 tons of wheat 'which we do not absolutely need

[1] Gilbert and Gott, *The Appeasers*, pp. 195-6.
[2] Cab. Memorandum: 'Central and South-Eastern Europe', 10 Nov. 1938, CP 257 (38), CAB 24/280.
[3] Campbell to Halifax, 10 Oct. 1938, R8228/957/92 (FO 434/5), f. 686.
[4] Cab. Minutes, 19 Oct. 1938, CAB 23/96.

at the present moment'.¹ Funk actually visited Yugoslavia, Turkey, and Bulgaria. His Turkish visit led to an accord on long-term credit, and a similar agreement was reached with Bulgaria.²

Chamberlain was absent from London when Halifax proposed his modest wheat-purchase scheme, and faced with opposition from both Simon and Oliver Stanley, the President of the Board of Trade, the Foreign Secretary took the issue straight to the Prime Minister, to whom he wrote:

> It is admittedly not a great thing to do, but is thought by those who know to have a symbolic value disproportionate to its intrinsic worth. My own feeling is that it is never likely in future to be possible for us to do a great deal in the Balkans, as compared with what is bound to be, for geographical and other reasons, the opportunity of Germany. None the less, I think it is of great importance that we should at this time of great unsettlement give some evidence of our existence and continued interest in those countries, and that we should not miss any reasonable opportunity which presents itself of keeping alive the small share of trade which we have with them.³

Halifax wished to know 'whether you might feel that any move on these lines cut across the general efforts at rapprochement with Germany that you are trying to make', and emphasized that unless Britain acted on the proposal 'the certain result would be to throw them [the Rumanians] wholly and rapidly into the German arms'. Chamberlain replied that he had no objections and that he did not think the proposal would cut across his policy.⁴

On 26 October 1938 Sir Frederick Leith-Ross sent Halifax the first report of the Inter-Departmental Committee on Central and South-Eastern Europe.⁵ The Committee believed that the ideal solution would be to increase the area's normal trade with Britain. Its trade

---

¹ Memorandum by Clodius, 13 Dec. 1938, *DGFP* v, no. 264.
² Ambassador in Turkey to the German Foreign Ministry, 11 Oct. 1938, ibid., no. 55. For a description of Dr. Funk's tour, see Toynbee, *Survey of International Affairs 1938*, i. 50–7.
³ Halifax letter to Chamberlain, 13 Oct. 1938, PREM 1/266B.
⁴ Minute by Chamberlain, ibid. The British effort was small in practice partly because the Government encountered spirited opposition from the National Federation of Corn Trade Associations, who objected that the Government were flooding the market with an unfamiliar product and disrupting prices (Board of Trade Memorandum: 'Wheat Storage Scheme', January 1939, R279/113/37, FO 371/23831). In fact the quality was good, and private traders later bought a further 150,000 tons (Leith-Ross to Sargent, 16 Jan. 1939, R496/113/37, ibid.).
⁵ Interim Report of the Inter-Departmental Committee on Central and South-Eastern Europe, 26 Oct. 1938, enclosure in FP (36) 54, CAB 27/627.

with Germany not only led to political control but also aggravated its shortage of foreign exchange. For these reasons 'practically all the countries of South Eastern Europe are most anxious to develop their export trade to the United Kingdom and several of them have appealed for credits which would facilitate increased purchases from the United Kingdom'. Increased Balkan exports would appeal to Britain for two additional technical reasons. First, she was not receiving a full return on her investments of about £100 million because of the foreign-exchange shortage.[1] Secondly, under the law governing its activities, the British Export Credits Guarantee Department could grant credits only if adequate security existed for repayment. Such security could be based only on increased foreign-exchange earnings, presumably from exports to Britain.

At that time, Britain's imports from the area averaged a little over 1 per cent of total imports, but in the Committee's opinion a 100 per cent increase 'would be a very substantial help to these countries and would materially assist to maintain our influence there'. The problem was that any attempt by Britain to stimulate such an increase would run counter to the Ottawa Agreement of 1932, which governed the system of Imperial preference on many products that the Balkan countries hoped to export, especially wheat and tobacco. Therefore the attempt would require 'some radical modification of our existing commercial policy'.

Four alternatives were considered: (1) modifications of tariffs, quotas, and preferences where they restricted British imports from the area; (2) direct purchases either by the Government or by some organization with Government backing; (3) increased purchases by the great trade interests of such commodities as wheat, oil, and particularly tobacco; (4) the grant of credits either on a frankly non-commercial or on a 'somewhat speculative' basis. The Committee favoured the first and third possibilities, since they were long-term solutions.

On 10 November Halifax presented the Leith-Ross Committee report to the Cabinet, along with a memorandum of his own which recapitulated the arguments about German hegemony outlined in May.[2] The consequences then envisaged as a result of the *Anschluss*

---

[1] The Greek Government were negotiating with the Council of Foreign Bondholders on this subject, and the Rumanian Government defaulted on the British coupon for the first time on 1 October 1938.

[2] Cab. Memorandum: 'Central and South-Eastern Europe', 10 Nov. 1938, CP 257 (38), CAB 24/280.

now seemed more likely than ever as a result of the German incorporation of the Sudetenland. He admitted that opinion differed on the degree to which German influence should be allowed to predominate, but he thought it would be generally agreed that the countries of central and south-eastern Europe 'should be actively encouraged to realize that a possible *point d'appui* other than Berlin does exist, and that British interest in them, both political or [sic] economic, will be maintained and developed'. He himself believed that it was 'essential to our ultimate security to promote our political influence by economic measures'.

Halifax outlined the alternative open to Britain: to allow Germany a free reign in developing the area economically, and to acquiesce in the political consequences. Those who argued in favour of this alternative stressed the benefits of increased trade between the area and Germany, not only for the prosperity and development of the whole of central and south-eastern Europe, but also for the derived prosperity of Britain and the rest of the world. Such benefits might even be sufficient to justify British participation in the development of the area, based on the London money market. After all, the pre-war economic alliance between Germany and the Austro-Hungarian Empire had been financed through 'short-term money regularly supplied by London'.

But Halifax rejected these arguments, and for reasons which are particularly significant because they illuminate the British Government's whole approach to the question of economic 'appeasement' after Munich. These arguments assumed, he wrote,

> that the trade between Germany and the South-Eastern European countries will be of an orthodox, liberal or free trade character, based on the free exchange of goods and payment by free exchange. But this has not been the case in the past and is unlikely to be the case in the future, unless, as is just possible, there is a fundamental change in Germany's economic and financial policy. It seems, at present, far more likely that any economic dominance that Germany may attain in these countries will result in their economic vassalage to Germany and to German economic doctrine, and that German foreign exchange restrictions and autarchic aims will become factors conditioning and moulding the economic life of each of them. This, in fact, seems certain so long as Germany refuses to envisage the depreciation of the mark and to relax her exchange controls, and so long as she insists that these countries shall receive payment for their exports in German goods, wanted or unwanted. Moreover, the

short-term credits by London to Germany, both before and since the war, have been frozen and have proved a source of great embarrassment and, indeed, of danger to the international credit of London. We could not afford to lock up further resources in Germany, so long as she maintains a system of exchange control; nor to advance funds to the Danubian countries so long as their trade with Germany only produces blocked marks. While, therefore, Germany, for one reason or another, is unwilling to lift her exchange controls, the arguments in favour of permitting her a free hand in these countries would seem largely to fall to the ground. It appears, indeed, as though no real progress could be made in economic conditions in Europe until exchange control is relaxed (a truth which has often been put forward in the past), and that meanwhile any increase in the economic predominance exercised by Germany in the countries in question will not redound in any way to the benefit of world trade in general or of British trade in particular.[1]

Here then were the arguments behind Chamberlain's attempts to wean Germany away from her economic isolation and autarky after Munich. By pressuring Germany to re-enter the free-currency trade network, Britain would reap two advantages: first, the German hold on central and south-eastern Europe would be weakened; secondly, Anglo-German trade would expand. Germany was after all Britain's single most important foreign, as opposed to Empire, market, and Britain was looking for relief from her serious trade deficit.[2]

There was a further argument for opposing German domination of south-eastern Europe. Italy feared German expansion on the one hand, but hoped on the other hand that co-operation with Germany would reward her with a North African Empire. If Germany were allowed to dominate the area completely, in Halifax's view, then Italy would be more inclined to co-operate with her than to oppose her.[3] This was in contrast to those, like Gladwyn Jebb, who thought that German penetration of central and south-eastern

---

[1] Cab. Memorandum: 'Central and South-Eastern Europe', 10 Nov. 1938, pp. 4–5.

[2] The trade deficit in 1938 was £284 million, in 1937 £339 million. Invisible exports were no longer covering these deficits. For further discussion of these ideas see Bernd Jürgen Wendt, *Economic Appeasement. Handel und Finanz in der britischen Deutschland-Politik 1933–1939* (Düsseldorf, 1971); also C. A. MacDonald, 'Economic Appeasement and the German "Moderates" 1937–1939, An Introductory Essay', *Past and Present*, 56 (Aug. 1972), 105–35.

[3] Cab. Memorandum: 'Central and South-Eastern Europe', 10 Nov. 1938.

Europe would eventually break the Axis and cause a revival of the Anglo-Franco-Italian Stresa Front.[1]

Halifax endorsed the Leith-Ross proposals, and added some recommendations of his own. He wanted military equipment and credits for Greece; an increase in imports of Greek tobacco; regular purchases of Rumanian wheat and oil, and help in building her naval base on the Black Sea. He advised credits wherever possible and increased trade with Yugoslavia, Bulgaria, and Hungary. The Cabinet referred the whole question to the Foreign Policy Committee.

In the meantime King Carol of Rumania, on a visit to London from 15 to 18 November, discussed several proposals with Chamberlain and Halifax. He pressed for assistance in building the Black Sea naval base, in developing Danubian trade and navigation, in developing the timber industry, and in building grain silos.[2] Chamberlain was extremely anxious for these proposals to be examined, and for Britain to send a commercial mission to Bucharest to discuss them.[3]

On 21 November the Foreign Policy Committee discussed assistance to Greece. Both Halifax and Leith-Ross had already tried to pressure Lord Dulverton, chairman of the Imperial Tobacco Company, into marketing a new brand of cigarette blended with Greek tobacco, but without success. The businessman in Chamberlain was sympathetic: 'Putting himself into Lord Dulverton's position he could not see any good answer to the suggestion that the Government were asking him to ruin his business and his tens of thousands of shareholders for a purely political object.'[4] The cost should be borne by the British taxpayer, not by an individual company. The second major objection to increasing Britain's imports of Greek tobacco was that if 'within a few weeks of the signature of the Anglo-American [Trade] Agreement the Americans saw the British Government encouraging another competitor they would think that we had played them a very dirty trick. Mr. Cordell Hull would be closely interested as he came from a tobacco growing State.'[5] In the end Halifax went away to think again.

[1] Minute by Jebb, 4 Apr. 1939, C4758/54/18 (FO 371/23016).
[2] Halifax to Palairet (Bucharest), 17 Nov. 1938, *DBFP* iii, no. 262.
[3] Memorandum by A. D. M. Ross (Southern Department), 9 Jan. 1939, R211/113/37 (FO 371/23831).
[4] FPC Minutes, 21 Nov. 1938, CAB 27/624.
[5] Ibid. The Anglo-American Trade Agreement was signed on 17 November 1938. The tobacco concessions requested by the United States Government had

Chamberlain did not object in principle to the Foreign Office policy. In the Cabinet next day he reaffirmed that 'it was desirable to stop Germany from obtaining complete economic control of this area', but that it was difficult to do so without giving the appearance of economic encirclement. He admitted that the Government 'had not yet been able to formulate any concrete proposals'.[1]

Nevertheless Oliver Stanley, President of the Board of Trade, had been studying means to widen the Government's powers to grant economic assistance. On 9 November and 7 December 1938 he obtained the Cabinet's approval for amendments to the Export Guarantees Act of 1937. He wanted to increase the limit allowed on outstanding guarantees; to extend the geographical scope of the Act; to remove the ban on guarantees for arms exports; and, most important, to include an arrangement for guaranteeing credits which could not be justified on purely commercial grounds, but which were necessary on political grounds.[2]

Meanwhile, the Government faced increasing pressure in Parliament to oppose German trade practices more forcefully, especially in the Balkans where they were most in evidence. Clement Attlee, the leader of the Labour Opposition, reminded the Government that 'the lesson in 1914–15 was that if you wanted to deal with the Balkan States, you had to give enough and you had to give it in time'.[3] Chamberlain cautioned that 'there is room both for Germany and for us in trade with those countries and . . . neither of us ought to try to obtain exclusive possession of their markets'.[4] R. S. Hudson, the Secretary of the Department of Overseas Trade, took a stronger line on 30 November 1938. He described the effects of German trading methods in south-eastern Europe and warned Germany that

> Unless you are prepared to put an end to this form of treatment, unless you are prepared to come to an agreement to sell your goods at

been denied, but the British Government had promised to review the situation before 1942, when the Ottawa Agreement came up for renewal (FPC Memorandum: 'Central and South-Eastern Europe', 30 Jan. 1939, FP (36) 79).

[1] Cab. Minutes, 22 Nov. 1938, CAB 23/95.
[2] Cab. Minutes, 9 Nov. and 7 Dec. 1938, CAB 23/96. Introduced in Parliament on 8 December 1938, the new Bill was enacted on 28 February 1939. The Foreign Office advised that the £10 million available under Clause 4 of the Act (for political credits) should be allocated as follows: £3 million for China, £2 million for Greece, £1 million each for Portugal, Rumania, and Egypt, £½ million for Iraq, and £¼ million for Afghanistan (Cab. Minutes, 18 Jan. 1939, CAB 23/97).
[3] 340 HC Deb., 5 s., col. 68.
[4] Ibid., col. 81.

prices which represent a reasonable return, then we will fight you and beat you at your own game. This country is infinitely stronger than, I was going to say, any other country in the world, but certainly stronger than Germany, and therefore we have great advantages, advantages which I believe will result in our winning the fight . . .[1]

Here was the threat of a subsidy war, a threat which also bore fruit when used in the Anglo-German negotiations for a coal cartel.[2]

During the course of the winter and spring various schemes designed to stall the German advance were critically examined in Whitehall.

In January 1939 Sir Frederick Leith-Ross submitted the Inter-Departmental Committee's second report to the Foreign Policy Committee.[3] It dealt with aid to Rumania and Greece. The Leith-Ross Committee made a number of recommendations for maintaining British influence, but was forced to the conclusion that

if His Majesty's Government are not prepared *either* to arrange for additional imports from these countries to facilitate the service of their existing debts or to repay any future credits that may be granted, *or* to grant credits on a non-commercial basis, it would be best to inform the Roumanian and Greek Governments that we see no possibility of giving them any substantial assistance.

Halifax, on the other hand, hoped that 'it will not be necessary to make such a choice'.[4] He wanted both solutions adopted, together with further political credits for war materials. The Leith-Ross Committee stressed the difficulties in the way of increasing oil and wheat imports from Rumania and tobacco imports from Greece. But Halifax was adamant on the question of Greek tobacco. He wanted to guarantee the British tobacco companies against any loss arising out of their marketing the commodity. He also wanted commercial missions to be sent out to Greece and Rumania, on

[1] 342 HC Deb., 5 s., col. 502.
[2] See below, pp. 57 and 79. In a memorandum of 7 November 1938 outlining the British complaint against German competition in the coal trade, the Board of Trade warned the Germans that 'there is already strong pressure on the Government to take decisive action to resist German competition. Indeed, a proposal that levy and subsidy should be met by levy and subsidy is already under consideration' ('The Problem of Coal Export Trade', FO 433/5, f. 193).
[3] Inter-Departmental Committee on Central and South-Eastern Europe, Second Interim Report, January 1939, enc. in FP (36) 79, CAB 27/627.
[4] Memorandum by Halifax: 'Central and South-Eastern Europe', 30 Jan. 1939, FP (36) 79, CAB 27/627.

condition that they took concrete proposals with them. He reminded the Foreign Policy Committee that the departmental experts under Leith-Ross were also studying policy towards Bulgaria, Hungary, and Yugoslavia. Turkey was being treated as a separate case. Halifax clearly thought that, despite its dictatorial regime, Greece was the most important country on the agenda:

> We must endeavour to ensure that Greece is capable of defending herself and ready to do so, for a weak and defenceless Greece would operate to the detriment of our security in the Mediterranean. Moreover, assistance to Greece is likely to prove of more political value than assistance to Roumania because, in present circumstances, Roumania is by reason of her geographical situation and her minority problems more susceptible to German pressure and threats than is Greece. It is, indeed, questionable whether the degree of encouragement which we are to-day in a position to give Roumania would in any case enable her to stand up to Germany politically.[1]

The Foreign Policy Committee, meeting on 8 February 1939, were sympathetic to Halifax's viewpoint. The exception was Sir John Simon, who naturally put the Treasury view against any increase in spending. Chamberlain, on the other hand, constantly overrode Simon's objections. He thought it was 'desirable to keep the pot boiling' by maintaining Britain's interest in the area. The Greek tobacco scheme was referred back for expert consideration. The Committee approved non-commercial credits for Greece and Rumania and the dispatch, in principle, of commercial missions to the two countries.[2]

The policy of countering German political and economic influence in central and south-eastern Europe by economic means was continued throughout the spring and summer, and eventually came under the aegis of the Ministry of Economic Warfare. It was designed by the Foreign Office above all as a means of keeping Britain's options open, and its relative importance as an instrument of foreign policy was accordingly reduced when military guarantees were given to Poland, Greece, Rumania, and Turkey. It could not be said that it was implemented with great urgency once it had been adopted, or that its effects were regarded with anything but scepticism by those

[1] Memorandum by Halifax: 'Central and South-Eastern Europe', 30 Jan. 1939, p. 2.
[2] FPC Minutes, 8 Feb. 1939, CAB 27/624.

more or less resigned to the inevitability of German hegemony in the area. The fact that in practice Britain concentrated on assistance to Turkey, Greece, and Rumania was characteristic of a reluctance to throw good money after bad. Nor, in practice, did British assistance amount to very much. But the aim was to achieve the maximum political effect with the minimum economic and political effort. Thus although Greece asked Britain for a treaty of alliance, which would certainly have ensured Greek friendship, the Foreign Office assumed that the British Government would not 'be anxious to increase their political commitments if they could achieve their object by different and less drastic means'.[1] This still leaves open the question why the British Government were prepared to increase their political commitments in March 1939. But the political commitment that was then made to Poland is at least more understandable if we accept that British policy in 1938 was not based on willingness to grant Germany a free hand in central and south-eastern Europe.

[1] Cab. Memorandum: 'Central and South-Eastern Europe', 10 Nov. 1938.

4

NEW APPROACHES TO GERMANY

NEVILLE CHAMBERLAIN saw in the Munich Agreement of September 1938 an opportunity to pick up where he had left off in March. The proposal he had then made for colonial concessions to Germany in return for German agreement not to upset the European *status quo* by force had been dashed by the *Anschluss*.[1] Thereafter he regarded British policy towards Czechoslovakia as a means of returning to an atmosphere suited to the resumption of negotiations. On 16 April 1938, after the decision to take the initiative over the Sudeten question, he wrote: 'We can't do anything with Hitler just yet but we are trying to get the Czechs to face up to realities and settle their minority problem and if we should be successful it might presently be possible to start again in Berlin.'[2]

Now that the Sudeten problem had been solved, he persuaded Hitler to subscribe to his own desire for co-operation. The Anglo-German Declaration of 30 September 1938 spoke of their determination 'to continue our efforts to remove possible sources of differences and thus to contribute to the peace of Europe'.[3]

Chamberlain's conception of Anglo-German co-operation was based on the assumption that Hitler did not harbour aggressive designs, that any alteration in the European *status quo* would come about by negotiation and not by force, and that Hitler's ultimate aim was not the domination of Europe. As he had told the Cabinet on 24 September 1938, the crucial question was

whether Herr Hitler was speaking the truth when he said he regarded the Sudeten question as a racial question which must be settled, and that the object of his policy was racial unity and not the domination of Europe. The Prime Minister believed that Herr Hitler was speaking the truth.[4]

That did not mean, however, that Chamberlain contemplated

---

[1] See above, p. 30.
[2] Quoted in Middlemas, *Diplomacy of Illusion*, p. 213.
[3] Record of Chamberlain–Hitler Conversation, 30 Sept. 1938, *DBFP* ii, no. 1228, p. 640.
[4] Cab. Minutes, 24 Sept. 1938, CAB 23/95.

granting unilateral concessions to Germany as a means to achieve the desired *rapprochement*. In his view, 'appeasement' could come about only as the result of a process of bargaining in which both sides made concessions in the political and economic spheres. In particular Chamberlain wanted an arms-limitation agreement, an end to Germany's efforts to secure economic (and hence political) hegemony in central and south-eastern Europe, and an end to unfair German economic competition in world markets, especially the practice of subsidizing exports. He was prepared in return to consider colonial concessions to Germany and to take steps to ease her economic difficulties, especially the foreign-exchange shortage, by allowing tariff concessions on German exports to the British Empire. He also hinted at an Anglo-German alliance against communist expansion.

Already during the September crisis, and increasingly during October, Chamberlain indicated the sort of agreement he had in mind. On 27 September 1938 his personal and 'Chief Industrial' adviser, Sir Horace Wilson, told Hitler that the Prime Minister contemplated 'arrangements for improving the economic position all round', and that many people in Britain had noted that Hitler 'regarded England and Germany as bulwarks against destruction, particularly from the East'.[1] This latter hint was taken up towards the end of October by Sir Samuel Hoare, the Home Secretary, who informed the German Ambassador in London, Herbert von Dirksen, that 'after a further rapprochement between the four European Great Powers, the acceptance of certain defence obligations, or even a guarantee by them against Soviet Russia, was conceivable in the event of an attack by Soviet Russia'.[2]

Chamberlain expressed his desire for disarmament and economic agreement more emphatically. He discussed these questions with Hitler on 30 September 1938, the day after the Munich Conference. The latter refused to be drawn on Chamberlain's proposal to abolish bombing aircraft. When the discussion turned to German economic relations with south-eastern Europe, Chamberlain began by assuring Hitler that Britain did not mean to encircle Germany economically. He did, however, want an improvement in international trade: 'Yesterday's proceedings would certainly ease the political tension,

[1] Record of Wilson–Hitler Conversation, 27 Sept. 1938, *DBFP* ii, no. 1129, p. 565.
[2] Dirksen to German Foreign Ministry, 31 Oct. 1938, *DGFP* iv, no. 260.

but something more positive was required in the economic sphere and he would particularly like to see a relaxation in the restrictions on international trade which now existed.'[1] Hitler likewise refused to be drawn on this question. No doubt he understood that to liberalize Germany's trading methods meant to abandon her hold over south-eastern Europe, a corollary which the Foreign Office Economic Relations Section had pointed out in August 1936.[2] But what Hitler feared above all was a devaluation of the mark, which would upset prices and wages and hence the stability upon which his regime based its strength and support.[3]

For these reasons the Germans also failed to respond to a significant unofficial approach made by Sir Frederick Leith-Ross, Chief Economic Adviser to the British Government and head of the Inter-Departmental Committee on Central and South-Eastern Europe. On 18 October 1938 he spoke to members of a German trade delegation, on its way to Dublin, of economic co-operation between the European Great Powers. He wondered

whether it might not be possible for Great Britain, France, and Holland to allocate to Germany a larger total of foreign currency—he mentioned a figure of 25 percent more. The foreign currency thus made available could then be used by Germany to pay for her imports from the Balkan countries. These countries would then in turn be in a position to buy colonial produce, and world trade would thus receive a stimulus.[4]

This proposal must be seen in conjunction with the other measures, described in Chapter 2, designed to undermine Germany's growing economic and political influence in south-eastern Europe. It makes

[1] Record of Chamberlain–Hitler Conversation, 30 Sept. 1938, *DBFP* ii, no. 1228, p. 639.
[2] See above, pp. 37–8.
[3] When Funk replaced Schacht as President of the Reichsbank in January 1939, Hitler instructed him to pay special attention to 'the maintenance of the stability of prices and wages, and of the value of the mark'. The British Financial Attaché in Berlin, G. H. S. Pinsent, commented: 'It is no accident that the first point in Hitler's letter [to Funk] is the maintenance of the stability of prices and wages. (The maintenance of the value of the mark probably means no more than this.) This is one of the main pillars of the whole Nazi economic system, without which it could never have worked. Its failure would involve so many problems—economic, social and political—that it might bring the regime to grief' (Memorandum by Pinsent, 1 Feb. 1939, C2015/8/18 (FO 371/22950)).
[4] Memorandum of Conversation between Leith-Ross, Rüter, and von Süsskind, 18 Oct. 1938, *DGFP* iv, no. 257. Britain could 'allocate' a larger percentage of foreign exchange to Germany by revising the Anglo-German Payments Agreement in Germany's favour. See below, p. 82.

no sense to interpret it, as some historians have done, as a British attempt to buy peace by payment of tribute or Danegeld.[1] For an injection of convertible currency into the Balkan economies would reduce their dependence on Germany and allow them to look elsewhere for their imports. The fact that Leith-Ross spoke of European co-operation on the basis of the van Zeeland plan is further evidence that this was the British aim. The Belgian statesman van Zeeland had published his 'Report on the Removal of the Obstacles to International Trade' on 26 January 1938. The report's main objective, according to Frank Ashton-Gwatkin, head of the Foreign Office Economic Relations Section, was 'a reconstruction and freeing of the economic situation in Central and South Eastern Europe', an aim with which he sympathized.[2] It was Ashton-Gwatkin who repeated the Leith-Ross proposal when it failed to draw a German response.[3]

The same German delegates who received the Leith-Ross proposal also discussed trade liberalization at the Board of Trade on 17 and 18 October 1938. The Germans, in pursuit of higher foreign-exchange earnings, wanted tariff concessions in the British and Empire markets, and offered similar concessions in return. But the British representative objected that German tariff concessions were meaningless, since German imports were governed not by tariffs but by Government allocation of foreign exchange. He suggested that German reciprocity might take the form of an end to 'uneconomic competition in the United Kingdom and in third countries', in other words an end to German export subsidies.[4] The British were particularly interested in reaching agreement on coal exports. The British coal industry had suffered most from German competition and consequently from a very high rate of unemployment. A coal cartel seemed to offer a favourable prospect of increasing Britain's coal exports while maintaining Germany's foreign-exchange earnings.[5] These trade negotiations got off the ground successfully. Further meetings in November confirmed the two sides' desire to negotiate, and talks

[1] This is the tenor of Gilbert and Gott, *The Appeasers*, Chapter 11.
[2] Memorandum by Ashton-Gwatkin, 27 Oct. 1938, C14471/41/18 (FO 371/21659).
[3] Conversation between Wienke (Reichsbank) and Ashton-Gwatkin, 6 Nov. 1938, *DGFP* iv, no. 262.
[4] Notes of Informal Meetings on 17 Oct. 1938 at the Board of Trade, C96/8/18 (FO 371/22950).
[5] Board of Trade Memorandum, 'The Problem of the Coal Export Trade', 7 Nov. 1938, FO 433/5, ff. 193-4.

were arranged between the Federation of British Industries and its German counterpart, the Reichsgruppe Industrie.[1]

Chamberlain's desire for disarmament did not fare so well. An important reason for this was that Hitler's superiority gave him no incentive for agreement, even though Britain intensified her rearmament efforts after Munich. Sir Alexander Cadogan, Permanent Under-Secretary at the Foreign Office, wrote soon after the crisis with regard to future policy that 'rearmament is a vitally necessary first step', without which 'it is difficult to have or to pursue a foreign policy'.[2] The British Government and their advisers were unanimous in their agreement with this judgement. The object was not only to remedy the weak situation in which Britain had found herself during the September crisis but also to provide a basis for negotiating with Germany from strength and to ensure a bargaining counter in disarmament talks. Chamberlain always believed that rearmament was essential to conduct a successful foreign policy, reading especially from the experience and admonitions of the nineteenth-century Foreign Secretary and Prime Minister, George Canning. On the other hand he was continually haunted by the expense. His remarks to the Cabinet on 3 October 1938 indicate his frame of mind:

> Ever since he had been Chancellor of the Exchequer he had been oppressed with the sense that the burden of armaments might break our backs. This had been one of the factors which had led him to the view that it was necessary to try and resolve the causes which were responsible for the armament race. He thought that we were now in a more hopeful position and that the contacts which had been established with the Dictator Powers opened up the possibility that we might be able to reach some agreement which would stop the armament race. It was clear, however, that it would be madness to stop rearming until we were convinced that other countries would act in the same way. For the time being, therefore, we should relax no particle of our effort until our deficiencies had been made good.[3]

So intensely did Chamberlain feel the necessity for mutual disarmament that he hinted at colonial concessions in return for German co-operation. On or about 11 October 1938 his Press Secretary, George Steward, told Dr. Fritz Hesse, the London representative of

---

[1] Notes of Meetings held on 8 and 9 Nov. 1938 to discuss German requests, C96/8/18 (FO 371/22950).
[2] Memorandum by Cadogan, 14 Oct. 1938, C14471/41/18 (FO 371/21659).
[3] Cab. Minutes, 3 Oct. 1938, CAB 23/95.

the Dienststelle Ribbentrop,[1] that the colonial question 'could only be solved parallel with the disarmament question and that the latter would have to have priority'.[2] But there was no response. As Baron Weizsäcker, State Secretary in the German Foreign Ministry, wrote to Dirksen on 17 October, 'things are moving rapidly but not in the direction of a German-British *rapprochement* at present'.[3]

The lack of German response confirmed the British in their desire to intensify the rearmament programme. Their efforts have been criticized as half-hearted, which they were in the sense that the Government did not make an all-out attempt to prepare for war with Germany. This would have involved conscription, a full-scale army expeditionary force, a Ministry of Supply to co-ordinate service requirements, the immediate adoption of the full two-power naval standard, and further measures to adapt industry to wartime production. The Conservative Opposition called for such measures, and Halifax favoured some of them. But Chamberlain was reluctant to give Hitler, not to mention the left-wing opposition, too obvious an opportunity to play on the contradiction between peaceful words and warlike preparations. Therefore he made every effort to present new measures in a defensive and non-expansionary light, which too many historians have taken at face value. In particular the belief that the Government allowed only acceleration, not expansion, and defensive rather than offensive measures, does not bear examination.[4]

The most important new measures were approved for the air force. On 7 November 1938 the Secretary of State for Air, Sir Kingsley Wood, proposed to the Cabinet an expansionary programme which came to be known as Scheme M. He recalled that under Scheme L, authorized in April 1938, the Air Ministry had ordered 12,000 aircraft for April 1940. He now revealed that in order to maintain the momentum 5,500 additional aircraft had been ordered, with Treasury sanction, for delivery after that date. In addition to this, he now proposed to work to a programme of

[1] Ribbentrop, German Foreign Minister since March 1938, had persuaded Hitler in 1933 that political reporting from abroad should not be left to Foreign Ministry diplomats. He established the Dienststelle Ribbentrop with Party funds as an unofficial rival of the Foreign Ministry, which it faced on the Wilhelmstrasse. According to Alan Bullock, 'it was staffed by journalists, business men out of a job, and by those members of the Party who were eager for a diplomatic career' (A. Bullock, *Hitler: A Study in Tyranny* (London, 1952), p. 322).
[2] Memorandum by Hesse, 11 Oct. 1938, *DGFP* iv, no. 251.
[3] Weizsäcker to Dirksen, 17 Oct. 1938, ibid., no. 253.
[4] Cf. Middlemas, *Diplomacy of Illusion*, p. 421.

3,700 fighters, 3,500 heavy bombers, and 4,800 other types. He wanted to order half of the total in each category immediately and to provide the necessary productive capacity for the rest.[1] As a result, Britain was to enjoy a front-line strength of 1,300 exclusively heavy bombers, 800 modern fighters, and 389 other types together with an increase in overseas air strength of about 30 per cent by the spring of 1942. The ratio of fighters to bombers was increased slightly, and priority in production and pilot training was given to fighter strength.

TABLE 2

Type	Top speed (m.p.h.)	Bomb load (lb.)	At cruising speed (m.p.h.)	Range (miles)
Stirling (G.B.)	327	10,000	280	2,000
Halifax (G.B.)	332	8,000	275	2,000
Manchester (G.B.)	320	7,520	280	2,000
Junkers 88 (G.)	286	5,510	—	1,553
Heinckel 111 (G.)	264	4,410	230	760
Dornier 17 (G.)	263	2,200	236	745

Sources: CP 218 (38); Peter Lewis, *The British Bomber since 1914* (London, 1967); William Green, *Famous Bombers of the Second World War* (New York, 1959); Kenneth Munson, *Bombers 1919–39* (London, 1970).

But the scheme also emphasized replacement of the medium bomber by the heavy bomber, which meant quite simply an expansion of offensive capacity in terms of bomb tonnage. It meant, as the figures in Table 2 show, that British bomb capacity would equal German capacity with about half the number of aircraft, and at longer range. As far as the Air Ministry knew, the Germans had no plans to develop the heavy bomber, 'a fact which underlies the need for preserving the utmost secrecy as to our own intentions'. Chamberlain and Sir John Simon were uncertain about this policy, mainly because of the expense and the difficulty of justifying it as defensive. They agreed to it nevertheless, and the ideal of superiority once more became a practical goal. In the words of the official historians: 'the Cabinet decided in favour of the heavy-bomber policy so that there might eventually come into being a striking force equal or even superior to that of Germany'.[2] As Chamberlain himself explained

[1] Cab. Memorandum: 'Relative Air Strengths and Proposals for the Improvement of this Country's Position', 25 Oct. 1938, CP 218 (38), CAB 24/279.
[2] Webster and Frankland, *The Strategic Air Offensive Against Germany*, i. 81. Hitler responded by ordering a fivefold increase in the expansion of the Luftwaffe, although this 'presupposed such astronomically high expenditures and

to Daladier, the French Prime Minister, on 24 November 1938, 'though His Majesty's Government had not said so, they were in fact increasing their bombing force in the same measure as their fighting force. Indeed, it was possible that they might presently increase the emphasis on the bombing side of their programme.'[1] In public the Government were able to say in truth that defensive rearmament was being accelerated, but omitted to say that both offensive and defensive capacity were being expanded.[2]

Expansion was not confined to the air force. On 7 November the Cabinet approved additional spending on the navy, and a review undertaken between November 1938 and February 1939 resulted in approval by the Committee of Imperial Defence of a new naval standard, which in August 1939 became the full two-power standard.[3] Army policy remained the same, however, and although the War Office intensified its demand for a full continental expeditionary force, the Cabinet abandoned the doctrine of 'limited liability' only in February 1939 under the pressure of the threat to the Low Countries.[4] Chamberlain apparently still thought of an expanded air force as a substitute for the army.

Most historians have given us the impression that Chamberlain's desire for *rapprochement* with Germany was not shared by the Foreign Office after Munich. This was of course true of some of its members. These included Sir Robert Vansittart, formerly Permanent Under-Secretary, and since January 1938 Chief Diplomatic Adviser to a Government that never called on his advice; Sir Lancelot Oliphant, Deputy Under-Secretary superintending the Eastern, Northern, and Egyptian Departments; Sir Orme Sargent, Assistant Under-Secretary superintending the Central and Southern Departments; Oliver Harvey, Halifax's Private Secretary inherited from

such generous allocations of raw materials that it was patently impossible to carry out' (Richard Suchenwirth, *The Development of the German Air Force, 1919–1939*, ed. Harry R. Fletcher, U.S.A.F. Historical Studies: no. 160 (New York, 1970), p. 83). Nevertheless, total output of aircraft rose by 60 per cent in 1939 (Burton Klein, *Germany's Economic Preparations for War* (Cambridge, Mass., 1959), p. 19).

[1] Record of Anglo-French Conversations, 24 Nov. 1938, *DBFP* iii, no. 325.

[2] Radar, or 'R.D.F.' as it was then known, was admittedly one defensive measure with absolute priority. By the spring of 1939 the early-warning system covered the approaches to the south-east of England, and was soon extended along the east and south coasts.

[3] Middlemas, *Diplomacy of Illusion*, p. 423.

[4] See below, p. 78.

Eden; Sir Reginald Leeper, head of the News Department;[1] and Laurence Collier, head of the Northern Department.

Perhaps more numerous, and certainly more influential, were those who did support Chamberlain's efforts. Sir George Mounsey, Assistant Under-Secretary superintending the Far Eastern, Western (General), and Treaty Departments, was one of these, and he resented the impression that was gaining currency that the Foreign Office opposed Chamberlain's policy. When Harold Nicolson, a former member of the Foreign Office and now a National Labour Member of Parliament, was reported in the press to have said in a speech at Manchester on 1 October 1938 that Chamberlain had been guided throughout the Czechoslovak crisis by Sir Horace Wilson ('whose advice was never inconvenient') rather than by Vansittart ('who was always right, but whose advice the Government found inconvenient'),[2] Mounsey objected that the functions of the Foreign Office were not only to advise the Government but also to execute policy 'whether it likes it or not'. 'To those of us here,' he continued, 'and there are others beside myself, who feel convinced that the policy of the Government is the right one, it is very disquieting to read such a statement of the case.'[3]

Among those who did support Chamberlain's policy were Sir Alexander Cadogan, Permanent Under-Secretary since January 1938; his Private Secretary, Gladwyn Jebb, inherited from Vansittart; Frank Ashton-Gwatkin, head of the Economic Relations Section; and William Strang, head of the Central Department, together with most of Strang's junior staff.

---

[1] Professor T. Desmond Williams is inclined to see Leeper at the centre of a Foreign Office conspiracy to feed the British press with exaggerated and alarming reports and rumours, particularly in May 1938 and March 1939 (T. Desmond Williams, 'The Historiography of World War II', in E. M. Robertson, ed., *The Origins of the Second World War* (London, 1971)). In the informative but apparently much censored collection of Private Office Papers, which deal with the internal affairs of the Foreign Office, there is the following reference to Leeper by Cadogan: 'Since [Eden's] departure (and before) I have had constant complaints from No. 10 of the handling of the Press by our News Department. Blame has been particularly attached to Leeper, not, I am bound to confess, without some reason. But he has been in a difficult position; I think he has tried to do his best: if he has failed, I attribute it to no base motives. I have got him off the Press work, and put him on to Propaganda' (Cadogan to Halifax, 28 Nov. 1938 (FO 800/396)).

[2] *The Times*, 3 Oct. 1938, p. 19.

[3] Mounsey to Cadogan, 2 Oct. 1938 (FO 800/396). In fact Nicolson expunged the offending words from his speech, but it had already been released to the press (Harold Nicolson, *Diaries and Letters 1930–1939* (London, 1966), pp. 373–4).

The views of some of these coincided remarkably closely with Chamberlain's and no doubt informed them. On 1 November 1938 Chamberlain told the House of Commons that he regarded the Munich Agreement and the Anglo-German Declaration as concrete achievements which should be 'properly and suitably followed up'.[1] Referring to this statement in a memorandum on 'The Future Course of Negotiations with Germany', William Strang asked himself 'along what lines this further effort at international appeasement should be conducted, and in particular what further grievances on the part of Germany remain to be redressed and what further revision of the peace treaty settlement with Germany is required to promote this end'.[2] During the course of the negotiations on the Sudeten question Hitler had personally assured Chamberlain that the Sudetenland was his last territorial ambition in Europe. If this assurance was to be believed, wrote Strang, then there would be little point in raising with Germany the question of further concessions. The question should be raised only if Hitler's intentions were thought to be aggressive. After an exhaustive tour of the German horizon, Strang concluded that it would in fact be wise to take Hitler at his word, and

that it would be a mistake for us to throw any part of that settlement [of Versailles] into the melting-pot in present circumstances. Germany will no doubt try to obtain modifications of the existing situation at Memel and Danzig, and even perhaps in respect of the Polish frontier, by direct action vis-à-vis the countries concerned. But for the present none of these questions appear to hold within themselves any imminent threat of war; and in this they differ from the situation which has faced us in Czechoslovakia during recent months.[3]

Although Strang recognized the possibility of a German-Polish conflict, he thought it very remote. Since the German-Polish Declaration of Non-Aggression in 1934, after all, 'Poland has moved appreciably into the German orbit'. Nevertheless the existence of the Franco-Polish Treaty of 1921 worried Strang, since it meant 'the possibility of our being drawn into a war as a result of action by France'.

If the policy of pre-empting German demands in Europe was to be rejected, what remained as a basis for future agreement with Germany? He concluded that negotiations should be picked up where

[1] 340 HC Deb., 5 s., col. 88.
[2] Memorandum by Strang, n.d., C14471/41/18 (FO 371/21659).
[3] Ibid.

they had been left off in March 1938, i.e. with Chamberlain's proposal for a colonial settlement based on German participation in the administration of a central-African belt, although 'there is little reason to believe that it would appeal to them'. Furthermore there had to be a *quid pro quo*. Hitler must give a formal assurance that 'the last of his territorial aims had been satisfied'; he must agree to disarmament; and lastly, 'Germany might well be asked to relax the regime of autarky and self-sufficiency which at present governs her economic policy'. There were to be no unilateral British concessions based on the hope that Germany would behave herself in future.

Cadogan's Private Secretary, Gladwyn Jebb, produced a draft policy summary based on Strang's and other papers.[1] He outlined four possible alternative policies for Britain to follow after Munich. First, there was 'collective security', by which he meant resistance to Germany, Italy, and Japan, in alliance with France and Russia. The trouble with this was that it would 'provoke a war in which defeat would be disastrous and victory hardly less so', since whatever the outcome it would 'place the whole of Europe at the mercy of Russia'. The second alternative was the policy of 'staying-put', which would mean no unilateral concessions to Germany but continued efforts to come to terms with Italy:

> Thus, we would leave the Germans to raise the question of colonies, and if they did so, take up the line that we could not discuss this question unless provided with a statement of the counterconcessions which the Germans would be prepared to make.

At the same time Britain would cement her relations with Greece and Turkey while countering German influence in the Balkans by economic means, so as to 'restrict the expansion of Germany to certain limited areas in Central and South Eastern Europe'.

The third possible policy was to press France to denounce the Franco-Soviet Pact (and presumably, though he did not say so, also the Franco-Polish Treaty) and to do nothing to maintain British influence north of Greece, thereby tacitly encouraging German expansion eastwards. Jebb conceded that this policy 'is reminiscent of Machiavelli, but should not perhaps be dismissed for that reason alone. If a real "Balance of Power" in Europe is desired, it would probably represent the best means of attaining it.' What Jebb

---

[1] Memorandum by Jebb, n.d., C14471/41/18 (FO 371/21659). Middlemas incorrectly attributes the authorship of this document to Strang and Cadogan jointly (Middlemas, *Diplomacy of Illusion*, p. 431).

presumably meant by this was that encouragement of Germany's expansion eastwards would bring her face to face with the Soviet Union in a confrontation which did not have to result in war to increase the security of the Western Powers. The problem was that to most of his colleagues this would seem to over-estimate the political reliability and the strength of Russia on the one hand, and to underrate the potential danger to the West of a predominant Germany on the other. In addition there was a moral undercurrent to British thinking, which Jebb acknowledged in his reference to Machiavelli.

The fourth possibility was for Britain to adopt the policy commonly referred to by Foreign Office officials as 'riding the tiger'. This 'would consist essentially in an attempt to come to even better and more permanent terms with Germany by what would in effect be unilateral concessions by us'. Even in this case only colonial concessions were contemplated, but they would not be made contingent on German counter-concessions. Britain would simply 'hand over the colonies and hope for the best'.

Jebb concluded that the decision as to which policy to adopt would depend on what further efforts in rearmament the Government were prepared to make. For example the policy of 'collective security' would 'necessitate our being armed to the teeth', whereas if no more rearmament was allowed, then Britain would probably have to fall back on the policy of 'riding the tiger'. Jebb preferred either of the two less extreme policies, and conceded that British policy 'must in any case be flexible and hence to some extent opportunist'.

He listed eight concrete proposals: (1) ratification of the Anglo-Italian Agreement;[1] (2) discussion between Chamberlain, Halifax, and the French Government on the best way to approach Germany; (3) announcement of further rearmament; (4) invitation to Göring to discuss a general agreement on arms limitation and trade liberalization, leaving him to raise the question of colonies; (5) agreement with France, Belgium, and Portugal on a collective colonial offer to be made 'in the event—but only in the event—of the Germans agreeing to satisfactory arms limitation (and some gradual liberation of the exchanges)'; (6) pressure on France to denounce the Franco-Soviet Pact; (7) announcement of Britain's intention not to encircle Germany economically and hence 'the taking of no *exceptional* measures to increase our trade with the Balkan States,

[1] See below, p. 73.

other than Greece and Turkey'; (8) final abandonment of partition in Palestine, so as to retain Arab loyalty.[1]

Cadogan agreed with Jebb's analysis of the four alternative policies and also with his conclusions. In his own summing up, he urged that Munich should be followed up with 'a frank discussion with a view to a settlement'. He agreed that a colonial offer should be considered, in return for disarmament, economic liberalization, and 'undertakings concerning stabilisation of frontiers'. Germany should be approached either direct or through a Four-Power conference, but in any event nothing should be done without French consent.[2]

The proposals that emerged from the Foreign Office were thus no different essentially from those made before March 1938. Although Foreign Office officials were unwilling to risk a Churchillian 'Grand Alliance', they were equally unwilling to adopt a policy of unilateral concessions to Germany in the hope that Germany would thereby be pacified. If there were to be concessions, they must be outside Europe (and not solely at Britain's expense) and must be accompanied by tangible German counter-concessions, namely, agreement to respect European frontiers, disarmament, and economic liberalization.

Where, then, was the difference between the 'hard-liners', such as Vansittart, and the rest? The difference lay essentially in their respective estimates of Hitler's intentions. Vansittart, Collier, Leeper, and others believed that Hitler was now in a position to obtain his aims by force and that he had no intention of allowing himself to be tied down to his purely tactical assurance that he had no further territorial ambitions in Europe. As Vansittart wrote, 'It is quite certain that the active elements in the Nazi Party, and they have become far more influential since Munich, are entirely opposed to any genuine "settlement" with this country and France. They are not in any real mood to bargain even about colonies.'[3]

On the other hand, those who controlled British foreign policy, namely Chamberlain, Halifax, and their chosen advisers, believed that Hitler should be taken at his word when he spoke of no further territorial ambitions, and that therefore European pacification on mutually acceptable terms was possible.

[1] Memorandum by Jebb, n.d.
[2] Memorandum by Cadogan, 8 Nov. 1938, C14471/41/18 (FO 371/21659).
[3] Quoted in Middlemas, *Diplomacy of Illusion*, p. 432.

During November doubts arose in the minds of those who wanted to believe in Hitler's good intentions, and Halifax in particular was perturbed. The Foreign Secretary's support of Chamberlain's policy of *rapprochement* with Germany is usually explained in terms of his 'sweet and Christian nature'.[1] (Hitler caricatured him as 'Christ's brother'.)[2] Halifax was a High Church Anglican, whose father had championed the cause of reunion with Rome, and there is no doubt that he took his religion very seriously.[3] But Halifax did not have the nonconformist conscience, and he was by no means a pacifist. In 1916 he regarded conscientious objectors 'with unmitigated contempt'.[4] In 1937 he attempted to shake Britain out of her pacifist stupor in an influential address to the congregation of St. Martin's-in-the-Fields.[5] He managed to justify the use of force in the best crusading tradition:

The pursuit of peace under all conceivable conditions might mean the acceptance of greater evils even than war, conducted with all the devilish resources of the twentieth century, and might therefore in itself be more reprehensible than war seriously and solemnly undertaken in defence of vital principles that would be denied and betrayed by a refusal to break the peace.[6]

Furthermore Halifax had what has been called a 'hard streak of Yorkshire ruthlessness' in him,[7] which enabled him as a Member of Parliament to write to his father in 1918:

I am dreadfully afraid of events turning out in a sense to let the Germans off, and it goes much against the grain not to burn some of their towns etc. But the great thing—in spite of Wilson—is to humiliate the German power beyond possibility of understanding.[8]

---

[1] Harold Macmillan, quoted in Correlli Barnett, *The Collapse of British Power*, p. 65.
[2] A. J. P. Taylor, *Beaverbrook* (London, 1972), p. 379.
[3] On at least two Good Fridays in his life he attended a three-hour Church service in spite of a diplomatic crisis. The first occasion was in 1939 when Mussolini annexed Albania (David Dilks, ed., *The Diaries of Sir Alexander Cadogan, O.M., 1938-1945* (London, 1971), 7 Apr. 1939, p. 170). The second was during the war, when he was Ambassador in Washington (Birkenhead, *Halifax*, p. 483).
[4] Ibid., p. 112.
[5] Halifax had been invited to speak by the pastor, Pat McCormick, successor to the arch-pacifist Dick Sheppard. His address from the pulpit was broadcast, and sold very well as a pamphlet (Alan Campbell Johnson, *Viscount Halifax* (New York, 1941), pp. 423-4).
[6] Quoted ibid., p. 423. [7] Birkenhead, *Halifax*, p. 299.
[8] Quoted ibid., p. 112.

This same ruthlessness allowed him, as Viceroy of India, to 'sign death warrants without remorse and without losing a moment's sleep'.[1]

But age, responsibility, and his experience in India, where he managed to placate the nationalists, at least for a while, strengthened his belief in the force of reason, and it was this that led him to an identity of views with Chamberlain. As he said in the summer of 1936, 'we want to build a partnership in European society in which Germany can freely join with us and play the part of Good Europeans for European welfare'.[2]

He was both fascinated and repelled by the Nazis. On his visit to Germany in 1937 he compared Göring to a 'modern Robin Hood: producing on me a composite impression of film-star, gangster, great landowner interested in his property, Prime Minister, party-manager, head gamekeeper at Chatsworth'.[3] On the other hand he could not dismiss the thought that Göring had been responsible for so much butchery during the 'Night of the Long Knives' in 1934.

As Foreign Secretary, Halifax subordinated his personal feelings to his loyalty to Chamberlain and to the need for a dispassionate outlook. But his dislike of the Nazi regime grew. He first openly disagreed with Chamberlain on 25 September 1938, in circumstances which are now familiar. Chamberlain had just returned from Godesberg where he had listened with incredulity to Hitler's latest terms for the annexation of the Sudetenland. Chamberlain proposed nevertheless to keep up the pressure on Czechoslovakia, but Halifax, on Cadogan's advice and after a sleepless night, explained to the Cabinet that he 'felt some uncertainty about the ultimate end which he wished to see accomplished, namely, the destruction of Nazi-ism. So long as Nazi-ism lasted, peace would be uncertain. For this reason he did not feel that it would be right to put pressure on Czechoslovakia to accept.'[4]

The peaceful outcome of the crisis gave him only momentary hope. He thought Munich 'a horrid business and humiliating ... but yet better than a European war'.[5] Although he did not openly dissociate himself from Chamberlain's policy he devoted himself

---

[1] Birkenhead, *Halifax*, p. 263.   [2] Quoted in Johnson, *Viscount Halifax*, p. 400.
[3] Quoted in Birkenhead, *Halifax*, p. 372.
[4] Cab. Minutes, 25 Sept. 1938, CAB 23/95.
[5] John Harvey, ed., *The Diplomatic Diaries of Oliver Harvey, 1937–40* (London, 1970), 1 Oct. 1938, p. 208.

NEW APPROACHES TO GERMANY 69

increasingly to furthering the Foreign Office policy of keeping Britain's options open. His Private Secretary, Oliver Harvey, summed up the change in February 1939:

H. now sees his way much more clearly; he has mastered his subject and speaks and acts with greater confidence and boldness. We may have trouble with the P.M. before long! H. . . . is carrying out his own line more and more. . . . He is almost unrecognisable from the H. of a year ago. He says bluntly 'no more Munich for me'.[1]

Halifax was responsive to Harvey's continual emphasis on the need for 'keeping our issue with the Nazis on the moral plane',[2] and he came to view the Nazis as a threat to Christian civilization, evidenced by the persecution in Germany not only of the Jews but also of the Christian Churches. Thus in the last resort Halifax was ready

to take up without quibble or mental reservation the supreme challenge of Nazism to the spiritual and moral integrity of mankind. Halifax's nature and experience were such that the only war supportable to him was a Holy War. If diplomacy could not teach Hitler to keep the peace, Halifax . . . [would find] the inner assurance he needed that the resultant war would in fact be a crusade.[3]

But the time had not yet come.

On 14 November 1938 the Foreign Secretary called a meeting of the Foreign Policy Committee. He had come to the conclusion that 'no useful purpose would be served by a resumption at the present time of the contemplated Anglo-German conversations'.[4] Secret information reaching the Foreign Office indicated that Hitler regarded the Munich Agreement as a disaster rather than a triumph, since it had prevented a show of German military strength. The September crisis had eroded Hitler's popularity in Germany, and the German people had credited Chamberlain with the prevention of a war that Hitler had been prepared to risk. Hitler was now apparently listening to extremists like Ribbentrop, the Foreign Minister, who believed that England would in fact never venture to go to war. Hitler therefore believed that he could pursue aggressive aims with impunity. Above all he now regarded Britain as his prime enemy. His intentions were summarized as follows:

(i) Going back on what was laid down in 'Mein Kampf' regarding the

[1] Ibid., 17 Feb. 1939, p. 255.
[2] Ibid., Harvey to Halifax, 8 Jan. 1939, p. 430.
[3] Johnson, *Viscount Halifax*, p. 520.
[4] FPC Minutes, 14 Nov. 1938, CAB 27/624.

desirability of friendship with England, Hitler now aims at the disintegration of the British Empire.
>   (ii) The methods by which he proposes to work towards this end are
>   (a) to break the Anglo-French Alliance by cultivating friendship with France.
>   (b) to maintain pressure against the British Empire in Spain and in the Far East through Italy and Japan. The Berlin–Rome–Tokio combination to be worked for all it is worth in order to reach a dominating position.
>   (c) to embarrass England by aggravating her difficulties in the Near East.
>
> (iii) There is to be no immediate open demand for Colonies in the near future since it is considered that when the time is ripe the Colonies will fall into Hitler's lap.
>
> (iv) Meanwhile Hitler will concentrate on extending and consolidating his position in South Eastern Europe.
>
> (v) Since the Naval Agreement with England automatically comes to an end in two years' time and as the Germans are still behind in their naval construction programme as defined in this Treaty, they have no immediate reason for raising the question of naval rearmament and of violating the Naval Treaty.
>
> (vi) German propaganda will represent all British measures for rearmament as directed primarily against the German people and under this excuse Hitler himself will press on his own armament to the limit.[1]

How far did this report correspond with reality? We know that Ribbentrop was stirring up the colonial question at this time, and that he was exerting pressure on Hitler.[2] However, Hitler was more preoccupied with the East. In mid-October he had said that 'the colonial question is to be handled with restraint until further notice'.[3] Thus although contingency plans for war with Britain were made in November by both the General Staff[4] and the Naval Staff,[5] Hitler planned to settle the outstanding questions in the East before turning his attention westwards, if he ever planned to do anything more than raise the colonial question.

Halifax wanted a compulsory National Register of wartime occupations and increased aircraft production, so as to help correct 'the false impression that we were decadent, spineless and could with

[1] FPC Minutes, 14 Nov. 1938, CAB 27/624.
[2] Klaus Hildebrand, *Vom Reich zum Weltreich. Hitler, NSDAP und Kolonial Frage 1919–1945* (Munich, 1969), p. 591. [3] Ibid., p. 583.
[4] Notes for Wehrmacht Discussions with Italy, 26 Nov. 1938, *DGFP* iv, no. 411. [5] Hildebrand, *Vom Reich zum Weltreich*, p. 592.

impunity be kicked about'.[1] Chamberlain, while he did not believe that Hitler 'contemplated any immediate aggressive action', was disappointed by the way in which Anglo-German relations had developed since Munich, and wanted 'a counter policy against German policy' together with 'the acceleration of our defence measures'. He proposed a visit to Rome, in order to give Mussolini 'greater freedom for manœuvre' and a chance to escape from Germany's clutches.

Perhaps just as significant as these secret reports about Hitler's anti-British attitude was the intensification of anti-Jewish measures in Germany at this time. On 7 November 1938 Herschel Grynszpan, a Polish Jew, murdered Ernst vom Rath, Third Secretary at the German Embassy in Paris. This gave the German extremists a pretext for widespread anti-Jewish rioting. On 12 November the German Government imposed a collective fine on the Jewish community, confiscated their insurance claims, and excluded them from economic and cultural activities. Although there is little reference to these excesses in the British Cabinet minutes, they were widely reported in Britain and affected public opinion deeply. According to Cadogan, writing much later, 'Hitler's open atrocities against the Jews in the autumn of 1938 certainly deeply impressed Chamberlain. . . . And of course Halifax was no less shocked.'[2] The German Ambassador in London, Herbert von Dirksen, reported 'pessimism among the most active supporters of Anglo-German friendship and a deterioration in Chamberlain's position, concluding that,

As long as this mood prevails, it will be impossible for Chamberlain to consider carrying out his plan of attempting a settlement with Germany on a broad basis. It remains to be seen whether, in addition to this, Chamberlain himself has changed his mind, as is asserted in well-informed circles.[3]

If Chamberlain had his doubts, he had not yet in fact abandoned his desire for *rapprochement* with Germany. But there was a change in emphasis, a new note of impatience. On 11 December 1938 he wrote that he was worried by the anti-British tone of the German press,

and the failure of Hitler to make the slightest gesture of friendliness. Unless this strong and virile people can be induced in partnership with

[1] FPC Minutes, 14 Nov. 1938, CAB 27/624.
[2] Quoted in Dilks, ed., *Cadogan Diaries*, p. 132.
[3] Dirksen to German Foreign Ministry, 17 Nov. 1938, *DGFP* iv, no. 269.

others to improve the general lot, there will be neither peace nor progress in Europe in the things that make life worth living . . . it takes two to make an agreement. . . . I am still waiting for a sign from those who speak for the German people . . . it would be a tragic blunder to mistake our love of peace and our faculty for compromise, for weakness.[1]

Chamberlain's misgivings were perhaps partly due to the continuing erosion of his Government's popularity. During October and November 1938 the Government suffered repeatedly at by-elections, fought largely on foreign-policy issues. They lost two seats and a large percentage of their majority elsewhere. The results have prompted one historian to conclude that 'it is in the two months after Munich that we are to find the key to the "sudden" change of opinion in March 1939'.[2] This is an exaggeration. As Dirksen pointed out in his report, 'experience has shown that trends, such as are to be seen in British public opinion at present, recede again after a very short time'.[3] His opinion seems to have been borne out on 21 December when the Duchess of Atholl lost an election at Kinross and West Perthshire, fought specifically on the issue of her opposition to Chamberlain's foreign policy. Nevertheless Chamberlain's comments to David Margesson, his Chief Whip, indicate his underlying uneasiness: 'I need hardly say that I was overjoyed at the result of the Perth Election which was far better than I had ventured to hope. It was a grand wind-up to a very difficult session.'[4]

During November and December the British Government were apparently uneasy about France. On 24 November 1938 Chamberlain and Halifax held wide-ranging talks in Paris with the French Prime Minister, Édouard Daladier, and the Foreign Minister, Georges Bonnet. Chamberlain regarded these talks as 'a means for renewing and strengthening mutual confidence'.[5] The British felt this need because they were suspicious about the Franco-German negotiations, in progress since October, for an agreement along the lines of the Anglo-German Declaration of 30 September 1938. Although Chamberlain told the Cabinet on 22 November that 'he had been assured that France was not proposing to sign a non-

[1] Quoted in Middlemas, *Diplomacy of Illusion*, p. 437.
[2] Roger Eatwell, 'Munich, Public Opinion, and Popular Front', *Journal of Contemporary History*, 6, no. 4 (1971), 122–39.
[3] *DGFP* iv, no. 269.
[4] Chamberlain to Margesson, 23 Dec. 1938, Viscount Margesson Papers, 1/3, Churchill College, Cambridge.
[5] Record of Anglo-French Conversations, 24 Nov. 1938, *DBFP* iii, no. 325.

aggression pact with Germany that would rule out help to this country',[1] he asked Daladier in Paris to confirm that France would help Britain in case of a German attack. Daladier gave his assurance, and Chamberlain seems to have been mollified by the terms of the Franco-German Declaration which were read out to him. He was less confident about French capacity to back up this promise. He urged them to intensify their efforts in air rearmament, to which Daladier retorted that he expected Britain to provide more than a two-division army expeditionary force. The two sides agreed to revive the Staff talks begun at a low level in March 1938. Still the British suspicion lingered on that the French might agree to a separate deal with Germany, especially in view of Daladier's reproachful attitude towards the doctrine of 'limited liability'. As Halifax told the Committee of Imperial Defence on 15 December 1938, 'a time might come when the French would cease to be enthusiastic about their relations with Great Britain if they were left with the impression that it was they who must bear the brunt of the fighting and slaughter on land'.[2]

Both Chamberlain and those Foreign Office advisers to whom he listened believed in the necessity of an approach to Italy. The Anglo-Italian Agreement of 13 April 1938, which gave Italy *de jure* recognition of her conquest of Abyssinia, and Britain a guarantee of the *status quo* in the Mediterranean area, awaited ratification. The British condition for ratification was a reduction of the Italian presence in Spain. In late October 1938 Mussolini proposed to withdraw 10,000 troops (actually under half the total), and on 2 November the Anglo-Italian Agreement was accordingly ratified. On 14 November the Cabinet Foreign Policy Committee endorsed Chamberlain's visit to Rome, planned for early January.

But in the meantime Franco-Italian relations worsened. On 1 December Deputies in the Italian Chamber staged an aggressive demand for French possessions, shouting 'Tunis, Djibouti, Corsica, Nice!'[3] The French suspected that this demonstration had been officially inspired, and in view of the terms of the Anglo-Italian

[1] Cab. Minutes, 22 Nov. 1938, CAB 23/96.
[2] Quoted in Howard, *The Continental Commitment*, p. 126.
[3] Lord Perth, the British Ambassador in Rome, reported that these cries 'were not distinguishable from the Diplomatic Gallery where I was seated' (Perth to Halifax, 30 Nov. 1938, *DBFP* iii, no. 461). On the other hand the German Ambassador seems to have heard them well enough (Mackensen to German Foreign Ministry, 1 Dec. 1938, *DGFP* iv, no. 412).

Agreement, the British were no less alarmed. Chamberlain threatened to cancel his visit to Rome, but Lord Perth, the British Ambassador, advised against such a drastic step.[1]

On 21 December Chamberlain told the Cabinet that he intended to 'make it plain that we could not support Italian claims to French territory'. He hoped to accomplish an end to the Spanish Civil War and to persuade Mussolini to 'prevent Herr Hitler from carrying out "some mad dog act" '.[2]

In fact the Rome visit achieved nothing except to confirm Italy's alignment with Germany. Mussolini maintained an aggressive stance *vis-à-vis* France, and assured Chamberlain of Hitler's peaceful intentions. Chamberlain, prompted by Cadogan,[3] was forced to warn Mussolini that 'the British position with regard to France was just like that which existed between Italy and Germany', and that 'it would be a terrible tragedy if aggressive action were taken under a misapprehension as to what lengths the democracies might be prepared to go'.[4]

The British Government had every reason to be concerned about German intentions. On 12 December 1938 Dirksen informed Cadogan that Germany intended to exercise her right under the Anglo-German Naval Treaty of 1935 to build submarines up to the full 100 per cent of British Empire tonnage.[5] On 15 December a member of the Berlin Embassy staff, Ivone Kirkpatrick, returned to London for Foreign Office duty with the news that Hitler was planning a surprise air attack on London.[6] Although his source never confirmed that Hitler had decided to act, the threat was taken seriously and gave rise to intensive preparations in London. All departments were instructed to ensure that war plans were ready before the end of March 1939.[7]

Chamberlain's confidence reached a low point. He took the apparently unprecedented step of asking the Foreign Office to draft a speech for him,[8] and Halifax's Private Secretary, Oliver

---

[1] Cadogan to Perth, 12 Dec. 1938, *DBFP* iii, no. 475; Perth to Halifax, 15 Dec. 1938, ibid., no. 477.
[2] Cab. Minutes, 21 Dec. 1938, CAB 23/96.
[3] Dilkes, ed., *Cadogan Diaries*, 12 Jan. 1939, p. 137.
[4] Record of Anglo-Italian Conversations, 11–14 Jan. 1939, *DBFP* iii, no. 500.
[5] Dirksen to Halifax, 10 Dec. 1938, ibid., no. 422.
[6] Dilks, ed., *Cadogan Diaries*, 15 Dec. 1938, p. 130. See also Sir Ivone Kirkpatrick, *The Inner Circle. Memoirs* (London, 1959), pp. 137–9.
[7] CID Minutes, 22 Dec. 1938, CAB 2/8.
[8] Dilks, ed., *Cadogan Diaries*, 19 Dec. 1938, p. 131.

Harvey, noted on 25 December: 'The old man seems definitely to have given up hope of Germany but clings to the hope of detaching Mussolini. He is certainly pressing on with rearmament.'[1]

On 3 January 1939 Sir George Ogilvie-Forbes, Chargé d'Affaires in Berlin, assessed the German scene. The beginning of 1939, he wrote,

witnessed Herr Hitler drunk with his resounding successes in Austria and Sudetenland and thirsting still more for political adventure, but at the same time handicapped by the strain which his very successes have imposed on the nation's moral and economic resources. In order, therefore, to secure contentment at home he is tempted to find some foreign diversion, and, moreover, the necessity of obtaining raw materials essential to the Four-Year Plan and to an overwhelming standard of rearmament also urges him to grasp for certain essential commodities. Germany is accordingly being mobilised and being made ready for action in any direction the Führer may command.[2]

In which direction was it to be? No sooner had Chamberlain and Halifax returned from their fruitless visit to Rome than they were faced with the prospect of an attack on the West. On 19 January Halifax circulated to his Foreign Policy Committee colleagues a lengthy compendium of memoranda by various members of the Foreign Office which indicated that Hitler was contemplating action early in the year. The most likely direction was towards the Ukraine, but recent reports showed that 'he may decide that the moment is propitious for dealing an overwhelming blow at the Western Powers'.[3] Cadogan judged that such an attack would be directed

---

[1] *Harvey Diaries*, 25 Dec. 1938, p. 229. Chamberlain's hopes were never far below the surface. In a New Year's message to the German nation, after affirming that German foreign policy was conditioned by the anti-Comintern Pact, Hitler said that 'we have as always only one desire, namely that in the coming year it may be possible to succeed in contributing to the general pacification of the world'. Chamberlain informed the Foreign Office that he thought this might be the sign he had been waiting for, but Cadogan assured him that the sentence was nothing more 'than the usual commonplace uttered on such occasions' (Minute by W. Strang, 5 Jan. 1939, C204/16/18 (FO 371/22988)). This rebuttal by the Foreign Office may have prompted the unofficial visit to Germany of a former M.P., Henry Drummond-Wolff. The German official whom he saw wrote that Drummond-Wolff was 'authorised to tell me that one of the Prime Minister's "principal advisers" had approved it' (Gilbert and Gott, *The Appeasers*, 2nd edn., rev., 1967, p. 201). If so, it was nothing more than an unsuccessful fishing expedition.

[2] Ogilvie-Forbes to Halifax, 3 Jan. 1939, *DBFP* iii, no. 515.

[3] FPC Memorandum: 'Possible German Intentions', 19 Jan. 1938, FP (36) 74, CAB 27/627.

either against Britain or against Holland, and that in the latter case Britain should intervene. There was also reason to fear a German attack on Switzerland and a simultaneous Italian attack on French territory.[1] Besides concrete evidence of such plans, the Foreign Office cited as significant indications Germany's economic difficulties, the growing supremacy of the Nazi 'extremists', the possibility that Hitler had made a deal with Poland to protect his rear, and his attempts to consolidate relations with Italy and Japan.

The Foreign Policy Committee, which met on 23 January 1939 to consider these reports, decided to ask the Chiefs of Staff whether Holland was a vital interest.[2] Their advice was that if Britain failed to defend Holland, 'at some later stage we should have to face the same struggle with Germany with fewer friends and in far worse circumstances'. Even now, Britain could hardly hope to win without help from other powers, in particular the United States.[3] On 26 January the Foreign Policy Committee decided that a German attack on Holland would indeed constitute a *casus belli*, though there were misgivings about undertaking a contractual commitment, particularly as the Dutch appeared reluctant to draw further attention to themselves,[4] and because the British were reluctant to repeat the mistake of May 1938, when they had reacted strongly to what turned out to be rumours about a German attack on Czechoslovakia.[5]

The rumours of an attack on the West proved illusory.[6] Some attributed them to the communists; most regarded them as a German *ballon d'essai*. As William Strang wrote to a colleague in Washington,

[1] Halifax to Mallet (Washington), 24 Jan. 1939, *DBFP* iv, no. 5.
[2] FPC Minutes, 23 Jan. 1939, CAB 27/624.
[3] FP (36) 77, CAB 27/627.
[4] Sir N. Bland (The Hague) to Halifax, 27 Jan. 1939, *DBFP* iv, no. 27.
[5] Minutes by F. K. Roberts and W. Strang, 1 Feb. 1939, C1402/15/18 (FO 371/22964).
[6] Unfortunately the files of the Secret Intelligence Service are not among those open to inspection at the Public Record Office, but the information emanated from sources which 'have all been tested over a long period. In most cases there is no doubt whatever that they expressed themselves as reported. Needless to say, if any reference to their remarks leaks out they will be in grave danger of "liquidation"', and, what is more important, we shall be deprived of their information' (Memorandum by G. Jebb: 'Summary of Information from Secret Sources', 19 Jan. 1939, FP (36) 74). Such reports probably derived from three types of sources: (i) the opposition to Hitler inside Germany (see below, pp. 188–92; (ii) Marxist groups anxious to stir up trouble between Britain and Germany, probably under the aegis of the Comintern; (iii) the German Government themselves, and especially the Ministry of Propaganda under Dr. Goebbels, who planted rumours as part of a 'war of nerves'.

the object . . . must have been to test the reactions of ourselves and the French. If we had 'registered' nothing but dismay, tempered by a desire to 'appease', it is quite possible that [the Germans] would have decided to embark on the scheme in earnest. Since, on the contrary, we have made it quite clear to our friends (and this fact must certainly have come back to the Nazis by indirect means) that we should resist a German attack on Holland by force of arms, there is now some hope that such a step on the part of Germany may have been averted.[1]

The British seemed to have lost their ability to assess the significance of these rumours, which were to play such an important part in determining their attitude during the coming months. Apparently no machinery existed for the co-ordination or collation of intelligence reports.[2] As Cadogan later admitted, 'we had no means of evaluating their reliability at the time of their receipt'.[3] At the time, Cadogan expected the politicians to be sceptical,[4] and there was an element of calculation in his presentation of all these reports to the Foreign Policy Committee. As he noted on 19 January, 'it won't do us any harm to brace ourselves to meet a shock in 6 weeks time—we shall be all the better for it'.[5]

The decision to fight for Holland was not the only outcome. Britain agreed to the French request to treat a German attack on Switzerland in the same way.[6] Georges Bonnet, the French Foreign Minister, told the Chamber of Deputies on 26 January 1939 that Britain and France would support each other to the hilt in case of

[1] Strang to Mallet, 16 Feb. 1939, C1789/15/18 (FO 371/22965).
[2] The British Intelligence establishment consisted of M.I.5, the 'Security Service', responsible for counter-espionage; M.I.6, the 'Secret Intelligence Service' (S.I.S.), responsible for clandestine information gathering abroad; the Intelligence Departments of the three Services; and the Industrial Intelligence Centre (I.I.C.), a Department of the Board of Trade responsible for economic intelligence. The Foreign Office received reports piecemeal from these and its own sources. After the guarantee to Poland the Government established a Situation Report Centre to evaluate intelligence. See D. McLachlan, *Room 39* (New York, 1968), p. 244; K. Strong, *Men of Intelligence* (London, 1970), p. 113.
[3] Quoted in Dilks, ed., *Cadogan Diaries*, p. 158.
[4] Some of them were. Sir Thomas Inskip, now Secretary of State for the Dominions, recorded in his diary: 'I find the reports unconvincing. . . . It is hard to believe that the reports are fabricated. Therefore they have to be taken seriously, but as I have said I find this difficult in the absence of any solid evidence of any sort . . . Cadogan seems to be persuaded they are important. So does Strang in the F.O. Halifax is I think sceptical' (Diary, 23 Jan. 1939, Inskip Papers 1/2, Churchill College, Cambridge).
[5] Dilks, ed., *Cadogan Diaries*, 19 Jan. 1939, p. 140.
[6] Halifax to Sir Eric Phipps (Paris), 10 Feb. 1939, *DBFP* iv, no. 98.

war, and Chamberlain confirmed this on 6 February. Further evidence of Italian designs on France also contributed to this show of solidarity. The Anglo-French staff talks were extended to cover war plans in every contingency and in every field of action. The British Government decided to take the United States and the Dominions more fully into their confidence, and initiated a series of very informative communications.

A further important result of the Dutch scare was the change in the size and role of the British army. Criticism of the doctrine of 'limited liability' had been mounting steadily since Munich, particularly from the French and from the War Office, who were apparently in collusion in their efforts to persuade the Government to abandon it.[1] But Chamberlain refused to be drawn into rash promises to the French in November 1938, and the War Office plan to stage a revolt of junior ministers on the issue in December was unsuccessful.[2] The threat to Holland finally resolved the conflict. On 25 January 1939 the Chiefs of Staff endorsed the War Office request, submitted in October 1938, for a continental expeditionary force of six Regular divisions (to be ready for action at two weeks' notice), an immediate reserve of four Territorial divisions, and full training equipment for the rest of the Territorial Army. The threat was that 'France might give up the unequal struggle unless supported with the assurance that we should assist them to the utmost'.[3] The Cabinet approved the measures on 22 February 1939, after consultation between Chamberlain, Simon, Inskip (now Secretary for the Dominions), and Leslie Hore-Belisha, the Secretary for War, on how to pare down the expense.[4]

Evidence that Hitler had no intention of responding to Chamberlain's desire for *rapprochement* had now steadily accumulated since November 1938. It appeared to substantiate the view that instead, Hitler now regarded Britain as his principal enemy. There was no secret about what Hitler wanted from Britain. As Ribbentrop was reported to have said on 9 November 1938, 'Germany demands an unrestrained hand in the East, and will suffer no English inter-

---

[1] See Brian Bond, ed., *Chief of Staff: The Diaries of Major-General Sir Henry Pownall* (Hampden, Conn., 1973), entry for 14 Nov. 1938.
[2] R. J. Minney, ed., *The Private Papers of Hore-Belisha* (London, 1960), pp. 161–5.
[3] COS Memorandum: 'State of Preparedness of the Army in Relation to its Role', 25 Jan. 1939, COS 827, CAB 24/283.
[4] Middlemas, *Diplomacy of Illusion*, p. 428.

ference in this sphere'.[1] But the British showed no desire to concede this wish. Hitler was reported to have said on the same occasion that 'conditions were all against an Anglo-German understanding. If Foreign Powers would not meet German demands, then Germany would take for herself what she could not get by negotiation.' Perhaps the clearest statement of the case came from a young Nazi press leader, who apparently reflected the view of 'important circles in Berlin' in saying that 'the English must come to an understanding with us on our terms if they do not—at least within the next two years—want to be involved in war with us'.[2]

Yet Neville Chamberlain, unlike the Foreign Office, seized on every opportunity to interpret German statements as indications of readiness to negotiate on British terms. The prospects for agreement seemed to be particularly good in the economic sphere. As a result of discussions between British and German officials in October and November 1938, the Federation of British Industries and the Reichsgruppe Industrie on 20 and 21 December found 'a common basis on which official discussions could usefully take place between the two organizations which might result in a mutual increase of trade between the two countries and in agreement with regard to Anglo-German competition in home and third markets'.[3]

Meanwhile the Board of Trade and the Colonial Office were studying the question of tariff concessions in British Empire markets, and progress was made in negotiating a coal cartel. The British and German delegates settled all their differences on the latter question on 28 January 1939, an achievement which the British Government took as a good omen for the future development of Anglo-German economic relations.[4]

On 30 January Hitler delivered an important speech to the Reichstag which seemed to confirm this optimistic assessment. He admitted that all was not right with the German economy and that 'we must export or die'. Germany would support Italy, but Germany's demands for colonial revision need not lead to war. The Foreign Office concluded that none of this was new, but feared that it had caused a 'surge of optimism'.[5] In Parliament on 31 January Chamberlain commented that the speech indicated a desire

[1] Quoted in FPC Memorandum: 'Possible German Intentions', 19 Jan. 1939, FP (36) 74, CAB 27/627.
[2] Quoted ibid. [3] *The Times*, 22 Dec. 1938, p. 8.
[4] Dirksen to German Foreign Ministry, 28 Jan. 1939, *DGFP* iv, no. 303.
[5] Dilks, ed., *Cadogan Diaries*, 31 Jan. 1939, p. 146.

to settle economic problems peacefully, and referred to the continuing industrial talks.[1]

These were not in fact proceeding smoothly. The British wanted agreement on price fixing, and were suspicious of the German emphasis on division of markets. Dr. Weber of the German Embassy told Frank Ashton-Gwatkin, head of the Foreign Office Economic Relations Section, that he hoped the industrial negotiations would result in 'a reduction of duty in the United Kingdom so as to allow German goods to compete over here; at the same time and in return for this certain third markets would be left to the British exporting industries so that in those markets they would be free from German competition'.[2] Ashton-Gwatkin was worried about the possible ramifications. In particular he did not favour a German monopoly in any one of Britain's export markets. He wrote to Guy Locock, Director of the Federation of British Industries: 'I doubt whether you would share this forecast of the negotiations. We would certainly be much concerned if we thought that they were going to lead to a surrender of any part of our commercial position (with which our political influence is so closely bound up) . . .'[3]

The Germans gained the impression that the British industrialists were no longer keen to negotiate. The Federation of British Industries had recently demanded protective measures against German competition, and the dismissal of Dr. Schacht from the Presidency of the Reichsbank had apparently prompted the belief that the German economy was in such dire straits that agreement was no longer in Britain's economic interest.[4] The British Government, on the other hand, were anxious that negotiations should succeed. Sir Frederick Leith-Ross, the Government's Chief Economic Adviser, told the German Ambassador on 23 January 1939 that the Government were interested in the discussions and that he 'hoped the impression given by the F.B.I. was based on some misunderstanding'.[5] The Board of Trade encouraged the Federation of British Industries to press on, and formal talks with German industrialists were planned to open on 15 March 1939.[6] Dr. Funk, German Minister

[1] 343 HC Deb., 5 s., cols. 42–3 and 80–1.
[2] Minute by Ashton-Gwatkin, 20 Jan. 1939, C877/15/18 (FO 371/22961).
[3] Ibid.
[4] Memorandum by Dr. Hipp (Reichsgruppe Industrie), 2 Feb. 1939, *DGFP* iv, no. 314.
[5] Leith-Ross to Stanley, 31 Jan. 1939, C1343/8/18 (FO 371/22950).
[6] Minute by Ashton-Gwatkin, 4 Feb. 1939, C1719/8/18 (ibid.).

of Economics (now also President of the Reichsbank), was invited to London 'to start informally a wider range of economic conversations'.[1] Funk was too busy, but Oliver Stanley, the President of the Board of Trade, was invited to Berlin instead.[2]

Economic negotiations were carried out mainly under the aegis of the Board of Trade. The Foreign Office were suspicious and kept a watchful eye. They wanted to use the prospect of economic agreement as an inducement for achieving their political requirements. When Ashton-Gwatkin visited Germany in February in order to find out 'what roads are still open to economic recovery and what roads are closed', he was instructed with Halifax's concurrence to 'make it clear that he will bring with him no proposals whatsoever'.[3] A more important object of Ashton-Gwatkin's visit was to re-establish contact with 'moderate' opinion in Germany and in particular with Hermann Göring, who appeared anxious to see him.[4] In his talks, Ashton-Gwatkin played on Göring's apparent desire for economic co-operation with Britain by stressing that 'political peace was the basis for economic confidence'. But Göring called this 'saddling the horse from the wrong end', and Ashton-Gwatkin concluded that 'the idea of armament limitation as a pre-existent condition to economic co-operation does not appeal to the Field-Marshal'.[5] Nothing very concrete emerged from his talks. He got the impression that Germany's economic difficulties might compel her 'to moderate her policy and reduce her expenditure on armaments', which was in complete contradiction to the hints dropped by both Ribbentrop and Ashton-Gwatkin's friend, Prince Max von Hohenlohe, that Hitler intended to 'deal further with the two "historic lands" ' of Bohemia and Moravia.[6]

The Foreign Office were by now thoroughly sceptical about the possibility of Anglo-German agreement. As the Financial Attaché in Berlin, G. H. S. Pinsent, reported on 27 February 1939:

Altogether these conversations hold out, in my opinion, little hope

[1] Dirksen to German Foreign Ministry, 24 Jan. 1939, *DGFP* iv, no. 299.
[2] Wiehl to Dirksen, 6 Feb. 1939, ibid., no. 308.
[3] Minute by Sargent, 1 Feb. 1939, C1195/16/18 (FO 371/22988).
[4] Minute by Ashton-Gwatkin, 1 Feb. 1939, ibid.
[5] Report by Ashton-Gwatkin on interviews with German statesmen, 19–26 Feb. 1939, *DBFP* iv, Appendix II.
[6] Ibid., and see the report of his interview with Hohenlohe, not printed, C2346/8/18 (FO 371/22950).

of progress in economic co-operation. The things which we want—particularly arms limitation, and, to some extent, freeing of the exchange—are not in reality practical politics. But the German mouth is wide open for concessions on debts, trade, etc., which would in reality merely serve to strengthen their rearmament position.[1]

His colleague, Magowan, the Commercial Attaché, stressed this danger in two memoranda to the Foreign Office which raised the whole issue of Anglo-German economic relations to the level of intense debate in Whitehall.

Anglo-German economic relations during the 1930s were governed by the Anglo-German Payments Agreement of 1934. Under this agreement, 55 per cent of the foreign exchange Germany earned from her exports to Britain was earmarked to pay for imports from Britain. A further 10 per cent was to be used for repayment of frozen trade debts, and Germany promised to service the Dawes and Young loans. The rest was free foreign exchange for Germany. In the spring of 1938 the agreement had to be revised to take account of the *Anschluss* with Austria. The Treasury wanted to increase to 60 per cent the proportion of foreign exchange devoted to purchases from Britain; to persuade the Germans to buy more finished, as opposed to re-exportable products; and also to persuade Germany to honour the Austrian debt. The British got what they wanted, but only after threatening to impose a unilateral clearing in Anglo-German trade.[2] The revised agreement was signed in June.

Six months later Magowan submitted his first memorandum. It was based on the assumption that German intentions towards Britain were now definitely hostile. The essence of his argument was that the terms of the Anglo-German Payments Agreement, by providing Germany with a surplus of free foreign exchange, allowed her to import materials essential for the rearmament programme. He suggested that Whitehall should examine ways to end 'a situation where we are strengthening German rearmament'.[3] In a second memorandum on 3 January 1939 he produced more evidence and suggested ways in which the agreement might be revised. Sir George Ogilvie-Forbes, the Chargé d'Affaires in Berlin, supported his colleague's views: 'the Nazi régime as at present constituted is

[1] Memorandum by G. H. S. Pinsent, 27 Feb. 1939, *DBFP* iv, Appendix II.
[2] C. A. MacDonald, 'Economic Appeasement', pp. 115–17.
[3] Memorandum by M. J. Creswell (Central Department), 20 Jan. 1939, C960/8/18 (FO 371/22950). Memorandum by Magowan, 6 Dec. 1938, C15187/30/18 (FO 371/21648).

NEW APPROACHES TO GERMANY 83

potentially hostile to British interests and is adjusting its economy to prepare for a war which might be waged against the United Kingdom'.[1]

The Foreign Office were impressed. Their reaction to the first memorandum had been to suggest that the subject should be discussed by an *ad hoc* inter-departmental committee. They now wanted it to go straight to the Committee of Imperial Defence.[2] But the Economic Departments had to be given a chance to air their views, and the Foreign Office found themselves fighting their way through what Sir Orme Sargent called 'the tangled undergrowth of Departmental obstructionism'.[3]

The Government's Chief Economic Adviser, Sir Frederick Leith-Ross, who had negotiated the Anglo-German Payments Agreement, pointed out that it 'represented the satisfaction practically in full of our requirements', and that it held several advantages. First, a proportion of the foreign-exchange proceeds from German exports to Britain returned to the City in debt service. Cutting off this source meant disorganizing the London money market and weakening the balance of payments.[4] Secondly, to the extent that Germany managed to switch her exports to non-creditor countries she would probably be able to realize their full value in real terms, i.e. in imports from them, without any foreign-exchange 'leakage' into debt service: 'I think the payment of this tribute is one of the best ways of strengthening ourselves and weakening Germany (as well as of satisfying financial morality!)'. Thirdly, the trade provisions of the agreement were extremely valuable. Any dislocation could mean 'another 100,000 unemployed'. Leith-Ross concluded that 'the abrogation of the Agreement would be almost, if not quite, as disadvantageous to us as to Germany, and I do not think that it is worth our while to cut off our nose in order to spite the German face'.[5] The Treasury

[1] Ogilvie-Forbes to Halifax, 3 Jan. 1939, C164/8/18 (FO 371/22950).
[2] Strang to Treasury, 20 Jan. 1939, ibid.
[3] Minute by Sargent, 19 Mar. 1939, C2581/8/18 (FO 371/22950).
[4] On the other hand W. B. G. Chisholm, of the Foreign Office Economic Relations Section, believed that the agreement merely permitted various London houses 'to derive certain relatively unimportant advantages in the shape of actual cash payments on account of interest' and 'to put their whole holdings on the credit side of their accounts', i.e. to treat German debts as good ones rather than what they were in reality—'bad debts that will have to be written off sooner or later' (Minute by Chisholm, 3 Feb. 1939, C959/8/18 (FO 371/22950), and enc. memorandum by Magowan).
[5] Leith-Ross to Sargent, 24 Jan. 1939, ibid.

and the Board of Trade shared these views,[1] and although Desmond Morton, head of the important Industrial Intelligence Centre, agreed with the thrust of Magowan's argument, he pointed out a further advantage that Britain derived from the agreement:

> Whereas Germany's most important imports from the United Kingdom are coal and textiles, with which, in the last resort, she might be able to supply herself from domestic resources, our most important imports from her are machine tools and machinery, much of which we should, under present conditions, find it very difficult to obtain elsewhere and without which our rearmament programme would be making even tardier progress than it is.[2]

He added the moral that Britain should 'make sure of an alternative source of supply before cutting off the existing one'.

This debate is significant because it demonstrates that the Economic Departments in Whitehall were not busily working, under the personal supervision of Neville Chamberlain, to undermine British interests in favour of concessions to Germany, which is the impression created by the orthodox interpretation. On the contrary, the argument against Magowan was that he underestimated the advantages of the agreement to Britain. Of course Chamberlain and the Economic Departments hoped that the imminent trade talks and Stanley's visit to Berlin would prove fruitful in the search for a *rapprochement*. But then so did responsible officials in the Foreign Office, however sceptical.

On 15 February 1939 the Duke of Saxe-Coburg, in a speech to the Anglo-German Society in Berlin, welcomed the progress made in Anglo-German economic relations, and referred expressly to the coal agreement and the industrial negotiations.[3] Sir Nevile Henderson, the British Ambassador in Berlin, was convinced that these references had 'received personal approval of Herr Hitler himself'.[4] Chamberlain wrote to him that the speech 'seems to come closer to that response for which I have been asking than anything I have seen yet'. He concluded:

> Things look as though Spain might clear up fairly soon. After that the next thing will be to get the bridge between Paris and Rome into working order. After that we might begin to talk about disarmament, preferably

[1] Minute by H. A. Hankey (F.O. Economic Relations Section), 13 Mar. 1939, C2581/8/18 (FO 371/22950).
[2] Morton to Sargent, 9 Jan. 1939, C353/8/18 (ibid.).
[3] *DBFP* iv, Appendix I (iii)n. [4] Quoted ibid.

beginning with Mussolini, but bringing in the Germans pretty soon. If all went well we should have so improved the atmosphere that we might begin to think of colonial discussions.[1]

Halifax saw the Prime Minister's letter and wrote separately to Henderson, obviously annoyed:

> I am afraid the business of getting the bridge built between Paris and Rome is likely to be more difficult than the P.M. appears to feel, and I confess that I think his last paragraph is generally optimistic.
>
> I do not myself feel there is any hope of making any sense of colonial discussions, as I think I said to you before you left England, unless and until your German friends can really show more than smooth words as evidence of friendly hearts.[2]

Halifax's annoyance reflected the change that had occurred since October 1938 in the opinion of those members of the Foreign Office on whom he and Chamberlain relied for advice. After Munich, Cadogan, for instance, had been quite prepared to believe that Hitler's intentions were peaceful, or at least that he harboured no aggressive designs against Britain. Now his whole attitude had changed. He wrote on 26 February 1939:

> I have the profoundest suspicion of Hitler's intentions: I believe they are strictly dishonourable, and I believe what he would like best, if he could do it, would be to smash the British Empire. . . . We must take every precaution we can to strengthen ourselves in the Mediterranean and in the West, and even to guard against possible trouble simultaneously in the Far East.[3]

Chamberlain's optimism on the other hand was fed not only by the apparent indications that Germany favoured economic co-operation but also by the approaching end of the Spanish Civil War. Once Britain and France had recognized General Franco, the worst hindrance to Franco-Italian friendship would be removed. On 9 March Chamberlain gave the Parliamentary Lobby correspondents a 'background' interview indicating that he was optimistic about the European situation and that he contemplated calling a European arms-limitation conference. If successful, its scope might be expanded to include economic problems and colonies, although 'any Colonial offer made by Britain would, of course, be part of a general

---

[1] Chamberlain to Henderson, 19 Feb. 1939, *DBFP* iv, Appendix I (iii).
[2] Halifax to Henderson, 20 Feb. 1939, ibid., Appendix I (iv).
[3] Minute by Cadogan, 26 Feb. 1939, C/2/39/3 (FO 800/294).

European settlement'.[1] Halifax, once again annoyed on hearing the source of this story (he had not been consulted), reproached Chamberlain, who apologized.[2] Halifax had been advised just three days earlier by Cadogan: 'I doubt whether it is good tactics at the present juncture for us to invite conversations at which we would be expected to place all our cards on the table.'[3]

On 10 March 1939 Sir Samuel Hoare took up the optimistic line, having consulted Chamberlain.[4] In a speech at Chelsea he stressed the potential economic benefits to be derived from European cooperation:

> Suppose that political confidence could be restored to Europe, suppose that there was a five-year plan, immensely greater than any five-year plan that this or that particular country had attempted in recent times, and that for a space of five years there were neither wars nor rumours of wars; suppose that the peoples of Europe were able to free themselves from a nightmare that haunted them and from an expenditure upon armaments that had beggared them, could they not then devote the almost incredible inventions and discoveries of the time to the creation of a golden age in which poverty could be reduced to insignificance and the standard of living raised to heights never before attained?[5]

He looked to 'the three dictators' of Europe and the Prime Ministers of Britain and France to work together to 'transform the whole history of the world'.

On 15 March the magazine *Punch* published its now famous cartoon showing John Bull waking from a nightmare (about the spectre of war, which was shown disappearing out of the window) with the relieved comment: 'Thank goodness that's over!' On the very same day, the first German troops crossed the Czechoslovak border.

---

[1] Diplomatic Correspondent, *Daily Mail*, 10 Mar. 1939, pp. 11–12.
[2] Feiling, *Chamberlain*, pp. 396–7; Halifax, *Fullness of Days*, p. 232.
[3] Minute by Cadogan, 6 Mar. 1939, C2560/16/18 (FO 371/22988).
[4] Templewood, *Nine Troubled Years*, p. 327.
[5] *The Times*, 11 Mar. 1939, p. 7. This theme was present in the speech drafted in the Foreign Office for Oliver Stanley to use at the Anglo-German trade dinner which he and R. S. Hudson were to attend in Berlin on 17 March: 'It is for political leaders to create an atmosphere in which contracts can be concluded, extensions planned, and initiative encouraged.' The draft also stressed the disadvantages for German business of autarky and armaments, while emphasizing that British rearmament was only defensive. Reference was made to conversations 'afterwards in political matters' (C2969/16/18 (FO 371/22988)).

It is commonly held that after Munich 'the policy of appeasement reached its apogee'.[1] But a study of British policy during the six months after Munich demonstrates the meaning of 'appeasement' as Chamberlain understood it. The policy he tried unsuccessfully to initiate was essentially no different from the numerous attempts made since 1934 to bring about a *rapprochement* with Germany on the basis of the *status quo* in Europe, i.e. on Britain's terms. The dictionary definition of 'appeasement', based apparently only on the atypical Munich episode, sees it as an attempt to buy off a potential aggressor by means of unwarranted unilateral concessions, frequently involving the sacrifice of principle. But after Munich, and perhaps in some measure because of it, there was no 'appeasement' of this sort. Chamberlain was not prepared to allow unilateral concessions. Before any discussion of colonies, he wanted concrete evidence of Hitler's desire to co-operate with Britain. He sought such evidence in Hitler's willingness to disarm and to abandon the autarkic economic system and exclusive trade relations with central and south-eastern Europe designed to monopolize the area economically and politically. If Chamberlain appeared optimistic to the last, it was because he was falsely encouraged by indications that Germany might be prepared to co-operate in the economic sphere. He apparently attached more importance than either his foreign-policy advisers or his critics to economic growth. In the final analysis, however, and although Chamberlain appeared to accept Hitler's peaceful assurances of September 1938 at their face value, he was not in fact prepared to make them the basis for further concessions without real as opposed to avowed willingness to co-operate with Britain.

[1] Gilbert and Gott, *The Appeasers*, p. 191.

5

THE IDES OF MARCH

THE question of Hitler's plans for the occupation of Bohemia and Moravia on 15 March 1939 is still hotly debated. A. J. P. Taylor believes that there was nothing 'sinister or premeditated in the protectorate' and that Hitler acted 'without design'.[1] Other historians see plans going back to October 1938, when Hitler warned the German army that it 'must be possible to smash at any time the remainder of the Czech State, should it pursue an anti-German policy'.[2] But this was no more than contingency planning, and it should be remembered that in November 1938 Hitler also ordered plans to be made in conjunction with Italy for war against Britain and France.[3]

At first Hitler's objective seems to have been as weak and dependent a Czechoslovakia as was consistent with her preservation as a unit. This meant a strongly autonomous Slovakia and Ruthenia, oriented towards Prague. This attitude was no doubt prompted by the German Army General Staff's assessment that 'it is in our *military interest* that Slovakia should not be separated from the Czechoslovak union but should remain with Czechoslovakia under strong German influence'.[4] Therefore Hitler supported the agreement reached between Czechs and Slovaks at Zilina on 7 October 1938, which gave Slovakia a long awaited autonomous Government and Diet with responsibility for most fields of administration and legislation except finance and foreign policy. Hitler apparently wanted no more than this, for although the Slovak separatists, Jozef Tiso (at the head of the new Government) and Ferdinand Ďurčanský, pleaded for German support for full independence in October, the German Foreign Ministry noted that 'at present Germany's official

---

[1] A. J. P. Taylor, *The Origins of the Second World War*, 2nd edn. (Penguin, 1963), p. 250.
[2] Directive by the Führer for the Wehrmacht, 21 Oct. 1938, *DGFP* iv, no. 81.
[3] Notes for Wehrmacht Discussions with Italy, 26 Nov. 1938, ibid., no. 411, enc.
[4] Supreme Command of the Wehrmacht to Foreign Ministry, 6 Oct. 1938, ibid., no. 39.

THE IDES OF MARCH

objective continues to be Slovakia and Carpatho-Ukraine (Ruthenia), with strong autonomy and orientation towards Prague, while it remains to be seen whether Slovak desires will one day develop from autonomy to independence as a state'.[1] In the meantime, Hungary appealed to Germany for arbitration in her frontier dispute with Czechoslovakia, and by the Vienna Award of 2 November Ribbentrop and Ciano, the Italian Foreign Minister, assigned a sizeable portion of southern Slovakia to Hungary.[2]

The German Government expected their relations with the Prague Government to follow the course agreed on 14 October 1938 between Hitler and František Chvalkovský, the Czechoslovak Foreign Minister. Hitler told him that Czechoslovakia 'must realize that she was in the German sphere and it was in her own interest to adapt herself to the conditions of this sphere'.[3] Chvalkovský, for his part, 'emphasized at length the firm determination of the Czech Government to comply with Germany's wishes'.[4] He promised to reduce the size of the army, the number of political parties, and the extent of Jewish influence, and also to co-operate with Germany in the economic sphere.

On 19 November the Czechoslovak Government agreed to the construction of a highway between Breslau and Vienna with extraterritorial rights across the Czechoslovak section, and to the construction of a canal between the Danube and the Oder. In November the German Foreign Ministry drafted a German-Czechoslovak treaty which called for the complete alignment of the two countries' foreign and economic policies in the German interest. In return Germany would guarantee Czechoslovakia.[5]

That this scheme was not followed through is at least circumstantial evidence that Hitler now had other plans for 'Czecho-Slovakia',[6] namely, the eventual military occupation of Bohemia and

[1] Under-Secretary Woermann to Consul Druffel (Bratislava), 17 Oct. 1938, ibid., no. 69.

[2] Circular of the State Secretary (Weizsäcker), 31 Oct. 1938, ibid., no. 98, and Documents on the Vienna Award, 2 Nov. 1938, ibid., no. 99.

[3] Conversation between Hitler and Chvalkovský, 14 Oct. 1938, ibid., no. 61.

[4] Ibid.

[5] See Vojtech Mastny, *The Czechs under Nazi Rule. The Failure of National Resistance, 1939-1942* (New York, 1971), p. 28; Radomir Luza, *The Transfer of the Sudeten Germans: a study of Czech-German relations 1933-1962* (New York, 1964), p. 167.

[6] The hyphen was inserted with the promulgation of the Slovak autonomy law of 22 November 1938, but was never consistently used, except perhaps by the Slovaks themselves.

Moravia, although there is no evidence that Hitler decided to act on such a plan until mid-February 1939. In December Hitler received reports of a revival of the anti-German 'Beneš spirit' in Bohemia and Moravia, which Chvalkovský had promised to curb. In January 1939 Hitler complained to the Foreign Minister that Czechoslovak policy had not yet been fully oriented towards Germany.[1] The complaint led to a flurry of reassuring activity in Prague, which prompted the Czech jibe that Chvalkovský was 'now learning shorthand to be able to keep up with the dictation more quickly'.[2] But by mid-February Hitler was beginning to doubt whether Chvalkovský measured up to his task. He told the Slovak separatist, Vojtech Tuka, on 12 February that he 'thought that Chvalkovský himself had the best intentions, but events do not stand and wait upon the good intentions of individuals'.[3] He went on to say that 'it would be a comfort to him to know that Slovakia was independent'.

It is probable that by this point Hitler had decided to subjugate Bohemia and Moravia. Operational plans had been issued to select military units beginning on 12 January, but without a set date for action.[4] Only on 13 February did Weizsäcker, State Secretary in the German Foreign Ministry, refer to the fact that 'Czechoslovakia will receive its death blow in approximately four weeks'.[5]

The German Government now actively encouraged the Slovak separatists, who began to make frequent visits to Berlin. In early March Göring apparently told two Slovak Ministers, Ďurčanský and Pružinský, that Germany 'was prepared to grant economic assistance to Slovakia only if the latter proclaimed herself an independent state'.[6]

The strained relations between the central Government in Prague and the autonomous Government in Bratislava, which had steadily deteriorated since October 1938, reached a crisis point during the first week in March. The Slovaks demanded a reduction in their

---

[1] Conversation between Hitler and Chvalkovský, 21 Jan. 1939, *DGFP* iv, no. 158, and conversation between Ribbentrop and Chvalkovský, 21 Jan. 1939, ibid., no. 159.

[2] Chargé d'Affaires in Czechoslovakia to Foreign Ministry, 27 Jan. 1939, ibid., no. 161.

[3] Conversation between Hitler and Vojtech Tuka, 12 Feb. 1939, ibid., no. 168.

[4] Mastny, *The Czechs under Nazi Rule*, p. 30.

[5] Quoted in Leonidas Hill, 'Three Crises, 1938–39', *Journal of Contemporary History*, 3 (1968), no. 1.

[6] Chargé d'Affaires in Czechoslovakia to Foreign Ministry, 9 Mar. 1939, *DGFP* iv, no. 184.

THE IDES OF MARCH

contribution to the joint budget, the dismissal from the central Government of the die-hard Defence Minister General Syrový, and greater Slovak participation in the central administration.[1] The negotiation of these issues finally broke down on 9 March, when the Slovaks refused to renounce formally their ultimate aim of complete independence. The Czechoslovak President, Emil Hácha, then dismissed the Slovak Government headed by Monsignor Tiso, sent troops into Slovakia, and imposed martial law on parts of the province. On 11 March he appointed the Slovak Karol Sidor to head a new Government. Sidor had been Deputy Premier in the central Government and was in favour of maintaining the union. On 13 March Tiso, who had fled to Vienna with some of his extremist followers, was persuaded to go to Berlin by Wilhelm Keppler, State Secretary for Special Duties in the German Foreign Ministry.[2]

In Berlin Hitler made it clear to Tiso that unless Slovakia proclaimed her independence he would no longer protect the province from the Hungarians, who at that very moment, he said, were moving troops up to the Slovak borders.[3] If there was any truth in this, it was because Hitler had the day before consented to the annexation of Ruthenia by Hungary.[4]

On 14 March the Slovak Diet assembled at Tiso's request and voted for the independence of Slovakia. Seeing his country disintegrate, Hácha turned to Berlin for guidance. There, in the early hours of 15 March, he told Hitler that 'he was convinced that the destiny of Czechoslovakia lay in the Führer's hands, and he believed that that destiny was in safe-keeping in the hands of the Führer'. Hitler told him that he had ordered 'the incorporation of Czechoslovakia into the German Reich', and asked the President to order the Czechs not to resist. This Hácha did, and signed a statement to the effect that 'he confidently placed the fate of the Czech people and country in the hands of the Führer of the German Reich'.[5]

The vital strategic area of Ostrava having been occupied during the afternoon of 14 March to pre-empt an expected Polish move, the invasion proper began at 6 a.m. on 15 March. German troops

[1] Chargé d'Affaires in Czechoslovakia to Foreign Ministry, 7 Mar. 1939, ibid., no. 180.
[2] Mastny, *The Czechs under Nazi Rule*, p. 36.
[3] Conversation between Hitler and Tiso, 13 Mar. 1939, *DGFP* iv, no. 202.
[4] The Regent of Hungary (Horthy) to Hitler, 13 Mar. 1939, ibid., no. 199.
[5] Declaration by the German and Czechoslovak Governments, 15 Mar. 1939, ibid., no. 229.

occupied Bohemia, Moravia, and, temporarily, some parts of Slovakia. On the same day Hungary began the occupation of Ruthenia, whose appeal for German protection was denied.[1] On 16 March Bohemia and Moravia were proclaimed an autonomous German protectorate, forming part of the Greater German Empire.[2]

The British Government's rather listless reaction to these events was implicit in the solution to the Czechoslovak crisis adopted in September 1938. As Sir Alexander Cadogan minuted on 6 March 1939, 'if in Sept.–Oct. last we couldn't save Czechoslovakia from what was then done to her, it is plain that we shall not be able to save her from further consequences'.[3] It would indeed have been illogical for Britain to fight for the remains of a country whose powers of resistance she had agreed to weaken.

This was the reason why the British Government had been so reluctant to guarantee the remainder of the Czechoslovak state in September 1938. They had been prepared to do so only in order to secure Czechoslovak and French acquiescence in British policy. On 14 September 1938, the day before he flew to Berchtesgaden, Neville Chamberlain had asked the Cabinet:

... supposing that part of Czechoslovakia were given to Germany, what would happen to the rest of the country? It might be said that there would be a helpless little strip of territory liable at any moment to be gobbled up by Germany. The Czechs might take that view and might prefer to die fighting rather than accept a solution which would rob them of their natural frontiers.

The only answer which he could find was one which he was most unwilling to contemplate, namely, that this country should join in guaranteeing the integrity of the rest of Czechoslovakia. This would be a new liability, and he realised that we could not save Czechoslovakia if Germany decided to over-run it. The value of the guarantee would lie in its deterrent effect.[4]

In the event it was not the Czechs but the French who caused the British the most embarrassment. On 18 September Daladier and Bonnet insisted on the guarantee as a condition of their agreement to British policy. The Anglo-French proposals presented to Prague the

[1] State Secretary to the Consul at Chust, 15 Mar. 1939, *DGFP* iv, no. 237.
[2] Proclamation by the Führer, signed 16 Mar. 1939, ibid., no. 246.
[3] Minute by Cadogan, 6 Mar. 1939, C2340/19/18 (FO 371/22992).
[4] Cab. Minutes, 14 Sept. 1938, CAB 23/95.

next day, for the cession of the Sudetenland, therefore contained an offer 'to join in an international guarantee of the new boundaries of the Czechoslovak State against unprovoked aggression'. Such an obligation could not be undertaken, however, until Czechoslovakia had abandoned her military alliances with France, Russia, and the Little Entente.[1] On 19 September Chamberlain explained to the Cabinet that the wording of the proposal had been deliberately left vague 'so that it would be open to us to introduce other conditions which might be found desirable on further reflection'.[2] At the Munich Conference on 29 September Hitler and Mussolini agreed that they would guarantee Czechoslovakia after the Polish and Hungarian minorities questions had been settled. Meanwhile, as the Minister for Co-ordination of Defence, Sir Thomas Inskip, announced in the House of Commons on 4 October, although the guarantee was not yet technically in force, the British Government 'feel under a moral obligation to Czechoslovakia to treat the guarantee as now being in force'.[3] This was intended not only to relieve the pressure of parliamentary questions on the subject, but also to deter Poland and Hungary from aggressive action in support of their respective claims.[4]

Once the last of these claims had been settled, with the Vienna Award of 2 November 1938, the British began to clarify their conception of the guarantee. There were two major alternatives: a joint, multilateral guarantee which envisaged collective action; or a several, unilateral guarantee which allowed the possibility of individual action. The British wanted a joint guarantee by Britain, France, Germany, and Italy, to operate only with the consent of three of them. Furthermore,

were Slovakia or Ruthenia to break away from Czechoslovakia and either establish independent States or else join Hungary or Poland it is clear that a new position would arise and it might be argued that the guarantee we have given to the new Czechoslovak State would no longer apply. It certainly would not apply to the territories which had broken away.

[1] Cab. Memorandum: 'British Guarantee for Czechoslovakia', 12 Nov. 1938, CP 258 (38), CAB 24/280, p. 1. The 'Little Entente' was the system of alliances between Czechoslovakia, Yugoslavia, and Rumania, brought together in one instrument in May 1929 and intended to maintain the *status quo* in central and south-eastern Europe.
[2] Cab. Minutes, 19 Sept. 1938, CAB 23/95.
[3] 339 HC Deb. 5 s., col. 303.
[4] German Minister in Hungary (Erdmannsdorff) to Foreign Ministry, 8 Oct. 1938, *DGFP* iv, no. 47.

Similarly a new position would arise were Czechoslovakia to join in a union with Germany which was so close as to amount to a virtual alienation of the independence of the republic. Even if this does not happen, it is possible that Czechoslovakia may move so much into the German orbit as to make the guarantee unnecessary and anomalous.[1]

When Chamberlain and Halifax discussed the subject with Daladier and Bonnet in Paris on 24 November, the French rightly thought the British idea worthless, since 'in actual fact there would never be three Powers against one, but always four against none, or two against two'. Chamberlain objected that it was a mistake to assume that German and Italian interests were always identical, and that in any case 'he had never conceived of a situation in which Great Britain might have to carry out her obligations alone', a situation which could arise if the alternative of a several guarantee were adopted.[2]

On 6 December Sir Alexander Cadogan reminded the Foreign Policy Committee of Britain's real objections:

> It had never been contemplated that we should give a several guarantee or that we should come to the help of Czechoslovakia either singlehanded or in conjunction only with France. There must be no repetition of the situation of last September, when France and ourselves had been faced with the alternatives of fighting, without any hope of saving Czechoslovakia, or of defaulting on the guarantee. We should therefore insist that if France, Germany, Italy and ourselves were the guarantor Powers, the assent of at least three of these should be necessary for the operation of the guarantee.[3]

But on that same day Ribbentrop, in Paris for the signing of the Franco-German Declaration, told the French that Germany would prefer not to guarantee Czechoslovakia because she 'might relapse at some future date into an anti-German policy'.[4]

Mussolini was no more forthcoming when Chamberlain and Halifax broached the matter in Rome on 12 January 1939.[5] The British themselves had an excuse up their sleeves. It was by now clear that Czechoslovakia was falling further and further within the German orbit. This the Foreign Office found inconsistent with the neutrality 'which in some form or another was, we have always

---

[1] 'British Guarantee for Czechoslovakia', CP 258 (38), pp. 6–7.
[2] Record of Anglo-French Conversations, 24 Nov. 1938, *DBFP* iii, no. 325.
[3] FPC Minutes, 6 Dec. 1938, CAB 27/624.
[4] Unsigned FO Minute, 9 Jan. 1939, C2580/17/18 (FO 371/22991).
[5] Record of Anglo-Italian Conversations, 12 Jan. 1939, *DBFP* iii, no. 500.

understood, to be an element in a new guarantee which Czechoslovakia was to receive'.[1]

Chamberlain now wanted to drop the whole subject. When Halifax proposed to broach it in Berlin, the Prime Minister objected, 'I was under the impression that the Foreign Secretary had agreed with me, that it was best to leave this matter alone for the present, and that there was a chance that if not stirred up the guarantee might fade out.'[2] In the event Halifax prevailed, but on 3 March 1939 he received the reply that the German Government were awaiting 'clarification of the internal development of Czecho-Slovakia' before further considering the question.[3]

By this time it was becoming obvious that the Germans were 'keeping their hands free to deal, as they think best, with any situation that may arise—or that they may provoke—in Czecho-Slovakia'.[4] This fact had also been clear for some time to the Czechoslovak Government, who in a circular to the four powers on 22 February 1939 had offered their neutrality in return for a guarantee.[5] But Sir William Malkin, the Foreign Office Legal Adviser, objected that 'legally Czechoslovakia cannot release herself from her existing obligations by a unilateral declaration, and this is not the sort of action which we want to encourage . . .'.[6] Since the Germans were obviously dragging their feet, the Foreign Office itself now wanted the question buried. Sir Orme Sargent recalled that Britain was still saddled with Inskip's 'moral obligation':

it is difficult to see how we are to rid ourselves of this dangerous commitment. All we can do is to assume that in the altered circumstances it is already a dead letter. But we cannot say this in Parliament without reopening the whole question and arousing an unpleasant and unprofitable controversy. I am inclined to think that there is nothing for it but tacitly to allow the present unsatisfactory situation to continue, in the hope that nothing will occur which might give occasion to the Czecho-Slovak Government to invoke this pledge and to call upon us to fulfil it.[7]

Cadogan agreed that 'one probably has to be cynical about this, and

[1] Minute by Strang, 9 Jan. 1939, C2580/17/18 (FO 371/22991).
[2] Minute by Chamberlain, 20 Jan. 1939, C659/17/18 (ibid.).
[3] Henderson to Halifax, 3 Mar. 1939, *DBFP* iv, no. 167.
[4] Minute by Strang, 11 Mar. 1939, C2657/17/18 (FO 371/22991).
[5] Troutbeck (Prague) to Strang, 20 Feb. 1939, *DBFP* iv, no. 126; Troutbeck to Halifax, 22 Feb. 1939, ibid. Note by Cadogan, 22 Feb. 1939, ibid., no. 138.
[6] Minute by Malkin, 2 Mar. 1939, C2340/19/18 (FO 371/22992).
[7] Minute by Sargent, 6 Mar. 1939, ibid.

to recognize that, with the passage of time, the question of the guarantee loses more and more of whatever it had of actuality'.[1]

Forecasts of a German occupation of Bohemia and Moravia went back to early February. Vansittart heard from many sources that Hitler meant to stir up the Slovak independence movement, and that 'Czech resistance to these claims will then give Hitler the opportunity to intervene "manu militari" '.[2] However, even Vansittart did not appear to be unduly alarmed by the prospect: 'While I confess that my gorge would rise if Hitler did it, it would not prevent me from considering the deed a confession of failure on his part.' These reports contrasted sharply with the tenor of those submitted by the British Ambassador in Berlin, Sir Nevile Henderson, who wrote on 18 February that 'My definite impression since my return here is that Herr Hitler does not contemplate any adventures at the moment and that all stories and rumours to the contrary are completely without real foundation.'[3] He reaffirmed this assessment on 28 February. Foreign Office reactions varied. Vansittart thought Henderson out of touch with reality and was thoroughly contemptuous of his political foresight. Sir Orme Sargent subjected his dispatches to ruthless criticism. Cadogan was sceptical: 'I shall continue to hope for a real change of heart in the German Govt., but I shall never believe in it until I see it proved.'[4] Meanwhile Britain must 'steer between the Scylla of ostrich-like complacency on the one hand and the Charybdis of "potential hysteria" on the other'. Halifax agreed with Cadogan's staunch and vigilant scepticism,[5] an attitude reinforced by assessments of military developments in Germany. Ivone Kirkpatrick, of the Central Department, put the Foreign Office view in a letter to the Admiralty on 24 February 1939:

All our most reliable information agrees that there is as yet no definite evidence of impending mobilization, nor is there any reliable military or political indication that Hitler has reached any decision as to the direction in which German policy should be guided this year. Meanwhile, the German army is working at high pressure and the training of reservists is being expedited. The position therefore seems to be that the German

[1] Minute by Cadogan, 6 Mar. 1939, C2340/19/18 (FO 371/22992).
[2] Minute by Vansittart, 20 Feb. 1939, C2209/15/18 (FO 371/22965).
[3] Henderson to Halifax, 18 Feb. 1939, *DBFP* iv, no. 118.
[4] Minute by Cadogan, 21 Feb. 1939, C2139/15/18 (FO 371/22965).
[5] Minutes by Cadogan and Halifax, 11 and 12 Mar. 1939, C2533/15/18 (ibid.).

General Staff was probably warned before Christmas to be ready for all eventualities in the spring, and has been making the necessary preliminary preparations.[1]

The uncertainty surrounding German intentions grew with the Slovak crisis. Nobody was quite sure how deeply Germany was involved, and although all officials agreed that the situation would help the Germans achieve their object of trying to bring Prague into the German orbit, opinion differed as to the means. Frank Roberts, Second Secretary in the Central Department, thought the most likely development would be 'a Slovakia either nominally independent or bound by even looser federal ties than at present to Prague and dominated in either event by German influence'. On the other hand Hitler might well 'decide to achieve his ambition, of which he was deprived last September, of a triumphal march upon Prague'.[2]

Roberts also discussed, on Sargent's instructions, whether Britain should take any initiative. He thought that it would be undesirable to make empty threats since 'there is nothing we can do to stop him, short of war'. The guarantee attached to the Munich agreement had never been implemented, and even if it were to serve as a pretext for attacking Germany, France would have to be willing to act too, a most unlikely possibility. He concluded that Britain 'would have no *locus standi* for taking any initiative in this matter and any attempt to check Herr Hitler by public statements or involving Signor Mussolini's support would only seem calculated to precipitate a solution unfavourable to Czecho-Slovakia'. His superiors agreed with him.[3] But nothing was certain yet. As Cadogan noted late on 13 March:

Slovak situation still v. obscure. We have S.I.S. news that the Germans are prepared to walk in. I showed this to P.M. this evening, observing that the one question that we couldn't answer was whether the Germans *would* put their plan into operation. Anyhow he's disillusioned with Hitler![4]

Even on 14 March Foreign Office officials found it difficult to believe that Hitler really intended, as R. L. Speaight of the Central Department pointed out, 'to take all the responsibility and risks of including 7 million Czechs in the Reich when, by allowing some

---

[1] Kirkpatrick to Captain G. C. Cooke, 24 Feb. 1939, C2335/13/18 (FO 371/22958).
[2] Memorandum by Roberts, 13 Mar. 1939, *DBFP* iv, no. 230.
[3] Minute by R. Makins, 14 Mar. 1939, C3381/7/12 (FO 371/22896).
[4] Dilks, ed., *Cadogan Diaries*, 13 Mar. 1939, p. 156.

semblance of independence, he could still make the Czechs themselves responsible for their future political and economic troubles'.[1] During the course of the day, however, the evidence became too strong to disregard. Halifax, Stanley, Cadogan, Vansittart, Sargent, Malkin, and Oliver Harvey met and agreed that

> we must make no empty threats since we are not going to fight for Czechoslovakia any more than for Danzig, although we would fight for Switzerland, Belgium, Holland, or Tunis. We should stop Stanley's visit to Berlin (due to start tomorrow) and perhaps recall Henderson to report. P.M. might also make a statement deploring this departure from the Munich spirit. We should not, however, regard ourselves as in any way guaranteeing Czechoslovakia.[2]

Chamberlain, against the judgement of the Foreign Office, wanted at least to register his disapproval in Berlin before the event. Cadogan and Halifax duly drafted a note referring to Britain's concern 'for the success of all efforts to restore confidence and a relaxation of tension in Europe', particularly at a time when economic discussions showed every sign of developing fruitfully.[3] Cadogan rightly thought this to be 'quite useless'.[4]

Cadogan was more concerned to prepare a defence against pressure to invoke the guarantee:

> at the time of the Anglo-French discussions in London in September last we had indicated that we should be prepared to take part in an international guarantee of these frontiers. We had confirmed this at Munich, where the German and Italian Governments had also said that they would join in a guarantee given by the four Munich Powers, but although we had made an approach to the other Governments we had not yet been able to obtain agreement on the terms of the guarantee. We were not, therefore, bound by any definite instrument.[5]

On the morning of 15 March the Cabinet was called to discuss Hitler's invasion of Czechoslovakia. Chamberlain preferred a different way out of the guarantee to Cadogan's:

> the fundamental fact was that the State whose frontiers we had undertaken to guarantee against unprovoked aggression had now completely broken up.... It might, no doubt, be true that the disruption of Czecho-

---

[1] 'Notes for Secretary of State on the Origins and Development of the Slovak Crisis', 14 Mar. 1939, C3243/7/12 (FO 371/22897).
[2] *Harvey Diaries*, 14 Mar. 1939, p. 261. The reference to Danzig is interesting in view of later developments. See below, pp. 169–70.
[3] Halifax to Henderson, 14 Mar. 1939, *DBFP* iv, no. 247.
[4] Dilks, ed., *Cadogan Diaries*, 14 Mar. 1939, p. 156.
[5] Minute by Cadogan, 14 Mar. 1939, C3156/7/12 (FO 371/22897).

Slovakia had been largely engineered by Germany, but our guarantee was not a guarantee against the exercise of moral pressure.[1]

Halifax added that Inskip's 'moral obligation' had been intended as 'a means of steadying the position during what was thought to be a purely transitory situation'. These were merely arguments for public consumption. The real reason for disregarding the guarantee was, as Cadogan had pointed out, that if Britain had not been in a position to help a much stronger Czechoslovakia in September 1938, the possibility of helping her now was still more remote.

Leslie Hore-Belisha, the Secretary of State for War, raised the very pertinent question of Hitler's further intentions. So far only Germans had been incorporated into the Reich, but 'the present step resulted in the establishment of German dominance over non-German peoples'. It all pointed to the *Drang nach Osten*. He thought that the Hungarian annexation of Ruthenia was in fact in Britain's interest, and that Britain should strengthen her relations with Turkey, Rumania, and, if possible, Hungary. But in one of those typical and frequent demonstrations of his complete control over the Cabinet, Chamberlain indicated that he was not interested in discussing these larger issues for the time being. He wanted the Cabinet to decide whether or not Stanley and Hudson should go to Berlin as planned; what he himself should tell the House of Commons that afternoon; and what should be done about the unused portion of the British loan to Czechoslovakia.[2]

The Cabinet agreed that the Berlin visit should be postponed,[3] but thought it would be 'premature' to recall Henderson from his post even for consultation. Turning to the subject of his statement, Chamberlain wanted to express the Government's regret at the military occupation of parts of Czechoslovakia, and to say that in the circumstances, Stanley and Hudson could not go to Berlin. Somebody questioned the wisdom of emphasizing the military occupation on the ground that 'the Czecho-Slovak Government had invited this step', but Chamberlain replied that Hitler 'had for some time past been working for a military demonstration'.

[1] Cab. Minutes, 15 Mar. 1939, CAB 23/98.
[2] A loan to Czechoslovakia of £10 million had been authorized by Act of Parliament in February 1939. £3¼ million of this sum had already been advanced in October 1938. The Government now froze the remainder.
[3] That is according to the final version of the minutes. According to the original draft, the visit was to have been cancelled. Presumably the decision was modified after the meeting. See draft minutes in C3353/19/18 (FO 371/22994).

Halifax took up Hore-Belisha's earlier remarks, thinking it important 'to find language which would imply that Germany was now being led on to a dangerous path. . . . Germany's attitude in this matter was completely inconsistent with the Munich agreement. Germany had deliberately preferred naked force to the methods of consultation and discussion.' Sir John Simon, the Chancellor of the Exchequer, wanted Chamberlain, who agreed, to make it quite clear that Britain was no longer bound by the guarantee. Chamberlain and Halifax were left to settle the terms of the statement on the lines of the discussion, which they did in consultation with Cadogan and Wilson.[1]

Neville Chamberlain's speech to the House of Commons that afternoon was unusually eclectic. It was a composite of all the points raised by his Cabinet colleagues, shaped mainly by Cadogan's hand, but it included an unexpected and, to many, unwelcome passage of his own at the end. He began with an account of the Czechoslovak crisis and the German and Hungarian military actions. He then informed the House that, since Czechoslovakia's existence had been 'terminated by internal disruption', the British guarantee no longer applied; that the balance of the British loan would remain in Britain; and that the Stanley–Hudson visit to Berlin was postponed. He went on to justify the Munich agreement, which, he said, 'has not proved to be final'. He would not 'today' associate himself with accusations of bad faith, but he could not believe 'that anything of the kind which has now taken place was contemplated by any of the signatories of the Munich agreement at the time of its signature'. The spirit of Munich had been violated. Furthermore, he recognized that for the first time the Germans were occupying territory inhabited by people with whom they had no racial connection. So far he had kept to the agreed line. But at the end he added:

Though we may have to suffer checks and disappointments, from time to time, the object that we have in mind is of too great significance to the happiness of mankind for us lightly to give it up or set it on one side. It is natural . . . that I should bitterly regret what has now occurred. But do not let us on that account be deflected from our course.[2]

Cadogan's ear was sufficiently attuned for this to strike him: 'Said he would base himself on statement, and did so, but added that he

---

[1] Dilks, ed., *Cadogan Diaries*, 15 Mar. 1939, p. 158.
[2] 345 HC Deb. 5 s., cols. 435–40.

would go on with his "policy" (?appeasement). Fatal!'[1] On the other hand one of the Prime Minister's critics in Parliament, Harold Nicolson, was not unfavourably impressed:

> The Prime Minister opens. He looks very haggard. He makes a very lame defence of his policy and a most jesuitical exegesis regarding the guarantee question. But he admits frankly that appeasement has failed and that the spirit of Munich has been violated.[2]

The historian Neville Thompson has written that the ensuing debate was 'a serious set-back for the Prime Minister' and that the House 'was in no mood for this kind of complacent acceptance'.[3] He gives the impression that Chamberlain was deserted wholesale by his supporters, with the sole exception of 'the ancient M.P. for Windsor', A. A. Somerville. In fact, of the ten main Conservative speeches, five were in support of Chamberlain's policy.[4] The *Manchester Guardian* Political Correspondent noted that Chamberlain's final words 'got a cheer from his own side', although 'it was not a strong cheer, not the sort of cheer it would have got a month ago'.[5] The other Conservatives were all members of the 'Eden group',[6] with the exception of Duncan Sandys, one of Churchill's clique. Eden himself spoke, denouncing the Prague coup in stronger terms than Chamberlain. He called for a 'truly all-Party Government', his old refrain, and for consultation with other powers 'to discuss with

[1] Dilks, ed., *Cadogan Diaries*, 15 Mar. 1939, p. 158.
[2] Balliol College, Oxford, Sir Harold Nicolson Papers, Diary, 15 Mar. 1939.
[3] Thompson, *The Anti-Appeasers*, pp. 204 and 202.
[4] In addition to Somerville, Chamberlain's supporters were Donner, De Chair, G. Nicholson, and Southby.
[5] *Manchester Guardian Weekly*, 17 Mar. 1939, p. 206.
[6] Also known as the 'Glamour Boys'. The group included Eden, Cranborne, J. P. L. Thomas, Mark Patrick, L. S. Amery, Commander Bower, Ronald Cartland, Anthony Crossley, H. J. Duggan, Paul Emrys-Evans, Sir D. Gunston, Sidney Herbert, Dudley Joel, Colonel Lancaster, Richard Law, Harold Macmillan, Harold Nicolson, Sir Edward Spears, Ronald Tree, and Lord Wolmer. They took a Burkean line towards the Government, preferring pressure and influence to direct confrontation and opposition in their attempts to alter policy. This tactic was no doubt partly inspired by Eden's desire to keep a record of respectability in case he was asked to return to power. The group opposed continued negotiation with Germany and Italy, thought largely in 'balance of power' terms, and saw in Eden a 'symbol of resistance to the dictators' (Thompson, *The Anti-Appeasers*, p. 168; Robert Rhodes James, *Churchill: A Study in Failure, 1900–1939* (London, 1970), p. 335; see also Nicolson, *Diaries and Letters 1930–1939*, which omits many interesting passages about the group's activities at this time.

those nations what our policy is to be and where we will make our stand'.[1] But he and his followers had previously concluded that

> We must support the Government but that we must prevent Oliver Stanley and Hudson from going to Berlin. That would be taken as an approval of Germany's action and would be exploited in Berlin in order to show that we in England really approved of their 'Einmarsch'. So we agree that A. [Eden] should speak approving the policy of the P.M.[2]

Thus at this point there was no question of a threat to Chamberlain's position as leader of the Conservative Party.

On the other hand the Labour and Liberal Opposition, in keeping with their usual practice, denounced Chamberlain and Hitler almost in the same breath. Thus they would have nothing to do with Eden's call for unity. They did, however, agree that Britain must rally the support of friendly nations, a demand which developed into the key issue of the debate. But Sir John Simon, replying for the Government, deprecated any extension of Britain's commitments as placing the control of her destiny outside her own hands.[3]

Likewise at the Cabinet meeting that morning Chamberlain had refused to discuss the question of what Britain should do to oppose any further extension of German power in Europe. At the same time it is clear from his remarks that he was in fact quite ready to charge Hitler with breach of faith. Why then did he not do so publicly, and why did he indicate his intention to continue his policy of *rapprochement* with Germany? Firstly there was the question of time. Chamberlain was personally identified with his policy and so deeply committed to it that he required time to weigh the evidence closely before considering future policy. This was bound up with his particular style of decision-making. As usual, he had not used the Cabinet that morning as a forum for debating long-term policy options. The limits of discussion were strictly defined to include only the most immediate questions. Once he had himself decided on policy, in consultation with his closest advisers, he would call the Cabinet together for its approval.

There was a second and more important reason for Chamberlain's restraint on 15 March. Although his hopes for disarmament and political agreement may have been dashed, he remained optimistic

---

[1] 345 HC Deb. 5 s., cols. 461–2.
[2] Nicolson Papers, Diary, 15 Mar. 1939.
[3] 345 HC Deb. 5 s , col. 557.

about the prospects for economic agreement with Germany, at least on the industrial level at which negotiations had begun that day. Chamberlain's concern for the success of the negotiations in Düsseldorf between the Federation of British Industries and the Reichsgruppe Industrie was evident from his speech. 'These discussions', he said, 'are still proceeding, and I believe are proceeding in a satisfactory manner.'[1] In fact they were not. Magowan, the British Commercial Attaché in Berlin, reported on 21 March that 'the Germans had been playing for position rather than making a genuine advance towards the British point of view',[2] and the Central Department minuted that 'it does not look as if the Germans ever intended these talks to succeed, quite apart from the Czech crisis'.[3]

By 17 March Chamberlain was rapidly losing support. Harold Nicolson wrote in his diary that

the feeling in the lobbies is that Chamberlain will either have to go or completely reverse his policy. Unless in his speech tonight he admits that he was wrong, they feel that resignation is the only alternative. All the tadpoles are beginning to swim into the other camp and we find ourself in the odd position of being Mr. Chamberlain's loyal supporters. The difficulty is that he himself cannot introduce conscription because he can only do so with a Coalition Government. The Opposition refuse absolutely to serve under him. The idea is that Halifax should become Prime Minister and Eden Leader of the House.[4]

On the same day the political correspondent of the *Spectator* reported that 'unless the Government can show very soon that they are fully alive to the German danger and are prepared to take the most drastic steps to meet it, it does really seem that there will be a revolt of Government supporters'.[5]

[1] Ibid., col. 438.
[2] C. A. MacDonald, 'Economic Appeasement', p. 126.
[3] Quoted ibid., pp. 126–7. There soon arose demands for British economic sanctions against German exports in reprisal for the German action (Weber to German Foreign Ministry, 28 Mar. 1939, *DGFP* vi, no. 116). On 23 March the leaders of the Labour movement asked Chamberlain about the possibility of an economic boycott (Minutes of meeting with Labour deputation, 23 Mar. 1939, C4317/15/18 (FO 371/22967)). It is only in this context that Chamberlain's statement to the House of Commons on the same day, that Britain did not want to 'stand in the way of any reasonable efforts on the part of Germany to expand her export trade', is understandable (345 HC Deb. 5 s., col. 1462). It is also likely that Chamberlain did not want to close the door completely to future trade negotiations, although on 24 May he was still against making any move (C. A. MacDonald, 'Economic Appeasement', p. 128).
[4] Nicolson, *Diaries and Letters 1930–1939*, p. 393.
[5] *Spectator*, 17 Mar. 1939, p. 431.

Halifax, whose political ear was closer to the ground than Chamberlain's at this point, mainly as a result of his contacts with Eden,[1] apparently warned Chamberlain that his position was seriously threatened, and that he must take advantage of his speech at Birmingham, long planned for 17 March, 'to make the policy of the Government plain'.[2] On 16 March Cadogan noted that Chamberlain had been 'binged up to be a bit firmer',[3] and Oliver Harvey confirms this.[4] On the other hand Chamberlain may not have needed much persuading, and it is possible that Halifax's influence was less decisive than is commonly believed. When R. A. Butler, Parliamentary Under-Secretary for Foreign Affairs, lunched with Halifax and Chamberlain at No. 10 on 16 March, 'the Prime Minister said with resignation, but with our solemn approval, "I have decided that I cannot trust the Nazi leaders again."'[5] Chamberlain himself told the Cabinet on 18 March that he had decided that 'Herr Hitler's attitude made it impossible to continue to negotiate on the old basis with the Nazi regime', and that 'no reliance could be placed on any of the assurances given by the Nazi leaders'. It was on the basis of this conclusion, he said, 'and after consultation with the Foreign Secretary, and others of his colleagues who were immediately available, that he had made his speech at Birmingham'.[6]

At Birmingham, his home and constituency, Chamberlain received a tumultuous welcome. His speech was broadcast to the Empire and to America. His delivery was slow and measured. He said that he had intended to talk about trade, employment, social service, and finance. But 'the tremendous events which have been taking place this week in Europe have thrown everything else into the background'. He explained that his speech on 15 March had been informed by incomplete and unofficial information. He had had no time to digest it, much less to form a considered opinion on it.

And, perhaps naturally, that somewhat cool and objective statement gave rise to a misapprehension, and some people thought that because I spoke quietly, because I gave little expression to feeling, therefore my

---

[1] *Harvey Diaries*, 18 Mar. 1939, p. 263.
[2] Birkenhead, *Halifax*, p. 432.
[3] Dilks, ed., *Cadogan Diaries*, 16 Mar. 1939, p. 157.
[4] *Harvey Diaries*, 16 Mar. 1939, p. 262.
[5] Lord Butler, *The Art of the Possible* (London, 1971), p. 77.
[6] Cab. Minutes, 18 Mar. 1939, CAB 23/98.

colleagues and I did not feel strongly on the subject. I hope to correct that mistake tonight.[1]

He then defended Munich at length, saying that he had hoped not only to avoid war but also to discover whether there existed any basis for agreement with Germany. He had been encouraged by Hitler's peaceful assurances, which he quoted. All these had now been broken. He dwelt on the sufferings of the Czechs, accused Germany of fomenting the crisis, and asked how Hitler's word could be trusted again. Was this 'the end of an old adventure' or 'the beginning of a new?' Was it, in fact, 'a step in the direction of an attempt to dominate the world by force?' He hinted at consultation with other powers:

We ourselves will naturally turn first to our partners in the British Commonwealth of Nations (cheers)—and to France—(cheers)—to whom we are so closely bound, and I have no doubt that others, too, knowing that we are not disinterested in what goes on in South-Eastern Europe, will wish to have our counsel and advice.[1]

On the other hand he was 'not prepared to engage this country by new unspecified commitments operating under conditions which cannot now be foreseen'.

Chamberlain's speech was a success, both at home and abroad. 'Chips' Channon, Private Secretary to R. A. Butler, the Parliamentary Under-Secretary for Foreign Affairs, wrote in his diary that 'the country is solidly behind Chamberlain just now: all criticism of him is temporarily stilled'.[2]

Meanwhile the Foreign Office was at a loss as to what to do. Cadogan minuted on 16 March that 'at the moment, it would be difficult to formulate anything. The S[ecretary] of S[tate] is consulting with the P.M. about the latter's speech at Birmingham tomorrow night and he [Halifax] will be speaking on Monday. We may have a clearer line by then.'[3] On the same day he and Halifax, Sargent, Leeper, and Harvey all discussed what Halifax should say in the House of Lords on 20 March. The fact that his speech paralleled Chamberlain's indicates that many of the latter's points must indeed have emanated from the Foreign Office.

Foreign Office officials were very aware of public opinion, of its pitfalls and its potential. Thus although they disliked the idea of a

[1] *The Times*, 18 Mar. 1939, and B.B.C. Record Library, London.
[2] R. Rhodes James, ed., *Chips. The Diaries of Sir Henry Channon* (London, 1967), 17 Mar. 1939, p. 186.
[3] Minute by Cadogan, 16 Mar. 1939, C3313/19/18 (FO 371/22993).

formal protest to Germany, first suggested by the French Ambassador in London, Charles Corbin, they recognized that 'it may be desirable for political purposes in this country'.[1] One was duly sent off on 17 March.[2] On the other hand at least one official wanted to make use of the anti-German feeling that was sweeping Britain.[3] Ivone Kirkpatrick, First Secretary in the Central Department, wrote on 17 March:

> The knowledge we possess of Herr Hitler's character and our experience of his methods makes it humanly certain that the present coup will be followed by a brief or very brief lull during which the optimists will tell us that Hitler has renounced his evil ways and that in consequence we have nothing to fear. It is during this period that public opinion, whom the Government have to consider, are difficult to move. Consequently if action to meet the German menace is to be taken a move should be made whilst the public are still under the influence of the latest coup. Accordingly there is no time to lose.[4]

Kirkpatrick (and many of his colleagues) wanted the introduction of conscription and Henderson recalled from Berlin. He also suggested a ban on all social intercourse between British and German army officers. He admitted that this idea seemed 'theatrical and fantastic' but thought that 'nothing would be such a blow to the self-esteem of the German officer than to be told... that he is supporting a disreputable régime and that he is not fit for the society of British officers'.

Henderson was in fact recalled that day 'to report', reversing the Cabinet's decision, but Halifax disliked Kirkpatrick's unique suggestion because he wanted to 'encourage a rift between the Army and the Party' in Germany rather than to lump them all together.[5] Nevertheless Halifax heeded his appeal for striking while the iron was hot, which indicates that the Government did not merely respond to the new mood in Britain at this time but sought to use it. All that was required was a pretext.

[1] Minute by Sargent, 17 Mar. 1939, C3102/15/18 (FO 371/22966).
[2] Halifax to Henderson, 17 Mar. 1939, *DBFP* iv, no. 308.
[3] The best description of this mood is by Robert Rhodes James: 'after the annexation of Czechoslovakia . . . the possibility of averting war with Germany was entertained only by a minority in Britain. By some strange process which is inexplicable to those who were not alive then, the fear of war which had been too evident in 1938 seemed to evaporate. The British did not want war, but the spirit in the air was not pacific. There was a weariness with procrastination, an aversion from false promises and wishful thinking, and a yearning for a simple, clear solution' (James, *Churchill: A Study in Failure*, p. 342).
[4] Minute by Kirkpatrick, 17 Mar. 1939, C3529/19/18 (FO 371/22994).
[5] Minute by Halifax, 19 Mar. 1939, ibid.

6

A TENTATIVE INITIATIVE

THE Anglo-German struggle for power and influence in central and south-eastern Europe was placed in stark relief by the German occupation of Bohemia and Moravia on the night of 14 March 1939. Three days later, when Virgil Tilea, the Rumanian Minister in London, was reported to have informed the British Foreign Office that Germany had presented his country with an ultimatum, the threat could not be ignored. In an atmosphere charged with rumour and alarm, the British challenge to German hegemony in Europe now shifted in emphasis from the economic to the political plane.

German policy in south-eastern Europe, as we have seen, was aimed at securing improved terms of trade with the area by means of the manipulation of exchange control, imposed first as a protective necessity but later used as a means of furthering German interests. Since November 1938, the key to the success of this policy was seen in Germany's relations with Rumania, whose economy the German Office of the Four-Year Plan sought to adapt to German needs. Trade negotiations took place in February and March 1939, and it was agreed that they should form the basis for 'large-scale, carefully planned cooperation over a long period of time'.[1] They were considered of the utmost importance in Germany. Helmuth Wohlthat, head of the German delegation, expected that 'orienting the Rumanian economy toward Germany by joint planning over a number of years will secure Germany the dominant position in south-eastern Europe, since similar treaties with the Balkan Powers could be expected to follow'.[1]

The British Government, as we have seen, were alarmed by this trend in German policy and attempted to counter it. In May 1938 they had accepted that the aim must be 'to ensure that this area of Europe shall look specifically for leadership to this country, and generally toward the Western Powers, rather than feel obliged in default of any other *point d'appui* to allow itself to be exploited by

[1] Wohlthat to Wiehl, 27 Feb. 1939, *DGFP* v, no. 306.

Berlin'.[1] While the British were unwilling to extend their commitments to include political guarantees, they were nevertheless ready to use their financial and commercial weight to help the countries of central and south-eastern Europe maintain their independence. With regard to Rumania, Britain favoured a number of *ad hoc* measures such as the wheat purchase made in November 1938,[2] rather than long-term schemes of the sort favoured by Germany. Such an approach would have been as alien to the pragmatic conduct of British policy as it would have been to the free-enterprise nature of the economy. It would also have been more difficult to justify in terms of national security to the signatories of the 1932 Ottawa Agreement, which established the system of Imperial Preference, and to the United States Government, with whom Britain had signed a comprehensive trade agreement in November 1938. Nevertheless certain long-term investment projects were worked out in Whitehall as a result of the London visit of King Carol of Rumania in November 1938. The Government proposed to send a trade mission to Bucharest to discuss these schemes, but kept their intention secret so as not to jeopardize the Anglo-German trade negotiations in progress. Meanwhile, Franco-Rumanian trade talks took place between January and March 1939, as a result of which Rumania received a tied loan of 500,000,000 francs and France increased her oil and grain purchases.[3]

The Rumanian Government were in a good position to exploit this great-Power rivalry, and their representatives in Paris and London constantly drew attention to the growing German influence. The western interest thus elicited was expected to influence favourably the course of the negotiations with Germany. German control of Czechoslovakia, however, altered both the balance of power and the significance of these negotiations, not only for Rumania but also for Britain and France.

According to the Rumanian Foreign Minister, Grigore Gafencu, the negotiations had begun well since Wohlthat 'appeared to accept the Rumanian thesis that a reasonable percentage of Rumanian trade must be with the strong-currency countries'.[4] But the establish-

---

[1] Cab. Memorandum: 'British Influence in Central and South-Eastern Europe', 24 May 1938, CP 127 (38), CAB 24/277.
[2] See above, pp. 44–5.
[3] A. and V. Toynbee, eds., *The Eve of War, 1939* (London, 1958), pp. 190–1. The Franco-Rumanian Trade Treaty was signed on 31 March 1939.
[4] Hoare to Halifax, 18 Feb. 1939, R1200/113/37 (FO 371/23831).

ment of a German protectorate over Bohemia and Moravia complicated matters. The Rumanians, plainly alarmed by the new implications of large-scale German participation in the economy, tried to stall the negotiations by raising new objections of principle.[1] They also asked for an assurance that there would be no interference with their previously ordered arms deliveries from Czechoslovakia. This was given only on 23 March, when the German-Rumanian Trade Treaty was duly signed.[2]

At the same time Rumania applied pressure in London. On 14 March Virgil Tilea warned the Foreign Office that acquiescence in Germany's designs on Czechoslovakia would have disastrous repercussions on Britain's prestige, and suggested among other things that the proposed commercial mission be sent at once to Bucharest and fully publicized.[3] On 16 March he told Sir Orme Sargent, Assistant Under-Secretary at the Foreign Office, that 'his Government, from secret and other sources, had good reason to believe that within the next few months the German Government would reduce Hungary to vassalage and then proceed to disintegrate Rumania ... with the ultimate object of establishing a German protectorate over the whole country'. He requested a £10 million loan for arms purchases from Czechoslovakia to replace those thought lost as a result of the German invasion.[4]

There appears to have been little immediate reaction to these proposals in the Foreign Office, although Sargent did press for the immediate dispatch of the British trade mission.[5] Firstly Tilea had stressed their unofficial nature. Secondly the Foreign Office was in a turmoil. As the Permanent Under-Secretary, Sir Alexander Cadogan, noted in his diary on 16 March: 'Don't know *where* we are.'[6] Thirdly, as Sargent explained to Tilea, they 'raised questions of high policy'.[7] Thus Cadogan minuted on 17 March that although he was due to see the Rumanian Minister that evening, 'of course I shall not be in a position to give him an answer'.[8]

But Tilea had already decided to make his *démarche* official. On

[1] Wohlthat to Weizsäcker, 30 Mar. 1939, *DGFP* vi, no. 131.
[2] Fabricius to German Foreign Ministry, 18 Mar. 1939, ibid., no. 31.
[3] Halifax to Hoare, 16 Mar. 1939, *DBFP* iv, no. 297.
[4] Minute by Sargent, 16 Mar. 1939, ibid., no. 298.
[5] Minute by Nichols, 17 Mar. 1939, R1814/113/37 (FO 371/23832).
[6] Dilks, ed., *Cadogan Diaries*, 16 Mar. 1939, p. 157.
[7] Minute by Sargent, 16 Mar. 1939, *DBFP* iv, no. 298.
[8] Minute by Cadogan, 17 Mar. 1939, C3857/3356/18 (FO 371/23061).

17 March he repeated his request for a loan to the Foreign Secretary, Lord Halifax, and raised the possibility 'that the German Government would make an almost immediate thrust upon Roumania'. For

during the last few days the Roumanian Government had received a request from the German Government to grant them a monopoly of Roumanian exports, and to adopt certain measures of restriction of Roumanian industrial production in German interests. If these conditions were accepted, Germany would guarantee the Roumanian frontiers. This seemed to the Roumanian Government something very much like an ultimatum.

Tilea then asked whether his Government could count on British support, and suggested that the situation might be saved 'if it was possible to construct a solid block of Poland, Roumania, Greece, Turkey, Yugoslavia with the support of Great Britain and France'. To this end the Polish-Rumanian Treaty of 1931, which envisaged mutual support against Russian aggression, and the Balkan Entente, which applied only to Bulgarian aggression, could both be made applicable to Germany.[1] Halifax undertook to put the question to the Cabinet.[2]

This information must have strongly impressed the Foreign Secretary, because just before his interview with Tilea he had heard from his Private Secretary, Oliver Harvey, that Princess Marthe Bibesco, a Rumanian writer living in London, 'had just been speaking to Bucharest to the President of the Council [Armand Calinescu] who had told her that Germany had presented an economic ultimatum to Rumania'.[3]

These alarming reports had to be evaluated in the context of Hungarian intentions, since German troops could only reach Rumania through Hungarian territory. Since 1920 Hungary had been intent on revision of the Treaty of Trianon, under the terms of which she had ceded, among other things, Transylvania to Rumania and most of Slovakia and Ruthenia (Sub-Carpathian Ukraine) to Czechoslovakia. Her aim had been partly achieved after Munich, when Germany and Italy, with the Vienna Award, allowed her to recover large areas in the south of Slovakia and Ruthenia. Hungary rapidly followed the German invasion of Bohemia and Moravia with the

---

[1] The Entente was signed in 1934 by Turkey, Yugoslavia, Rumania, and Greece.
[2] Halifax to Hoare, 17 Mar. 1939, *DBFP* iv, no. 395.
[3] *Harvey Diaries*, 18 Mar. 1939, p. 263.

A TENTATIVE INITIATIVE 111

annexation of Ruthenia, and concentrated her troops on the Rumanian border, maintaining a state of tension until 24 March, the day after the signing of the German-Rumanian Trade Treaty. The British Minister in Budapest, Sir George Knox, later thought that Hungary's mobilization 'had been inspired and used by Germany to wring economic concessions from Roumania'.[1] But on 17 March the threat seemed more immediate. On that day Sir Robert Vansittart, formerly Permanent Under-Secretary and now Chief Diplomatic Adviser to the British Government, reported that in case of a European conflict the Hungarian Government had undertaken on 14 March 'to allow German troops to pass through Hungary on their way to occupy the Roumanian oil-fields' and 'to place the Hungarian army at the disposal of the German General Staff' in case of Rumanian resistance.[2] Gladwyn Jebb, Cadogan's Private Secretary and in charge of Foreign Office liaison with the Secret Intelligence Service, concluded on 18 March on the basis of S.I.S. information that 'it seems therefore clear that, from the purely military point of view, Germany may be preparing for a drive through Hungary to Roumania, in concert with Bulgaria, accompanied by defensive action only in the West'.[3] This sort of report confirmed the Foreign Office in its suspicion that Hungary would do Germany's bidding. The alleged German threat to Rumania was therefore seriously considered in the Foreign Office, although when Tilea returned for his interview with Cadogan, he told the Permanent Under-Secretary that the Rumanian Government 'had refused these proposals, and that further proposals had subsequently been received from the German Government, but that of these he had not particulars'.[4]

It is hard to judge whether this heightened or lessened the tension, but Tilea's earlier news presented Britain with an ideal opportunity to regain the initiative. As Cadogan had asked in exasperation in October 1938, 'Can we take any initiative? Can we make the Germans guess, and so reverse the process, under which we have suffered for years, of the Germans "keeping us guessing"?'[5] The international atmosphere was charged with nervous apprehension. For example it

[1] Knox to Halifax, 24 Mar. 1939, C3995/3356/18 (FO 371/23061).
[2] Minute by Vansittart, 17 Mar. 1939, C3749/3356/18 (ibid.).
[3] Memorandum by Jebb: 'Summary of S.I.S. military information regarding Germany', 18 Mar. 1939, C3565/13/18 (FO 371/22958).
[4] Halifax to Hoare, 17 Mar. 1939, *DBFP* iv, no. 395.
[5] Minute by Cadogan, 14 Oct. 1938, C14471/41/18 (FO 371/21659).

was virtually certain that Memel, the German city seized by Lithuania in 1923, would be annexed within the next few days,[1] Danzig was threatened;[2] an attack on the West was intimated;[3] news had just been received that Italy was about to act with regard to her claims on France or on Albania.[4] Public opinion was now thoroughly aroused, but more important to the Foreign Office, reports from around the world indicated that British prestige had suffered a serious blow. If Britain did not face the issue of German predominance in Europe now, her actual and potential allies might resign themselves to continued isolation or increased reliance on Germany, whereas her potential enemies would draw the conclusion that they had little to fear in testing the weak points of the British Empire. This applied particularly to Italy and Japan, whose lack of concrete commitment to Germany held out continual hope to British policy-makers.

While Neville Chamberlain was speaking in Birmingham on the evening of 17 March, Halifax, Cadogan, and Sargent dispatched telegrams to France, Russia, Poland, Turkey, Greece, and Yugoslavia 'referring to this threat to Roumania, and asking them, more or less, what they will do about it'.[5] No doubt they hoped to receive confirmation of Tilea's report as a by-product of these inquiries, for it would have been hard to believe, as was later pointed out, that the Rumanians had failed to approach their allies first.[6]

On the next morning, 18 March, the head of the Secret Intelligence Service, Admiral Sinclair, informed the Foreign Office that the news of the ultimatum might be false.[7] At 12.30 p.m. Sir Reginald Hoare, the British Minister in Bucharest, advised London to cancel the previous night's telegrams, a copy of which he had also received, and at 3.40 p.m. followed this up with the explanation that the story of an ultimatum had appeared so improbable that he had sought confirmation of it from the Rumanian Foreign Minister.[8] Gafencu had confirmed his impression 'that economic negotiations with the Germans were proceeding on completely normal lines as between

---

[1] Halifax to Phipps, 18 Mar. 1939, *DBFP* iv, no. 413.
[2] Kennard to Halifax, 17 Mar. 1939, ibid., no. 391.
[3] Minute by Roberts, 14 Mar. 1939, C2994/15/18 (FO 371/22966).
[4] Minute by Nichols, 17 Mar. 1939, FO 371/22967, f. 206 (no registry no.).
[5] Dilks, ed., *Cadogan Diaries*, 17 Mar. 1939, p. 160.
[6] Waterlow to Halifax, 19 Mar. 1939, *DBFP* iv, no. 425.
[7] Minute by Leeper, 18 Mar. 1939, C3563/3356/18 (FO 371/23060).
[8] Hoare to Halifax, 18 Mar. 1939, *DBFP* iv, nos. 397, 399.

A TENTATIVE INITIATIVE

equals' and that '*for the moment* there was no threat to Roumania's political or economic independence'. Gafencu 'was distressed that the Roumanian Minister should in an excess of zeal have misrepresented the situation'.

Tilea, when confronted by Cadogan with this *démenti*, continued to maintain that the ultimatum had been presented. He had, however, received his information from a private source, 'the general manager of a big Roumanian industrialist, who had come specially to Paris to pass the news on to him'. Tilea had urged the rejection of this ultimatum in a letter to the Rumanian Minister of Economics, Ion Bujoiu, who had telephoned him that morning (18 March) 'to say that discussions with the Germans were continuing on questions of principle: that they were not discussing details and that he hoped to continue discussion of general principles in order to gain time'. Cadogan diplomatically suggested to Tilea that there might be some truth in both stories, but said that it was not clear that Tilea 'had at any time obtained knowledge of the ultimatum directly from his Government'. Tilea replied that Bujoiu had not denied the ultimatum, to which Cadogan retorted that neither had he confirmed it. Cadogan must have registered surprise at Tilea's further confession, that he had not informed his Government of his request for an armaments loan of £10 million because he felt that a refusal 'would dishearten his Government and might have a very bad effect'. Cadogan minuted on his report that 'on the whole I do not think that my interview with M. Tilea increased my confidence in him'.[1]

The explanation for Tilea's *démarche* has been hotly debated. There are five possibilities. The first is that he acted purely on his own. The Rumanian historian, V. Mosiuc, has written that there is no reference to a German ultimatum either in the instructions on which Tilea acted or in his own account of his conversation with Halifax.[2] Theo Kordt, the German Chargé d'Affaires in London, reported on 19 March that he had learned 'from a reliable informant' that Tilea had acted 'on his own initiative' because 'German-Rumanian economic negotiations appeared to be producing favourable results, and, in consequence, his own plans for developing Anglo-Rumanian economic relations would come to nothing'.[3] The American Minister in

[1] Minute by Cadogan, 18 Mar. 1939, C3538/3356/18 (FO 371/23060).
[2] D. Irving, ed., *Breach of Security, The German Secret Intelligence File on Events leading to the Second World War* (London, 1968), Introduction by D. C. Watt, p. 28.
[3] Kordt to German Foreign Ministry, 19 Mar. 1939, *DGFP* vi, no. 42.

Bucharest, Gunther, reported on 20 March that 'when taken to task Foreign Minister Gafencu says Tilea replied that he was merely trying to be helpful'.[1] Gunther's British colleague, Sir Reginald Hoare, judged that before leaving for London Tilea had received some sort of general instruction from King Carol to use every effort to convince the British Government 'of the necessities of the situation in South-Eastern Europe and that he set about his task with impulsive naïveté'.[2]

The second possibility is that Tilea was used by the most virulently anti-German group in the Foreign Office, and specifically by Sir Robert Vansittart, to persuade the British Government to commit themselves to resist further German aggression. The British Embassy in Berlin reported that the official Nazi newspaper, the *Völkischer Beobachter*, had on 20 March published an article by its London correspondent, Dr. Boetticher, which included the following:

Panic was artificially raised on Saturday in London and later also in Paris by reports issued by British news agencies to the effect that Germany had presented a trade ultimatum to Bucharest. This was followed a few hours later by the news that King Carol had appealed for help to the British and French Governments . . .

In the opinion of diplomatic circles it is incontestable that M. Tilea in agreement with Sir Robert Vansittart, is the author of these panic reports. M. Tilea obviously thinks it would be detrimental to his career if his country should increase its exports owing to the results of German–Roumanian trade conversations now being held although he has at the same time failed in his efforts to bring about closer trade relations between Roumania and England. Sir Robert Vansittart, according to London opinion, had looked upon the invented ultimatum as a suitable means to win over British public opinion and also British Ministers to the policy of military co-operation between England and the states of the East and South East.[3]

Halifax immediately suppressed the distribution of this report inside and outside the Foreign Office. This need not be taken as an indication that he knew or suspected it to be true, but must be seen in the context of Vansittart's already controversial reputation. There is no doubt that there existed a faction in the Foreign Office that now opposed all efforts to reach agreement with Germany, associated in

[1] Gunther to Hull, 20 Mar. 1939, U.S. Department of State, *Foreign Relations of the United States. Diplomatic Papers, 1939* (Washington, D.C., 1956), i. 75. This series is cited hereafter as *FRUS*.

[2] Hoare to Halifax, 20 Mar. 1939, *DBFP* iv, no. 443.

[3] Quoted in Ogilvie-Forbes to Halifax, 20 Mar. 1939, C2/39/— (FO 800/294).

A TENTATIVE INITIATIVE

particular with Vansittart. He was the *bête noire* of German propaganda, which placed him at the head of a Foreign Office 'war party', at best resisting any sort of settlement with Germany, at worst advocating preventive war against her. Halifax was aware that Foreign Office influence on policy-making in these crucial days must not be jeopardized. It had already suffered enough from internal division and a reputation for opposition to the Prime Minister's ideas. He was also possibly in favour of Vansittart's role of devil's advocate, for although when in a bad temper he would ask Cadogan how to get rid of him, he seems to have favoured his presence at Foreign Office meetings.[1] Halifax therefore prevented the distribution of the article in the circles where it was calculated to undermine both Vansittart's influence and the British diplomatic initiative which Tilea's information had engendered.

Tilea's own explanation is that the Foreign Office already knew about an economic ultimatum from secret sources and conveniently attributed the information to the Rumanian Minister.[2] He denies the accuracy of the Foreign Office archives where they allege that he spoke of a *specific* German ultimatum to Rumania. He maintains that he spoke in general terms only, saying that the German economic demands were virtually an ultimatum in the sense that the threat of direct German action was always in the background. Thus the threat was implied, not expressly stated. What, then, was the source of the ultimatum report? Vernon McKenzie, a journalist at the time, has written that 'it can be unequivocally stated that such an ultimatum was sent from Berlin and arrived in Bucharest but it was intercepted by espionage agents and never reached Rumanian officials in the form in which it had been intended'.[3] McKenzie explains that the cipher clerk in the German Legation in Bucharest, Gustav Schmidt, was the only member of the Austrian Legation in Bucharest to have been retained by Germany after the *Anschluss*. Having decoded the ultimatum message, and before showing it to his superiors, he passed it to agents of an anti-German secret service with whom he cooperated. It is possible that in this way the Foreign Office in London

[1] Dilks, ed., *Cadogan Diaries*, 12 Apr. 1938, p. 68, and *passim*.
[2] Author's interview with Tilea, 30 May 1972. Certainly there had been previous Secret Intelligence Service reports about Hitler's intention to dominate Rumania. See, e.g., Memorandum by F. K. Roberts, 'Evidence of German military Measures and Preparations for supporting Italy', 14 Feb. 1939, C2058/13/18 (FO 371/22958).
[3] V. McKenzie, *Here Lies Goebbels* (London, 1940), p. 154.

learned about it before Tilea's *démarche*. Schmidt, according to McKenzie, was shot on orders from Berlin when his action was discovered. McKenzie gives us an unsubstantiated glimpse into what Cadogan once called 'the missing dimension' of international history,[1] but the facts are supported to some extent by Sir Reginald Hoare, who wrote to the Foreign Office on 23 June 1939 that he had 'heard an interesting version of the death last April of a secretary of the German Legation here, called Schmidt, who had formerly been a member of the Austrian Legation and had been taken over by the Germans after the Anschluss'. Most rumours agreed, according to Hoare, that he had committed suicide.

> I now hear . . . that Schmidt had been ordered to commit suicide because he had chattered about the famous 'Tilea ultimatum' to Roumania while in his cups in a night club, and that in the event of his failure to do so, he had been warned that a worse fate might be in store for him.

Hoare confirmed that Schmidt had 'received an urgent summons to the Legation during a lunch party, after which he was never seen again', and concluded that the 'long and the short of it seems to be that Tilea was perhaps not so wide of the mark!'[2] F. Brown, of the Foreign Office Southern Department, commented that this evidence was 'fairly circumstantial, but not conclusive', an opinion with which we can only concur.[3]

The fourth possibility is that Tilea acted on instructions from his Government, anxious to strengthen their bargaining position in the economic negotiations with Germany. Tilea's *démarche* on 17 March was made officially, and he was not dismissed from his post. According to a report from the Yugoslav Chargé d'Affaires in London, Milanovič, intercepted by the Germans, Tilea told him that he had been directed by the Rumanian Government to tell Halifax about the ultimatum and to ask for British aid. The Rumanian Government were using the German demands to increase tension and to safeguard Rumania's security in every possible contingency. Tilea had accordingly 'made the utmost possible use of his instructions'. Halifax had apparently replied that Rumania could in principle count on Britain's support.[4] Naturally the Rumanian Government would disclaim responsibility for Tilea's action after the event.

[1] Dilks, 'Appeasement Revisited', p. 34.
[2] Hoare to Ingram, 13 June 1939, R5123/464/37 (FO 371/23847).
[3] Minute by Brown, 28 June 1939, ibid.
[4] Irving, ed., *Breach of Security*, p. 62.

A TENTATIVE INITIATIVE

The fifth and most likely explanation is that the episode reflects division in Rumanian political circles as to the attitude to be adopted towards the German demands in the light of Germany's renewed thrust in central Europe. More specifically, Tilea probably acted on instructions from King Carol, whose goal was to maintain Rumanian independence and to strengthen his hand against the pro-German elements in his Government and in the country by demonstrating that the Western Powers offered an alternative to Rumania's falling completely into the German orbit. His aim on assuming dictatorial power in February 1938 had been to bring about a true 'national rebirth' in order to 'cope with the essential problem of national unification and welding together of the forces of resistance to fascism'.[1] Drastic anti-Fascist measures taken on 30 November 1938 included the murder of Codreanu, leader of the Iron Guard. Carol's attack on the Iron Guard increased his difficulties with the pro-German elements in his *entourage*, because it demonstrated his determination to thwart their influence and his refusal to side overtly with Germany. But the German attack on Czechoslovakia lent further weight to those who advocated acceptance of the German economic demands while undermining the King's power to oppose them openly without jeopardizing his own position. To strengthen his hand he would have to point to Western support for Rumanian independence. We have noted Hoare's judgement that Tilea received general instructions from the King to intensify Britain's interest in Rumania. Sir Lewis Namier says, with some understatement, that 'Tilea may have acted without instructions from Gafencu, but King Carol is supposed occasionally to have taken a hand in foreign affairs'.[2] Tilea confirms that his source was an industrialist close to the King, without whose consent the information would not have reached him.[3] Lord Lloyd, President of the British Council and one

---

[1] S. Fischer-Galati, *Twentieth Century Rumania* (New York, 1970), p. 59.

[2] Namier, *Diplomatic Prelude*, p. 82. This view is shared by Andreas Hillgruber, *Hitler, König Carol und Marschall Antonescu* (Wiesbaden, 1954), p. 35, and by Sidney Aster, *1939: The Making of the Second World War* (London, 1973), p. 72. Harold Nicolson believed that the story was true and emanated from King Carol. The British reaction would then have forced the Germans to retract (Nicolson Papers, Diary, 20 Mar. 1939).

[3] Author's interview with Tilea, 30 May 1972. The industrialist was probably the pro-Western Max Auşnit, the biggest of the Big Four Rumanian industrialists and a friend of King Carol. Auşnit worked closely with Tilea during early 1939 to establish an Anglo-Rumanian Trading Corporation (Board of Trade Minute, 22 Feb. 1939, R1219/113/37 (FO 371/23832)).

of the best informed Englishmen on the subject of Rumania as a result of his numerous official and semi-official visits there, discussed the situation with Tilea on 19 March and reported to Halifax that

> Tilea is very anxious that you should realise the delicacy of the internal situation in Roumania, but cannot tell you so officially. I think that Gafencu is not a strong man and has all along been in favour of concessions to Germany, whilst the King is surrounded by people having German economic interests pressing him in the same direction. Personally, I think the King will stand very steady, especially if he gets encouragement from here, but I know that Tilea is right about the pro-German influences that play upon the King from industrialists and other business people in Roumania.[1]

There seems clearly to have been some official Rumanian sanction behind Tilea's *démarche*. It is also clear that whatever the terms in which he couched his warning of the threat to Rumanian independence,[2] it served to emphasize the fact that if Britain were to maintain her policy of countering German expansion in south-eastern Europe, some political initiative must be taken. The story of an ultimatum to Rumania, whether true or false, presented the Foreign Office with an ideal pretext for beginning the search for support in Europe which it considered essential to secure before making the British challenge to Germany explicit.

Thus it was that on the morning of 18 March the Minister for Co-ordination of Defence, Lord Chatfield, asked the Chiefs of Staff to advise him on the prospects of giving military support to Rumania in preparation for an emergency Cabinet meeting scheduled for 5 p.m. They reported that German control of Rumania would give Germany virtual immunity from the effects of economic warfare (i.e. blockade), the principal weapon in Britain's strategic arsenal, but that with only France as an ally 'we can't take any immediate action which would stop Germany going south east and ultimately reaching the Mediterranean'. The only hope therefore would be to defeat Germany herself by attacking her in the west, which would

---

[1] Lloyd to Halifax, 20 Mar. 1939, C4105/3356/18 (FO 371/23062).
[2] There was no mention of the word 'ultimatum' in the report of the German threat to Rumania published in *The Times* on 18 March, for which Tilea was also the source (author's interview with Tilea, 30 May 1972). The Diplomatic Correspondent drew attention to this point on 20 March (*The Times*, 20 Mar. 1939, p. 14). Either Tilea was trying to cover his tracks or the word 'ultimatum' was emphasized in the Foreign Office as a peg on which to hang their approach to the 'threatened States' of eastern Europe.

A TENTATIVE INITIATIVE

probably fail unless Germany were engaged on two fronts. On the other hand, 'if we could get an alliance between Great Britain, Russia, Poland and France now and issue an ultimatum, we might deter Germany from her intention to absorb Rumania'. Therefore 'we should at once take diplomatic action *vis-à-vis* Russia and Poland'.[1]

In response to further questions, the Chiefs of Staff advised definitely against challenging Germany if Russia and Poland were neutral. Even supposing Poland to be an ally, that conclusion held good. They wrote that 'we should expect the Poles to fight stoutly, but surrounded as they are on three sides by Germany, they would be confined to the defensive and with their inferior communications it is improbable that they would contain any considerable portion of the German Army or Air Force'. With Russia as an ally and Poland neutral the prospects were more favourable, but even so the Chiefs of Staff would not recommend challenging Germany over the Rumanian question.

Britain's only hope of success in a war against Germany, therefore, lay in mutual Russian-Polish co-operation in engaging Germany on her eastern front. To emphasize their view of the vulnerability of Britain's position, the Chiefs of Staff repeated the conclusion they had reached in November 1937, 'which still holds good today', that

> war against Japan, Germany and Italy simultaneously . . . is a commitment which neither the present nor the projected strengthening of our defence forces is designed to meet, even if we were in alliance with France and Russia, and which would, therefore, place a dangerous strain on the resources of the Empire.[2]

It has been said that one of the main factors behind the British decision to challenge Germany openly in March 1939 was the Government's optimistic assessment of the progress made in rearmament, particularly in aircraft production.[3] If this was in some Ministers' minds, it certainly was not the view of the Chiefs of Staff, who showed their views to have changed little since the end of 1937. Furthermore it is clear that the British guarantee to Poland at the end of March was given against the advice of the Chiefs of Staff, who placed little value in Polish resistance without the active help

---
[1] COS Minutes, 282-3, 18 Mar. 1939, CAB 53/10.
[2] Ibid.
[3] W. N. Medlicott, *Contemporary England* (New York, 1967), p. 395.

of Russia. The decision to guarantee Poland, however, was not taken on the basis of strategic considerations alone. For instance neither the professional diplomats nor the politicians shared the assumption that Russia would in fact help when the time came. Intentions had to be judged as well as capabilities, and the ideal strategic configuration was not always politically feasible.

We have seen that while the Chiefs of Staff were deliberating, the ultimatum story was officially denied by the Rumanian Government. Nevertheless when the Cabinet met that afternoon, Halifax thought his colleagues should take the opportunity to consider Britain's position in the event of a future threat to Rumania. Chamberlain agreed, saying that a 'German attempt to dominate Roumania was ... more than a question whether Germany would thereby improve her strategic position; it raised the whole question whether Germany intended to obtain domination over the whole of South Eastern Europe'. But the Prime Minister refused to contemplate a British commitment. He emphasized that 'he was not asking the Cabinet to determine there and then whether we should declare war on Germany if Germany invaded Roumania'. Instead, he thought that 'the real point at issue was whether we could obtain sufficient assurances from other countries to justify us in a public pronouncement that we should resist any further act of aggression on the part of Germany'. He went on to say that 'such an announcement might deter Germany, at any rate for the period', and that 'we should take full advantage of the breathing-space thus offered'.[1]

This proposal clearly did not go far enough for the majority of the Cabinet, whose general view was that they would favour a commitment to defend Rumania provided Britain could get concrete support from France, Poland, Turkey, Russia, and preferably the rest of the Balkan countries as well. But Chamberlain, whose main support came as usual from Sir John Simon, the Chancellor of the Exchequer, had already laid down the limits of discussion. Besides, the others, and especially the Service Ministers, admitted that there would be great advantages from the point of view of rearmament in 'postponing the issue for another six or nine months'.

While the Cabinet were prepared to challenge Germany, they were not prepared to challenge the Prime Minister, and agreed, in concert with France, to ask Russia, Poland, Yugoslavia, Turkey, Greece, and Rumania whether they would join Britain in resisting 'any act

[1] Cab. Minutes, 18 Mar. 1939, CAB 23/98.

of German aggression aimed at obtaining domination of South-East Europe'. If these countries agreed, then 'we should make a public pronouncement of our intentions to resist any such act of German aggression'. Chamberlain, Halifax, Simon, and Stanley, the President of the Board of Trade, were authorized to meet next day to discuss the terms of the telegrams to be sent out.

Thus not only the Chiefs of Staff but also the Cabinet were more conscious of British weakness than strength, and were therefore prepared to agree to Chamberlain's idea of a warning declaration rather than a specific commitment to resist Germany. This added to the confusion that now reigned. Vague, ill-defined, and hackneyed formulations were aimlessly bandied about. Had the Cabinet been contemplating a specific commitment, their thinking would no doubt have been more precise.

A noteworthy feature of this meeting was that Chamberlain already believed, despite the Chiefs' of Staff appreciation, that 'Poland was very likely the key to the situation'.[1] He did not elaborate, but his remark indicates that, unlike the Chiefs of Staff, he was looking at the problem primarily in terms of politics rather than military strategy. Poland was the most powerful state in central and south-eastern Europe. The German-Polish Non-Aggression Pact of 1934 guaranteed her against the forcible redress of German grievances against her while serving as a counterweight to Russian revisionist aims. But after September 1938 (when Poland, with German approval, demanded and received Teschen from Czechoslovakia), Germany opened the question of her claims and Poland tentatively sought to revive her old policy based on the Franco-Polish Alliance of 1921, which had never been allowed to lapse. Nevertheless Britain and France could not be absolutely sure that Colonel Beck, Polish Foreign Minister and architect of Poland's association with Germany, would not come to some further agreement with Hitler. Polish support in resisting German aggression would therefore be highly significant not only in itself but also, as Chamberlain explained, because 'the attitude of other countries would obviously be affected if Poland decided to join with us'.[2] Fear of Russia was widespread in eastern Europe, and Chamberlain, who also distrusted Russian intentions, had no desire to play into Germany's hands.

Before the four Ministers met on the morning of 19 March, a

[1] Ibid.   [2] Ibid.

Sunday, replies were received from the various Governments whose views on the threat to Rumania the Foreign Office had requested on the evening of 17 March. They all doubted whether an ultimatum had been given, and all without exception threw the ball back into Britain's court. Thus Aléxis Léger, Secretary-General of the French Foreign Ministry, hoped that the British Government 'did not mean to subordinate their attitude to the views expressed by the Governments they were now consulting... That would be to put the cart before the horse.'[1] The Russian Foreign Minister, Maxim Litvinov, suggested that this difficulty could be overcome if a conference of Britain, Russia, France, Poland, and Rumania were to meet 'to discuss the possibilities of common action'.[2] The ministerial 'Inner Cabinet'[3] meeting that day decided to reject the Russian conference proposal. Chamberlain refused to be drawn into entanglements. As he had explained with reference to a similar Russian proposal just under a year before, following the *Anschluss*, 'the object would appear to be to negotiate . . . mutual undertakings in advance to resist aggression'.[4] Halifax, while sympathetic to this object, objected to the means of achieving it. Plenipotentiaries would have to telephone to their Governments for instructions 'over wires which would certainly be tapped'. Furthermore, 'it would be fatal for a conference to be summoned unless it was certain in advance that it was going to be a success, and this involved precisely those soundings through the diplomatic channel which were now being undertaken'.[5]

The Ministers then drafted the warning declaration to Germany. Chamberlain proposed that only France, Poland, and Russia be asked to co-sign with Britain a statement that they 'were interested in maintaining the political independence of the States of South Eastern Europe, and that if this independence was threatened at any time, they undertook to consult together'.[6] The smaller states, envisaged as signatories the day before, were now left out because it was important to publish the warning as soon as possible, and be-

[1] Phipps to Cadogan, 18 Mar. 1939, *DBFP* iv, no. 418.
[2] Seeds to Halifax, 19 Mar. 1939, ibid., no. 421.
[3] This term usually refers to Chamberlain, Halifax, Simon, and Hoare, the Home Secretary, who met as an 'Inner Cabinet' during the crisis in September 1938. Hoare was now ill, and this is apparently the only occasion during the March crisis when such a meeting was held.
[4] 333 HC Deb. 5 s., 24 Mar. 1938, col. 1400.
[5] Minutes of Meeting between Halifax and the Dominions High Commissioners, Dominions Office, 22 Mar. 1939, C4415/15/18 (FO 371/22968).
[6] Minutes of Ministerial Meeting, 19 Mar. 1939, C3858/15/18 (FO 371/22967).

A TENTATIVE INITIATIVE

cause Chamberlain disliked the prospect of consulting with the smaller Powers since they might claim to consult over 'minor matters' and 'this might precipitate the very situation which we wished to avoid'.[1] There was another important reason for excluding them. Chamberlain did not want Italy to feel that the declaration was directed at her.[2]

But while the number of signatories decreased, the scope of the declaration was widened, first to include eastern Europe (because Poland herself, and Lithuania, might be threatened), then to cover all European states. This was intended to weaken, rather than strengthen, the warning. It now lost any specificity and began to look like a weak version of Article 10 of the League of Nations Covenant.[3] Sir John Simon viewed it as 'a Regional Covenant in which the states in a given area bind themselves to consult together in the event of any case of unprovoked aggression against one of their numbers'.[4] This was precisely what Chamberlain wanted. He 'emphasized that the first essential was to secure a public warning. There was no harm done in his view if this warning was in somewhat general terms and kept people guessing.'[5] Thus not only did Britain's concrete obligations remain as they had been defined in 1936 by the then Foreign Secretary, Anthony Eden, but the Government were back to Eden's favourite policy of trying to keep Germany guessing. Furthermore, Chamberlain insisted that the declaration must not refer to the violation of frontiers, only to the independence of states, leaving the way open for revision of the status of Memel and Danzig.

Though Chamberlain regarded his proposal as 'pretty bold and startling',[6] when the Cabinet were asked to approve it next day (20 March), there were some who objected that the declaration was not specific enough to inspire confidence. On the other hand the Ministers appeared to have accepted Chamberlain's refusal to undertake new commitments.[7] The Prime Minister hoped to deter Germany with a

---

[1] Cab. Minutes, 20 Mar. 1939, CAB 23/98.   [2] Ibid.
[3] Article 10: 'The Members of the League undertake to respect and preserve as against external aggression the territorial integrity and existing political independence of all Members of the League. In case of any such aggression or in case of any threat or danger of such aggression, the Council shall advise upon the means by which this obligation shall be fulfilled.' Cf. the declaration, pp. 124–5, below.
[4] Minutes of Ministerial Meeting, 19 Mar. 1939, C3858/15/18 (FO 371/22967).
[5] Ibid.
[6] Quoted in Feiling, *Chamberlain*, p. 401.
[7] Cab. Minutes, 20 Mar. 1939, CAB 23/98.

warning. But he knew perfectly well that consultation between states was not a sound basis for deterrence. He admitted that

> the real issue was that if Germany showed signs that she intended to proceed with her march for world domination, we must take steps to stop her by attacking her on two fronts. We should attack Germany, not in order to save a particular victim, but in order to pull down the bully.

Though the purpose was clear, the means were lacking. As Chamberlain went on to say, 'it was undesirable that we should be too specific as to the nature of our collaboration or use words which would tie us down'.[1]

Halifax, though recognizing that the formula was not 'very heroic', at this stage does not appear to have tried to convince Chamberlain that a warning without a commitment would serve no constructive purpose. Nor did Cadogan, who thought it 'seemed a good idea'.[2] Others in the Foreign Office were certainly contemptuous, the formula being described by one official, Roger Makins, as 'amateur collective security'.[3] Oliver Harvey noted that although the Government 'seemed to be taking position seriously at last', it was 'still doubtful how far we will commit ourselves to *action*'.[4]

But it was the French Ambassador, Charles Corbin, not members of the British Foreign Office or Cabinet, who succeeded in stiffening the declaration to a certain extent. When Cadogan read him the draft, 'he expressed horror—and there is *some* force in his objection'.[5] With the approval of Halifax and Chamberlain, Cadogan changed the wording to include the purpose of consultation—to decide 'what steps should be taken to offer joint resistance'.[6] On the evening of 20 March the declaration was sent for approval to Moscow, Paris, and Warsaw. It read as follows:

> We the undersigned, duly authorized to that effect, hereby declare that, inasmuch as peace and security in Europe are matters of common interest and concern, and since European peace and security may be affected by any action which constitutes a threat to the political independence of any European State, our respective Governments hereby undertake

[1] Cab. Minutes, 20 Mar. 1939, CAB 23/98.
[2] Dilks, ed., *Cadogan Diaries*, 19 Mar. 1939, p. 161.
[3] *Harvey Diaries*, 21 Mar. 1939, p. 266.
[4] Ibid., 20 Mar. 1939, p. 265.
[5] Dilks, ed., *Cadogan Diaries*, 20 Mar. 1939, p. 161.
[6] Halifax to Phipps, Seeds, and Kennard, 20 Mar. 1939, *DBFP* iv, no. 446.

A TENTATIVE INITIATIVE

immediately to consult together as to what steps should be taken to offer joint resistance to any such action.[1]

This first British initiative was clearly the outcome of a desire to warn Germany that she could no longer threaten aggression with impunity, and of continued preoccupation with British weakness. During the course of discussion and decision-making over the week-end of 18–19 March, the British Government explicitly confirmed their belief that German domination of south-eastern Europe threatened British interests and must be resisted. But they were still not prepared to confront Germany directly with this appraisal. What they did hope to gain, however, if only in a declaration of intent, was the potential of an eastern front on the basis of common interests with Poland and the Soviet Union.

British concern was not limited to Germany. Policy towards Italy and the Far East was also discussed over the week-end. We have seen that on 17 March the Foreign Office received news not only of a German threat to Rumania but also of an Italian threat to France or Albania. The Foreign Office proposed to deal with this possibility by warning Mussolini privately that Britain would immediately support France.[2] The idea of a personal letter from Chamberlain to Mussolini originated in the Foreign Office, and Halifax ascertained on 18 March that the Prime Minister was 'not unfavourable to the idea'.[3] But Chamberlain's conception of its purpose was radically different. He objected that a warning 'might expose him to a rebuff from Signor Mussolini, who might think that we were interfering in his business'.[4] If Chamberlain believed that French security was Britain's business, he was not prepared to say so, or even to repeat his statement to that effect of 6 February 1939.[5] His idea was to refer to his talks with Mussolini in January 1939, when the latter had assured him of Hitler's peaceful intentions, and to ask Mussolini now to use 'his good offices for peace' in Berlin. Cadogan thought this would convey the impression that the Prime Minister 'was seeking another Munich' and that Mussolini would infer that 'we and the French have lost our nerve'.[6] But Chamberlain had his way, and Cadogan's fears were borne out. Ciano, the Italian Foreign

[1] Ibid.
[2] Minute by Nichols, 17 Mar. 1939, FO 371/22967, f. 206 (no reg. no.).
[3] Minute by Halifax, 19 Mar. 1939, ibid.
[4] Minutes of Ministerial Meeting, 19 Mar. 1939, C3858/15/18 (FO 371/22967).
[5] See above, pp. 77–8.
[6] Minute by Cadogan, 20 Mar. 1939 (FO 371/22967).

Minister and Mussolini's son-in-law, noted in his diary on 23 March that Mussolini regarded the letter as 'another proof of the inertia of the democracies'.[1] Mussolini answered on 1 April that he would not help until Italy's claims against France had been recognized. The Foreign Office view did not differ from Chamberlain's in recognizing the need to separate Italy from Germany, only in how it should be done. Chamberlain's approach to Mussolini reduced the value of his warning of 6 February. In this way he allowed British diplomatic signals to become confused, and Italy was left to conclude that British policy lacked determination.

As for the Far East, the British Government decided that in case of war in Europe the United States must be called upon to move a fleet into Pacific waters 'as a gesture *vis-à-vis* Japan'.[2] On the morning of 19 March the Australian Prime Minister, J. A. Lyons, asked Chamberlain by telephone whether Britain still planned to send a fleet to Singapore. Chamberlain confirmed this, but with the qualification that he could not be sure how soon after a Japanese intervention or in what strength the fleet would be sent. This reflected the Naval Staff's appraisal and pointed to the importance of some action by the United States. Accordingly Halifax explained to Joseph Kennedy, the American Ambassador in London, on 21 March, that

> In 1936, when the trouble was on with Italy, Great Britain had promised Australia that, in the event of any trouble, they would send a fleet to Singapore. Under present conditions, they do not feel they can spare a fleet to Singapore and they wonder if the United States would consider, at the psychological moment, transferring the American fleet back to the Pacific. ... This would be perfectly satisfactory to Australia and would permit the British Navy to function in the Mediterranean.[3]

Lord Chatfield, who also saw Kennedy, got the impression that the American Ambassador was not receptive to the idea. But when Halifax met the Dominions High Commissioners in London on 22 March for a background 'briefing', he told them that

> President Roosevelt was very anxious to help as far as he could and (though this was very private and he asked the High Commissioners to

---

[1] H. Gibson, ed., *The Ciano Diaries, 1939–1943* (New York, 1946), 23 Mar. 1939, p. 51.

[2] Minutes of Ministerial Meeting, 19 Mar. 1939, C3859/15/18 (FO 371/22967).

[3] Kennedy to Hull, 22 Mar. 1939, *FRUS*, 1939, i. 88. The response was that on 15 April the fleet returned from the Atlantic to the West Coast. In October 1939 part of it moved to Pearl Harbour, the rest following in April 1940.

A TENTATIVE INITIATIVE

'forget it') might be able to arrange, if necessary, for the United States fleet to be moved into the Pacific . . . in order to keep Japan quiet if war broke out in Europe.[1]

There was perhaps an element of calculated optimism about this statement, since it was only on 22 March that Kennedy even reported his conversation with the Foreign Secretary. Halifax had been impressed with the isolationist attitude of the Dominions in 1938,[2] and he now wanted their unequivocal support for the challenge to Germany.

At first the prospects seemed good. Sir Thomas Inskip, the Dominions Secretary, saw the High Commissioners on 18 March[3] and reported to the Cabinet that they all approved Chamberlain's Birmingham speech.[4] On 20 March Halifax went so far as to say, in what was obviously a calculated indiscretion designed to give the appearance of Empire solidarity, that Britain was in 'close and practical consultation' with the Dominions.[5] However the Prime Minister of Canada, Mackenzie King, very quickly pointed out that the Dominions had not been consulted at all, but merely informed.[6] When he met the High Commissioners on 22 March, furthermore, Halifax discovered that the views of the Dominions had not in fact come very far since Munich. The Canadian and South African in particular were opposed to European involvements, and the New Zealander took his Government's old line about reviving the League of Nations.[7] All these views were confirmed in communications direct from the Dominions.[8] Only the Australian Government were able to

---

[1] Minutes of Meeting, 22 Mar. 1939, C4415/15/18 (FO 371/22968).
[2] *Harvey Diaries*, 4 Oct. 1938, p. 208.
[3] Minutes of Meeting at Dominions Office, 18 Mar. 1939, C4318/15/18 (FO 371/22967).
[4] Cab. Minutes, 18 Mar. 1939, CAB 23/98.
[5] Viscount Halifax, *Speeches on Foreign Policy*, ed. H. H. E. Craster (London, 1940), p. 248.
[6] U.K. High Commissioner in Canada to Dominions Office, 24 Mar. 1939, H/IX/116 (FO 800/310), and covering letter from W. C. Hankinson (D.O.) to Harvey (F.O.), 28 Mar. 1939, H/IX/120 (FO 800/310). Chamberlain had also referred to 'consultation' with the Dominions in his Birmingham speech, but he assured the Cabinet that he had not intended this 'to be a prelude to some new form of consultation' (Cab. Minutes, 22 Mar. 1939, CAB 23/98).
[7] Minutes of Meeting at D.O., 22 Mar. 1939, C4415/15/18 (FO 371/22968).
[8] U.K. High Commissioner in New Zealand to D.O., 20 Mar. 1939, C4228/3356/18 (FO 371/23862); U.K. High Commissioner in South Africa to D.O., 22 Mar. 1939, C4229/3356/18 (ibid.); U.K. High Commissioner in Canada to D.O., 24 Mar. 1939, H/IX/117 (FO 800/310).

say, having overcome the opposition of the Labour Party, that 'there can be no doubt about Australia supporting Britain in any development that might occur'.[1] Despite these views, the attitudes of the Dominions were not vital factors in determining British policy over the next two weeks, as they are alleged to have been in September 1938. The British seemed confident that in the final analysis the Dominions Governments would recognize the logic of Empire interdependence, which J. A. Lyons had expressed at the Imperial Conference in 1937:

> There could be no possible doubt that if some great disaster happened to Britain, there could be no hope or future for any of the other members of the Commonwealth and it was, therefore, in the supreme interests of every one of them . . . that the component parts of the Commonwealth should stand firmly and solidly together.[2]

This British confidence was reflected in Britain's war plans, which were drawn up on the assumption that the Empire's total resources would be available.[3]

Neville Chamberlain had sought agreement with Germany on the basis of disarmament, the relaxation of her effort to obtain exclusive control over south-eastern Europe, and respect for European frontiers. The German invasion of Bohemia and Moravia made nonsense of such terms, although the British were in a worse position to stop it than they would have been in September 1938. The invasion demonstrated that Hitler did not feel bound by his pledge to consult Chamberlain about revision of the European *status quo* and that he felt powerful enough to behave as he pleased in eastern Europe. We have seen that despite the search for agreement with Germany, British policy-makers nevertheless sought to maintain British influence in south-eastern Europe on the assumption that once Germany obtained a predominant position in the area politically, British interests would be threatened.

The invasion of Bohemia and Moravia was one thing, the threat to Rumania quite another, for German control of Rumania's

---

[1] Quoted in R. Ovendale, 'The Influence of United States and Dominion Opinion on the Formation of British Policy, 1937–39' (unpublished D.Phil. thesis, University of Oxford, 1971), p. 245.

[2] Quoted ibid., p. 50.

[3] CID Memorandum, 'The Position of the Dominions in the Event of War', May 1939, DP (P) 54, CAB 16/183A.

resources, as the Chiefs of Staff pointed out, would go a long way to neutralize the effects of one of Britain's major strategic weapons, economic warfare. The means of British resistance to German expansion towards the south-east therefore changed from economic pressure to open challenge. If this was at first muted, it was because the British were still embarrassingly conscious of their military weakness. It was this consciousness that led them into the search for allies. They knew in their hearts, however, that to secure allies they would be required to put their weakness on the line. 'But that is a risk that must be taken,' wrote Cadogan on 20 March, 'this country has taken risks before.'[1]

[1] Dilks, ed., *Cadogan Diaries*, 20 Mar. 1939, p. 161.

7

A CONDITIONAL COMMITMENT

AT 11.05 p.m. on 20 March 1939 the Foreign Office sent off the proposed Four-Power Declaration for approval by the French, Russian, and Polish Governments.[1] The prospects for Russian and Polish co-operation were not good.

Speaking on 10 March 1939 to the 18th Communist Party Congress in Moscow, Stalin had warned that the Russians intended 'to be cautious and not allow our country to be drawn into conflicts by warmongers who are accustomed to have others pull the chestnuts out of the fire for them'.[2] The British Ambassador, Sir William Seeds, warned 'those innocents at home who believe that Soviet Russia is only awaiting an invitation to join the Western democracies' to take heed.[3] The British interpretation of Stalin's words was that there was no reason to expect anything but Russian interests to determine Russian foreign policy. This was reasonable enough,

---

[1] Halifax to Phipps, Seeds, and Kennard, 20 Mar. 1939, *DBFP* iv, no. 446.

[2] Seeds to Halifax, 20 Mar. 1939, ibid., no. 452, p. 413, n. 3.

[3] Ibid., p. 419. During the course of his speech Stalin reiterated what has become the standard Soviet historical explanation of 'appeasement': that Britain and France were seeking to turn German aggression eastwards against Russia. See Ivan Maisky, *Who Helped Hitler?*, trans. Andrew Rothstein (London, 1964). For a recent restatement of the Soviet case, based on the British documents now available, see V. Sipols and M. Pankrashova, 'Preparation of the Munich Deal. Britain's Road to Munich', *International Affairs* (Moscow, 1973), no. 4, pp. 78–87; no. 6, pp. 81–8; no. 7, pp. 70–9. According to this account, the essence of the British Government's policy was to 'mend their fences with Nazi Germany, in order to divert fascist aggression from the British Empire and to direct it against the USSR'. The 'deal' contemplated by British ruling circles was for 'Germany to commit herself not to touch Britain and her colonial Empire. In exchange, they were prepared to meet Hitler's demand that Central and Eastern Europe be recognized as the Nazi Reich's "sphere of influence" and that Germany's colonial possessions be returned, mainly at the expense of France, Belgium, and Holland. The documents show that step by step Chamberlain conceded all these points to Hitler' (ibid., no. 4, p. 78). In fact the documents show nothing of the sort. As we have seen, the British Government refused to concede Hitler a free hand in eastern Europe and were willing to make colonial concessions only in return for German agreement to abandon their claim to the area as an exclusive sphere of influence.

but it was its very reasonableness that infuriated the directors of British foreign policy over the next five months.

Seeds's warning turned out to be justified. On 21 March he reported that the Soviet Foreign Minister, Maxim Litvinov, was still pushing for a conference and doubted in any case whether the Poles would sign.[1] The next day the Russians answered definitively: they would only sign the declaration after both France and Poland had promised their signatures.[2] This was a good move. If Poland did sign, then she served securely as a buffer state. If she did not sign, as Litvinov expected, then Russia's hands were left free.

The second anticipated difficulty about the Four-Power Declaration was the attitude of Poland. The French proposal for an 'Eastern Locarno' in 1934 had foundered among other things on Poland's reluctance to align herself with the Soviet Union.[3] In particular, the Poles objected to allowing Russian troops across territory so recently won from them, for fear that they would never leave. Furthermore the Poles had only just negotiated the 1934 Declaration of Non-Aggression with Germany. This was the second main pillar on which Poland's policy of 'equilibrium' between her two more powerful neighbours was based.

The first was a similar agreement with Russia in 1932. On 20 March 1939 Roger Cambon, Counsellor at the French Embassy in London, reminded Sir Orme Sargent that 'even threatened as they are at present, it is very doubtful whether either Poland or Roumania would ever withdraw the opposition which they have always maintained to allowing Russian troops on to their territory, even as allies'.[4]

The fact that these problems were known to exist has prompted the suggestion that Chamberlain's idea of a Four-Power Declaration

[1] Seeds to Halifax, 21 Mar. 1939, *DBFP* iv, no. 461.
[2] Seeds to Halifax, 22 Mar. 1939, ibid., no. 490.
[3] Although couched in the form of a 'regional covenant' of mutual assistance, the 'Eastern Locarno' was a thinly disguised design by Louis Barthou, the French Foreign Minister, to maintain the *status quo* in central and eastern Europe against German revisionism. Poland, Russia, Germany, Czechoslovakia, Finland, and the Baltic States were to join the pact which was to be supplemented by a Franco-Soviet mutual assistance agreement. The Poles disliked the fact that Russian troops would have to cross Polish and formerly Russian territory to help France, and also the fact that they would be abandoning the cherished policy of equilibrium. The British, who were consulted, disliked the fact that the scheme was obviously aimed at the encirclement of Germany. The Germans disliked it for the same reason.
[4] Minute by Sargent, 20 Mar. 1939, C3735/3356/18 (FO 371/23061).

was never intended seriously, that it was merely a manœuvre calculated to take the wind out of the sails of public opinion.[1] This is too Machiavellian. Admittedly the plan was not very daring; but for that very reason the British did not expect serious opposition to it. Sir Alexander Cadogan accepted that Cambon's point should be borne in mind in any discussions that followed the signature of the declaration, but argued that

> for the moment . . . we are only inviting Poland and the Soviet [Union] to join with us and France in *consultation* in face of any threat. It will be in course of further exchanges of view that we shall attempt to define what, in given circumstances, any of the consultants might be prepared to do.[2]

Chamberlain's idea was to face Germany not with the actuality but with the potential of an eastern combination of Russia and Poland, thinking that this would 'in itself be a valuable contribution to the stability of Europe'.[3] He was still reluctant to enter into new commitments, as the Russians and the Poles were quite aware. Yet within ten days the proposed 'consultation' had turned into a unilateral and unconditional guarantee of Poland's independence, which in practical terms meant a guarantee of the *status quo* in Danzig, the most volatile area in Europe.

On 21 March the Polish difficulties began to materialize. The Vice-Minister for Foreign Affairs, Miroslaw Arciszewski, revealed to Sir Howard Kennard, British Ambassador in Warsaw, the two critical Polish objections to the plan: first, its possible effect on the attitude of Germany towards Poland; secondly, the difficulty of military or political co-operation with Russia.[4]

On 22 March the Polish Foreign Minister, Colonel Jozef Beck, emphasized the second objection:

> He said that the Four Power Declaration clearly demanded very serious consideration. His chief preoccupation was the suggested participation of Soviet [Russia]. Hitherto Poland had kept the balance between Germany and Soviet Russia and had avoided coming down on one side or the other. The proposed declaration would definitely place

---

[1] R. J. Richards, 'British Policy in Europe from the Munich Agreement to the Polish Guarantee, September 29, 1938 to March 31, 1939' (unpublished M.A. thesis, University of Durham, 1967), pp. 309 ff.
[2] Minute by Cadogan, 20 Mar. 1939, C3735/3356/18 (FO 371/23061).
[3] Halifax to Phipps, Seeds, and Kennard, 20 Mar. 1939, *DBFP* iv, no. 446.
[4] Kennard to Halifax, 21 Mar. 1939, ibid., no. 459.

Poland in the Soviet camp and the reaction in Germany, especially given the Führer's mentality, would undoubtedly be serious.[1]

He could not yet give a definite answer but implied that Poland might associate herself with England and France if Russia were left out.

Kennard commented that the British plan confronted the Poles 'with the necessity of a crucial decision'. The Poles, fearing German retaliation against an open Polish alignment against Germany, would have to ask themselves

(1) whether there is any actual threat to their independence which would justify them in provoking German displeasure, (2) whether other signatories are prepared and in a position to see them through not only eventual war but also [the] period of uneasy peace which might follow such a declaration.[2]

Here was the crux of the matter. Before entering such an anti-German coalition Poland would obviously want a firm commitment from Britain to save her from the possible consequences. This was certainly the view of Juliusz Lukasiewicz, the Polish Ambassador in Paris, who told his American colleague on 24 March:

it is totally impossible for any state of Central or Eastern Europe . . . to consider seriously any British proposals unless England decides to commit those acts which without doubt would demonstrate its readiness to endanger its relations with Germany . . . all diplomatic negotiations will have no possibility of success so long as the British Government decides not to accept definite and precise obligations supported by all those armed forces which it has at its disposal.[3]

The Polish attitude lent itself easily in British and particularly in French minds to the interpretation that Colonel Beck was pro-German, since he was apparently unwilling to be anti-German. The truth, wrote Sir Robert Vansittart, was that he 'doubted Western resolve'.[4]

[1] Kennard to Halifax, 22 Mar. 1939, ibid., no. 479. According to the diary of Count Jean Szembek, Under-Secretary in the Polish Foreign Ministry, Beck thought the proposal had 'seductive aspects' to it and gave it serious thought (Jean Szembek, *Journal 1933–1939*, trans. into French by J. Rzewuska and T. Zaleski (Paris, 1953), 22 Mar. 1939, p. 433).
[2] Kennard to Halifax, 21 Mar. 1939, *DBFP* iv, no. 465.
[3] Lukasiewicz to Beck, 29 Mar. 1939, in Waclaw Jedrzejewicz, ed., *Diplomat in Paris 1936–1939. Papers and Memoirs of Juliusz Lukasiewicz, Ambassador of Poland* (New York, 1970), p. 181. For the effect that these strong words may have had in London, see below, p. 152.
[4] Lord Vansittart, *The Mist Procession* (London, 1958), p. 536.

Halifax now felt that the British initiative was threatening to lose it momentum. The whole world was watching London, and panic reigned in the Foreign Office. Cadogan was almost hysterical: 'we must have a moral position, and we shall lose it if we don't do something now. P.M.'s speech was all right on sentiments, but the country—and other countries—are asking "What are you going to *do*?" '[1]

It was Georges Bonnet, the French Foreign Minister, who supplied the answer. On 21 March he accompanied the French President on a State visit to London.[2]

The French were vitally interested in preserving Rumania's independence. Aléxis Léger, Secretary-General of the French Foreign Ministry, explained that

> we now found ourselves on the basis of the preservation of the balance of power, and it was incumbent upon us to concern ourselves in the first place with matters which definitely affected that balance and, therefore, our vital interests. . . . It was because Roumania could supply Germany with the means of carrying on . . . a war [against France and Britain] (means which she at present lacked), that it was necessary to protect that country.[3]

French policy was to secure a Polish guarantee for Rumania in case France became involved in war with Germany on her behalf. On 18 March Colonel Beck had asked Daladier, the French Prime Minister, whether Poland could expect help from France in case the Germans seized the Free City of Danzig.[4] Daladier assented, but with the proviso 'that Poland concluded a defensive alliance with Roumania'.[5] However, as was shown by Bonnet's talks with Chamberlain and Halifax on 22 March, the French naturally wanted British

---

[1] Dilks, ed., *Cadogan Diaries*, 20 Mar. 1939, p. 161. Oliver Harvey continually stressed the need for keeping the issue with Germany on a moral plane (see above, p. 69), and on 22 March Duff Cooper, First Lord of the Admiralty until his resignation after Munich, wrote to Halifax that the United States would fight for Britain '*on one condition*: It must be an ideological war—a war based on moral principle' (Cooper to Halifax, 22 Mar. 1939 (FO 800/315, f. 57)).

[2] Vansittart organized a magnificent *soirée de gala* at the India Office at which he proclaimed the greatness of France in his own verse, but for busy officials the visit was an unwelcome distraction: 'The French visit has made this week a nightmare. Superimposed upon a crisis, it has rendered everything impossible' (Dilks, ed., *Cadogan Diaries*, 21 Mar. 1939, p. 162). He was writing on 25 March.

[3] Campbell (Paris) to Halifax, 22 Mar. 1939, *DBFP* iv, no. 493.

[4] For the background to the Danzig question, see below, pp. 164–5.

[5] Phipps to Halifax, 18 Mar. 1939, *DBFP* iv, no. 402.

backing for this scheme. On the other hand they were conscious of the need to cultivate the new mood in Britain with extreme caution. On 21 March Daladier advised Lukasiewicz, the Polish Ambassador in Paris, not to 'seek a precise spelling-out of [British] commitments, since this could weaken the nascent trend in London to take the first step in this direction'.[1] Bonnet must have been surprised at the attitude he found there, for Halifax was now prepared to go to war with Germany without even bothering to secure the eastern front.

Bonnet opened his talks with Halifax on 21 March. Bonnet clearly did not think the Four-Power Declaration went far enough: it was important, he said, 'to think of the practical aspect'.[2] The problem was how to help Rumania in case of a German attack, and Poland was the only country in a real position to do so. Given this fact, it would be

> insupportable if, Germany having attacked Roumania, and France having attacked Germany in her support, the Poles were to say that their pact with France did not apply, it being remembered that Poland had a greater interest in Roumania's fate than had France, as well as having a treaty with Roumania. It was desirable, therefore, to go to the utmost limit, even to the extent of threats, to bring Poland in.[3]

In Halifax Bonnet found a ready listener. He recognized 'the capital importance of Poland, and even the need for using something in the nature of a threat'.[4] But much to Bonnet's surprise, Halifax was prepared to go much further than this. He thought that 'even if no assurance of Poland's collaboration could be obtained in advance . . . it would still be very difficult for France and Great Britain to take no action if there was a further act of aggression by Germany'.[5]

---

[1] Jedrzejewicz, ed., *Diplomat in Paris*, p. 178.

[2] Record of Anglo-French Conversations, 21 Mar. 1939, *DBFP* iv, no. 458, p. 425.

[3] Ibid., p. 426. The Polish-Rumanian Treaty of 1931 envisaged Russia, not Germany, as the aggressor. Under the terms of the Franco-Polish Treaty of 1921, the Poles undertook to assist France only in case of an unprovoked German attack on her.

[4] Draft Minutes of Anglo-French Conversations, 21 Mar. 1939, C4194/15/18 (FO 371/22967). Halifax deleted the words 'something in the nature of a threat' from the draft and substituted the much quoted words which appear in the final version printed in *DBFP*: 'very plain language to the Polish Government'.

[5] Record of Anglo-French Conversations, 21 Mar. 1939, *DBFP* iv, no. 458, p. 427.

He was prepared to take a 'very firm line' even without the certainty of Polish support at the outset because in his view 'this very fact would be likely to bring Poland in'. This, he thought, was an essential prerequisite for conducting 'a successful war against Germany'.

Here, appearing for the first time, was the fateful idea of a unilateral guarantee to Poland. Halifax's position makes sense on two assumptions: that Germany was bent on dominating Europe, and that unless Poland and other states in eastern Europe were prevented by unilateral and unsought-for guarantees from making their own accommodations with Germany, the British means to resist German domination would be fatally undermined. What value the British at this stage, or at any stage, attached to the military assistance of Poland is doubtful. Although the 'second front' argument was considered important, it was probably never the decisive consideration. What Halifax feared above all was that unless Britain 'took the lead' in challenging any further German expansion, the moral and psychological balance would shift so drastically in favour of Germany—not only in Europe but throughout the world—that Britain's ability to go on functioning as a Great Power would be irretrievably destroyed.

It is hard to pass judgement on this line of reasoning, for in so far as Britain felt herself confronted with the alternative of fighting or abdicating as a Great Power, that position was largely the product of the failures of previous British diplomacy. It is one thing to retreat in orderly fashion from an untenable position; it is another thing to conduct one's foreign policy in such a way that one is constantly humiliated and shamed by squaring up for battle and then backing down. This had been the British posture over both Abyssinia and Czechoslovakia. Thus the critical decisions in March 1939 were made in an atmosphere of panic, humiliation, and moral hysteria. A frantic urgency to do something—anything—replaced a calm consideration of the alternatives. There arose a clamour for action to cut off the possibility of another surrender to the forces of evil. Lord de la Warr, for example, a Cabinet colleague, wrote to Halifax that he wanted commitments 'so watertight that he [Hitler] (and we!) cannot get round them'. He noted that 'our intentions are the same'.[1] Vansittart likened the Nazis to 'criminals whose hands are still dripping with blood and who have just slapped our embarrassed

[1] De la Warr to Halifax, 25 Mar. 1939 (FO 800/315, f. 70).

faces before the world'. To do nothing 'will be held, very comprehensibly, not only in Europe but in the United States, as a degradation. And . . . the effect on Mussolini will be grave and dangerous.'[1]

Bonnet managed to inject a dose of realism into this situation. Once he realized that Halifax was ready to challenge Germany he used all his skill to persuade him to induce Poland to guarantee Rumania. His success, though it turned out to be only temporary, was a triumph for French diplomacy.

At 5 p.m. on 22 March Halifax and Bonnet resumed their talks in the company of Chamberlain.[2] This meeting was one of the most important events leading up to the guarantee to Poland. For the first time the British acquiesced in the principle of an eastern-European commitment, although as a result of Bonnet's skilful diplomacy that commitment was not to be unconditional.

Halifax opened by asking what the next step should be, assuming, as all expected by this time, that the 'Polish reply to our recent approach was evasive or negative'. He produced information to show that Rumania was still very much threatened.

Bonnet stressed again that Germany must be faced with Polish and Rumanian resistance, and thought it vital 'not to give Poland (or indeed, Roumania) a pretext for running out on account of Russia'. He pointed out that Britain and France were in a position to induce the Poles to co-operate:

Poland still attached importance to her treaty with France, and she desired assistance from Great Britain. Both these facts could be used as a lever to secure her participation in the organisation which we were trying to build up for the defence of Roumania.

Halifax, prompted by Bonnet's insinuation, outlined the logic of the situation:

The first step would be to think of the particular case of Roumania, and to assure ourselves (1) that Roumania would resist, and (2) that, if Roumania resisted, Poland would support her. In order to persuade Poland to commit herself to support Roumania, Great Britain and France would have to give Poland a private undertaking that, if Poland came in, they would come in also. Having reached this understanding with Poland, it might be suggested to both Poland and Roumania that they

[1] Memorandum by Vansittart: 'Impending German occupation of Czechoslovakia', 13 Mar. 1939, C3234/15/18 (FO 371/22966).
[2] Also present were Cadogan, Strang, Phipps, Corbin, and Bonnet's Private Secretary, Bressy (Record of Anglo-French Conversations, 22 Mar. 1939, *DBFP* iv, no. 484).

should not raise any objection to our doing our best, both in their interest and in our own, to secure Soviet participation.[1]

Bonnet agreed. The Poles did not like vague obligations, and 'if something precise could be put before them, they would probably accept'. This prompted Halifax to go a stage further. He thought that Poland would no doubt expect to be covered by the same sort of guarantee that Britain and France were now contemplating for Rumania. Out of a sense of caution, the French had now managed to persuade the British to throw their weight behind the French scheme to persuade Poland to help Rumania. But they had also helped to precipitate a British commitment, though it was to be conditional, to a highly unstable situation in eastern Europe. Paradoxically, French diplomacy increased the likelihood of war.

Chamberlain acquiesced in the demise of his own plan, agreeing that 'if the Polish reply, as was to be expected, was negative or evasive, the intention would not be to press them any further, but to try the new procedure now proposed'. However, the Foreign Office did not proceed at once with the new scheme. They gave careful thought to one of the central issues now facing British policy: what to do about Russia?

Apart from ideology there were strategic and above all political arguments for and against including Russia in an anti-German coalition. Many of the Government's critics, both on the Left and on the Right, had been advocating some sort of association with Russia since before Munich. As Basil Liddell Hart, the military strategist, later recalled: 'There was little chance of checking Hitler except by securing the support of Russia—the only power that could give Poland direct support and thus provide a deterrent to Hitler.'[2] Chamberlain and Halifax were of course aware of this strategic problem. It was, after all, also the view of the Chiefs of Staff. During the Anglo-French talks Halifax had observed that 'it would be unfortunate if we were now so to act as to give . . . [Russia] the idea that we were pushing her to one side'.[3] Chamberlain suggested a secret agreement whereby Russia would agree to help

---

[1] Record of Anglo-French Conversations, 22 Mar. 1939, *DBFP* iv, no. 484, pp. 459–60.

[2] B. H. Liddell Hart, *The Memoirs of Captain Liddell Hart* (London, 1965), ii. 222.

[3] Record of Anglo-French Conversations, 22 Mar. 1939, *DBFP* iv, no. 484, p. 459.

Poland or Rumania if Germany attacked either of them.[1] None of the east Europeans need even know about it. Chamberlain's suggestion is surprising in view of his much cited 'profound distrust of Russia',[2] but it was probably made with a view to placating the British Left wing. In any case nothing came of it. Instead Chamberlain and Halifax were swayed by arguments on the other side, which all derived from the diplomatic, intelligence, and military professionals.

The first argument was strategic: Russia lacked offensive capability. Admiral Sinclair, head of the Secret Intelligence Service, thought she 'could do nothing of real value'.[3] The British Military Attaché in Moscow, Colonel Firebrace, thought the Red Army incapable of undertaking a major offensive, despite its large size.[4] The problems were mainly related to inefficient command and supply. They would, however, 'prove a formidable obstacle' to an invasion of Soviet territory.[5] The Air Attaché, Wing Commander Hallawell, reached similar conclusions about the air force: 'The Soviet air force is capable of developing little offensive power against Germany unless operating in concert with Poland. This power would even then be limited.'[6]

The Military Attaché in Warsaw, Colonel Sword, confirmed this view on 22 March:

while still seriously to be reckoned with in the defence, it is doubtful whether an offensive war would, or could, be undertaken by the Red army with any hope of final success. In any event, the Polish General Staff have stated categorically that Soviet troops would not be allowed to penetrate into Polish territory—though the entry of war material would be permissible.

On the other hand he thought highly of the Polish army, 'well led and trained, tough and of great endurance'. He reckoned that

[1] Draft Record of Anglo-French Conversations, 22 Mar. 1939, C4194/15/18 (FO 371/22967). Chamberlain's suggestion is omitted from the final version printed in *DBFP*.
[2] Feiling, *Chamberlain*, p. 403.
[3] Minute by Oliphant, 29 Mar. 1939, C3968/3356/18 (FO 371/23061).
[4] The peace strength of the Red Army was put at approximately 110 infantry divisions, 35 cavalry divisions, and 5 mechanized corps: a total of about 1,600,000 men with 9,000 tanks. The Chiefs of Staff later estimated that Russia could maintain only 30 divisions in the field (FPC Minutes, 25 Apr. 1939, CAB 27/624).
[5] Memorandum by Colonel Firebrace, 6 Mar. 1939, *DBFP* iv, no. 183.
[6] Memorandum by Wing Commander Hallawell, 6 Mar. 1939, ibid.

Poland could put about fifty-four divisions in the field, although 'her material resources are insufficient to maintain these forces for a war of long duration'.[1] Sir Howard Kennard, the British Ambassador in Warsaw, reported that the Poles 'can be depended upon to fight for their independence and territorial integrity, even if they knew that resistance was almost hopeless'.[2] In any case the vital factor was geography. No doubt the Russians would fight equally valiantly, but they were at one remove from Germany.

But the decisive objections to Russia's inclusion were political. Foreign Office officials, on the basis of information reaching them from all over the world, concluded that the open inclusion of Russia would undermine potential support.

On 21 March the British Ambassador in Rome, Lord Perth, warned that an association with Communist Russia would have a disastrous effect in Fascist Italy.[3] He followed this up with a further warning on 24 March:

> My Hungarian colleague told the Counsellor yesterday that in his opinion, if Great Britain linked up with Soviet Russia on European security, she would be cutting her own throat as this would automatically indispose a large number of other countries who, whatever else they were, were violently anti-Soviet. *He thought Poland would be included amongst these and that some of them would even prefer German domination to Russian assistance.*[4]

Frank Roberts of the Foreign Office Central Department thought there was 'great force in these views', and his colleague in the Northern Department, A. S. Halford, agreed that Britain 'could hardly make a bigger mistake'.[5]

On 22 March T. M. Snow, British Minister in Finland, reported that 'the rumours of an Anglo-Soviet alliance have caused a very noticeable cooling off in sympathy and highly placed Finns are astonished that His Majesty's Government could believe that the Soviet Union would honour its pledge'.[6] On 23 March a Japanese diplomat in London expressed similar feelings to Ivone Kirkpatrick,

---

[1] Sword to Kennard, 22 Mar. 1939, *DBFP* iv, no. 498, enc.
[2] Kennard to Halifax, 22 Mar. 1939, ibid., no. 498.
[3] Perth to Halifax, 21 Mar. 1939, ibid., no. 376.
[4] Perth to Halifax, 24 Mar. 1939, ibid., no. 509. Author's emphasis.
[5] Minute by Roberts, 25 Mar. 1939; minute by Halford, 31 Mar. 1939, C3907/3356/18 (FO 371/23061).
[6] Snow to Halifax, 22 Mar. 1939, C3849/3356/18 (ibid.).

A CONDITIONAL COMMITMENT 141

First Secretary in the Central Department.[1] The Foreign Office, who feared that the dreaded military alliance between Germany and Japan was possibly imminent, were reluctant to hasten the event by lining up Russia as a threat to Japan.[2]

The South Africans and the Canadians also expressed reservations. The Canadian Prime Minister, Mackenzie King, regretted

> that it should apparently have become necessary for the United Kingdom to associate herself with the USSR. From the Canadian point of view particularly that of French Canadians and other Roman Catholic communities that association would still be regarded as very unfortunate.[3]

The Rumanians were no more helpful. Although they still feared a German-inspired attack by Hungary, they 'deprecate suggestion of general pact of mutual assistance as possibly provocative to Germans and also because opinion in Poland, Yugoslavia and, to some extent, in Rumania would be opposed at any rate for the present to inclusion of Russia'.[4] The Portuguese Ambassador, Dr. Monteiro,

> noticed that in the early stages of [Britain's] approaches to Soviet Russia and Poland use had been made in the Press of the expression 'an alliance of the Democracies against the Totalitarian States'. [He] thought that this form of expression would have a most unfortunate effect not only in his own country and Spain but in Brazil and other South American countries and many of the Balkan States.[5]

A minute by the head of the Foreign Office Central Department, William Strang, indicates that all these objections to the inclusion of Russia had been effective:

> We are about to approach the Polish and Roumanian Governments with a proposal which, while it does not totally exclude the participation of

---

[1] Minute by Kirkpatrick, 23 Mar. 1939, C3942/3356/18 (ibid.).
[2] Summary of military information no. 6 (New Series) for 48 hours ending 1200 hrs. 27 Mar. 1939, War Office, C4234/15/18 (FO 371/22967). See below, pp. 179–80.
[3] U.K. High Commissioner in Canada to D.O., 24 Mar. 1939, C4470/3356/18 (FO 371/23062).
[4] Hoare to Halifax, 21 Mar. 1939, *DBFP* iv, no. 464. The Rumanian attitude towards Russian assistance was never as clear cut as the Polish, however. On 17 March Cadogan's Private Secretary, Gladwyn Jebb, asked Virgil Tilea whether his Government would accept Russian help. He replied that 'of course they would. There was no question about it' (Minute by Jebb, 18 Mar. 1939, C3576/3356/18 (FO 371/23060)).
[5] Halifax to Selby (Lisbon), 25 Mar. 1939, C4213/3356/18 (FO 371/23062).

Soviet Russia, puts them in the second rank. In the formulation of this scheme, the observations of Mr. Snow and others in a similar sense have been taken into account.[1]

Besides, there was the objection that the Russians were politically unreliable. On 16 March the Foreign Office had asked Sir William Seeds to comment on the likelihood of Russian assistance to Rumania. His answer, received on 24 March, was that the Red Army might possibly go out to meet a German invasion of Rumania if they anticipated an attack on Russian territory, but that if the Russians interpreted an attack on Rumania as a prelude to a move westwards, then

it seems certain that the Soviet Union would do everything in their power to keep out of the resulting struggle, and would, indeed, feel considerable satisfaction at the prospect of an international conflict from which all of the participants would be likely to emerge considerably weakened, and which would thus furnish the Soviet Union with an opportunity of greatly strengthening its own position.[2]

Furthermore, he had the impression 'that Poland and Roumania distrust and dislike the Soviet Union no less than they do Germany, and that a Soviet offer of assistance might in certain circumstances be almost as unwelcome to them as a threat of invasion'.

Frank Roberts, of the Foreign Office Central Department, thought that all this 'brings out very clearly the danger of relying upon Russian support and Polish and Roumanian objections to receiving such support, even if it were forthcoming'. Seeds's arguments provided 'powerful justification for our present approach to the problem of collective security'.[3] Strang and Kirkpatrick agreed. D. W. Lascelles, First Secretary in the Northern Department, wrote that 'we fully realize—I hope we do—the completely unreliable character of the Soviet Government', and believed that the Russians would act only according to their own interests,'—the only interests which they will ever consult when it comes to the point'.[4] Strang, Sargent, Oliphant, and Cadogan all agreed. Sargent thought it more important to get Poland in than Russia, since Poland was Germany's neighbour and had a direct motive for co-operating. He was not in favour of accepting 'anything more than the offer of economic assistance at

[1] Minute by Strang, 28 Mar. 1939, C3849/3356/18 (FO 371/23061).
[2] Seeds to Halifax, 21 Mar. 1939, *DBFP* iv, no. 476.
[3] Minute by Roberts, 28 Mar. 1939, C3968/3356/18 (FO 371/23061).
[4] Minute by Lascelles, 27 Mar. 1939, C3849/3356/18 (ibid.).

A CONDITIONAL COMMITMENT 143

this stage'.¹ The only dissenting voice, apart from Vansittart's, was that of Laurence Collier, head of the Northern Department, who thought that the Russians might be persuaded to help as long as there was no question of Britain and France holding back, but even he questioned 'how much their help would be worth'.²

The preponderant view therefore was that to choose Russia as an ally would be a mistake. It would risk undermining too much potential support, especially in central and south-eastern Europe, in return for too little in the way of firm benefits. If any of these countries had thought Germany even slightly reasonable—and perhaps some still did—they would have preferred German to Russian domination.³ They would also have preferred an Anglo-German understanding to having to take sides in an Anglo-German war. Furthermore the assessment of Russia's offensive capabilities, judging from her performance against Finland in 1940, was perhaps not so wide of the mark. Hitler's estimate appears to have been identical, and the French certainly shared it.

A further insight into the pressures on British foreign policy is given by Chamberlain's interview with a Labour Party delegation on 23 March. Germany had reoccupied Memel the day before, and on 23 March signed both a treaty of protection with Slovakia and the Trade Treaty with Rumania.⁴ British public opinion was further

---
¹ Minute by Sargent, 20 Mar. 1939, C3735/3356/18 (ibid.).
² Minute by Collier, 29 Mar. 1939, C3968/3356/18 (ibid.).
³ Cf. Professor Barraclough: 'Resistance to Hitler from within Europe was incomparably weaker in 1939 than resistance to Germany had been in 1914. The reason was that the national spirit which had sustained Europe from 1914 to 1918 had lost its *élan* and Fascist ideas had won a following in most European countries' (Geoffrey Barraclough, *An Introduction to Contemporary History* (London, 1967), p. 33).
⁴ Treaty of Protection between Germany and Slovakia, 23 Mar. 1939, *DGFP* vi, no. 40; German-Rumanian Economic Treaty, 23 Mar. 1939, ibid., no. 78. The signature of the latter at least was deliberately timed to undermine morale in eastern Europe and hence the British efforts to organize support (Wohlthat to Weizsäcker, 30 Mar. 1939, ibid., no. 131). British interpretations of the German-Rumanian Treaty varied. Chamberlain's view was that its importance 'very largely depended on how it was worked in practice. In certain circumstances the existence of this Treaty might strengthen Rumania's power to resist German aggression.' Oliver Stanley, President of the Board of Trade, thought it was 'either eyewash or complete surrender'. Two facts supported the first alternative: there had been no alteration of the exchange rate within the German-Rumanian Clearing, and Rumania had not agreed to any definite obligation as to the minimum amount of trade to be done with Germany each year. Lord Chatfield, Minister for Co-ordination of Defence, believed the Treaty presaged an attack elsewhere (FPC Minutes, 27 Mar. 1939, CAB 27/624). The Foreign Office took

aroused and Chamberlain was forced to take account of it. At 9.45 a.m. on 23 March he received Hugh Dalton, David Grenfell, Emmanuel Shinwell, and representatives of the Trade Unions. Horace Wilson and Alec Cadogan were also present, the latter because 'it had been impossible to get Halifax there so early in the morning'.[1]

Dalton asked Chamberlain to explain the Government's position. The Labour Party thought that Hitler's 'onward march' had brought war closer than ever and that the only satisfactory policy was collective security, which meant

> gathering together a body of peace-loving nations who could unite in the face of German aggression. They were glad to learn from Lord Halifax's speech in the House of Lords earlier during the week that the Government were now inclining in this direction but, from such information as was available to them from the Press, they feared that time, which was the essence of the problem, was being wasted in debate and interchange of communications. They would call attention to reports in the 'Daily Telegraph' of the same day, that the difficulties of the present discussions with certain foreign Governments might be attributed to the vagueness of His Majesty's Government's proposals.[2]

Chamberlain, in a remarkably frank and apparently not unfriendly interview (he had a reputation for insulting Labour in parliamentary debates), said that he was trying to halt German aggression by facing Germany with the certainty of having to fight a war on two fronts. He explained why he had rejected the Russian suggestion of a conference and said that he thought that in any case, 'the key to the position in the East was not Russia, which had no common frontier with Germany, but Poland, which had common frontiers with both Germany and Roumania'. The trouble was that the Poles were frightened of abandoning their precarious balance between Germany and Russia. Chamberlain

> was convinced that they would never sign the joint declaration, no matter what assurances [the British] and the French . . . might give them of assistance in the event of German aggression on Poland, for such assurances could never effectively operate until Poland had undergone a

a grave view. Oliver Harvey thought the Treaty gave away almost all Rumania's economic freedom (*Harvey Diaries*, 24 Mar. 1939, p. 267).

[1] Hugh Dalton, *The Fateful Years. Memoirs 1931–1945* (London, 1957), p. 231.
[2] Minutes of meeting with Labour deputation, 23 Mar. 1939, C4317/15/18 (FO 371/22967).

violent invasion by Germany. It was true that at one stage the Poles had suggested that it might help them if the Soviets were omitted from the signatory powers, but [Chamberlain] did not feel that this would, in fact bring them in.[1]

Therefore the problem had to be approached from a different angle. The French thought Rumania to be in immediate danger. The British had agreed with them that

> if an arrangement could be concluded which was limited to the case of Roumania, it might be possible for Poland to accede to it in a way in which she could not accede to a more general declaration. . . . [Britain and and France] were therefore now attempting to work out whether Poland would be prepared to join [them] in assisting Roumania if she were attacked and were prepared to defend herself.

As for Russia, he explained that both Poland and Rumania objected to her inclusion, and that 'any attempt to bring the Soviet [Union] into an arrangement dealing with the specific case of Roumania would probably wreck it'. They were not overlooking the possibility of Russian assistance in the form of supplies. He went on to say that Yugoslavia and Turkey had been left out for the time being so as not to antagonize Italy. Mussolini was obviously worried by Hitler's latest success and Chamberlain hoped to take full advantage of this opportunity 'to loosen the bonds between Berlin and Rome'. When asked whether, in the event of other powers being unwilling to co-operate, the Government contemplated making a unilateral declaration of their intention to resist German aggression, Chamberlain 'said that he did not think that this was possible, and the members of the deputation assented'.

Meanwhile the Foreign Office were trying to put these ideas into practice. But a Polish counter-proposal held up their efforts. On 24 March Count Edward Raczynski, the Polish Ambassador in London, proposed the conclusion of a 'confidential bilateral understanding' whereby Britain and Poland would undertake to consult in accordance with the terms of the Four-Power Declaration.[2] He also suggested that something might be included about Danzig, perhaps on the lines of Halifax's assurance to him on 21 March that should the Danzig question develop in such a way as to threaten Polish independence, then the British would be 'gravely concerned'.[3]

[1] Ibid.
[2] Halifax to Kennard, 24 Mar. 1939, *DBFP* iv, no. 518. See above, pp. 124–5.
[3] Halifax to Kennard, 21 Mar. 1939, ibid., no. 471.

Raczynski explained that the secrecy of the Polish proposal was intended to prevent a hostile reaction in Germany; to prevent any leakage by the notorious French; and to avoid linking Poland and the Soviet Union in a public declaration. Count Jean Szembek, Under-Secretary in the Polish Foreign Ministry, wrote in his diary that Beck's idea was to leave out France and Russia 'so as not to give the impression of pursuing a broad scheme for Germany's encirclement'.[1]

Raczynski explained Beck's proposal to Halifax in deliberately involved and enigmatic terms. We know, however, what Beck had in mind. The head of the Western Department in the Polish Ministry of Foreign Affairs, Jozef Potocki, had instructed Raczynski that Beck wanted 'a bilateral agreement providing for British support, especially in the case of Danzig, in return for which [Poland] would undertake to consult with Great Britain'.[2] Halifax put his first-class brain to work. He asked Raczynski whether the Polish proposal meant that 'while we should undertake to assist Poland in the event of a threat to Poland's independence, Poland in similar fashion would support Great Britain if she were the object of attack, or join Great Britain in the event of attack upon any other country?'[3] Raczynski thought not. He now put the proposal more simply: Britain would be bound to support Poland in case of trouble over Danzig, while Poland would be bound to consult with Britain. Halifax thought that this 'was not quite the same thing'. He gave the Polish Ambassador no answer, but raised the difficulty that the secret nature of the agreement might embarrass Anglo-French relations. Nevertheless he repeated his assurance that should any threat to Polish independence arise over the Danzig question, 'then this would be a matter of the gravest concern to ourselves'.

On the next day, 25 March, Halifax summoned Cadogan, Vansittart, Sargent, Malkin, Strang, and Harvey for a long and important meeting to discuss future policy, in view of the Polish attitude and in view of the German-Rumanian Trade Treaty.[4] By now

---

[1] Szembek, *Journal*, 22 Mar. 1939, p. 434.

[2] Quoted in Anna M. Cienciala, *Poland and the Western Powers 1938–1939, A Study in the Interdependence of Eastern and Western Europe* (London, 1968), p. 217.

[3] Halifax to Kennard, 24 Mar. 1939, *DBFP* iv, no. 518.

[4] This was one of the very few high-level Foreign Office meetings to have been recorded, and even then the record took the form of a memorandum rather than minutes (PREM 1/321). It was drafted by Strang and revised by Cadogan (Dilks,

the Four-Power Declaration was dead. The Poles objected to an openly anti-German and pro-Soviet declaration without, and perhaps not even with, a commitment from Britain. Halifax was 'sure that we cannot possibly agree to any secret understanding with Poland because of our Geneva pledge and because of Parliament'.[1] He also objected that it would have to be concealed from France and that it would deprive British diplomacy of one of its main objectives, an openly proclaimed challenge to Germany.

It was now clear that Russia's inclusion would

(1) impede [the] construction of [a] front against aggression, since a number of our potential associates are extremely reluctant to be associated with Russia, even for the purpose of resisting Germany;

(2) tend to consolidate the relations of the parties to the anti-Comintern Pact and make it less likely that we should be able to exercise influence on, and establish good relations with, the weaker members of the Pact, namely Italy and Japan;

(3) excite anxiety in such countries as Portugal, Spain, some South American republics.[2]

Halifax thought it particularly important to avoid committing Italy irretrievably against Britain by the inclusion of Russia, but 'both for internal reasons and because of her ultimate military value, if only as our arsenal, we must keep [Russia] with us'.[3]

If Britain could not build on to a Russian coalition, the only alternative was to build around Poland, whose inclusion was vital 'since Germany's weak point is her inability at present to conduct a war on two fronts, and unless Poland is with us, Germany would be able to avoid a war on two fronts'. Contrary to Halifax's earlier willingness to wage war regardless of Polish adhesion, he now recognized the importance of the fact that Polish neutrality would secure Germany on her eastern front and leave her free either to attack Rumania through Hungary or to attack the West, a possibility that was by no means ruled out.

Halifax now proposed to ask Poland and Rumania whether they would resist German aggression, and to say that if so, then Britain and France would support them. The commitment to Rumania would be unconditional, but three conditions would attach to the

ed., *Cadogan Diaries*, 26 Mar. 1939, p. 163). Cf. *Harvey Diaries*, 25 Mar. 1939, p. 268.

[1] Ibid.
[2] Memorandum by Strang and Cadogan, 26 Mar. 1939, PREM 1/321, p. 2.
[3] *Harvey Diaries*, 25 Mar. 1939, p. 268.

commitment to Poland. First, Poland must agree to support Rumania. Second, she must agree to help Britain and France in case they were attacked by Germany. Third, she must agree to help Britain and France 'if they go to war with Germany to resist German aggression anywhere in Western Europe or in Yugoslavia'.[1] Rumania was thought too weak to enter such a wide-ranging commitment.

Halifax must have been impressed with the potential leverage of a British commitment to Poland, for he was now proposing to extract from the Poles not only a pledge to support Rumania but also a pledge to support Britain and France, whatever their reason for going to war with Germany. This was optimistic, indeed possibly dangerous, as Halifax later recognized.[2]

As for Russia, Halifax wanted to explain the difficulties frankly to her and to suggest that she and France should turn the Franco-Soviet Pact of 1935 into a straight defensive alliance.[3] The argument to be used to explain this to Poland was that it was impossible to get British and French left-wing support unless Russia was 'in some way' associated with the scheme.

The whole plan was based on the assumption that apart from western Europe, the line to be held against further German aggression must be the frontiers of Poland, Rumania, and Yugoslavia. Yugoslavia was to be informed only after Poland and Rumania had agreed, and Turkey and Greece would then fall automatically into place. The balance of power determined the fundamental importance of this line. First of all German control of the physical resources beyond the line would give Germany the strength to turn against the West without fear of defeat. Secondly, the countries beyond the line had to be capable of attacking Germany on her eastern front.

These points were strongly emphasized by the British Military Attaché in Berlin, Colonel F. N. Mason-MacFarlane, who argued that because Poland, Rumania, and Yugoslavia were so apprehensive about further German territorial aspirations,

> we may be practically certain that if the Western Powers show a strong front, adequate allies will be available in the East to force Germany to employ more troops than she can afford from her Western defences if she

---

[1] Memorandum by Strang and Cadogan, 26 Mar. 1939, PREM 1/321, p. 5.
[2] See below, p. 152.
[3] The Franco-Soviet Pact had been left full of loopholes to take account of French obligations under the Locarno Treaties.

is to capture and hold the areas necessary to free her from the effects of a blockade. . . .

Germany's strategic situation on interior lines is undeniably favourable, but neither the total ground forces nor the present state of her communications offer much hope of achieving the swift Napoleonic successes which can alone save her from the comparatively rapid collapse which must follow failure. In no respect is Germany's 'home front' as a whole capable of sustaining an effective blockade for any length of time.[1]

Mason-MacFarlane argued in addition that it would take time for the German army to absorb the military resources gained as a result of the occupation of Bohemia and Moravia. At present Germany was able to put about 100 divisions in the field, a figure which he reckoned would reach at least 175 in two years. He concluded that

if a trial of strength is regarded as inevitable, from the point of view of *War on the ground* the situation *at the moment and for the next* few months is very distinctly more unfavourable to Germany than it is likely to be in the course of the next decade, unless events develop on unforeseen lines. It will actually be at its most unfavourable from now for another couple of months; will then probably improve somewhat till October; and will then again be worse, in some respects, till the Spring of next year.

Mason-MacFarlane's views and their effect on British policy-making at this time are further examined in Chapter 9. Suffice it to say here that the Foreign Office were impressed. Cadogan believed that

if we want to stem the German expansion . . . we must try to build a dam *now*. Of course, as to whether, if Germany really does gobble up S.E. Europe, she will really be stronger to attack us, I still have some doubts. But Mason-MacFarlane thinks she will, and he ought to know more about it than I. If we are set on this course, we must set about it quickly and firmly. It *might* act as a deterrent to avert war, though I confess I think the chances of that are rather slight.[2]

Thus whether or not Chamberlain believed that war with Germany could be avoided at this point,[3] the Foreign Office appears to have been resigned to it, and wished to ensure that it was waged on as favourable terms as possible.

[1] Memorandum by Mason-MacFarlane, n.d., C3954/13/18 (FO 371/22958).
[2] Dilks, ed., *Cadogan Diaries*, 26 Mar. 1939, pp. 163-4.
[3] He wrote to his sister on 19 Mar. 1939 that 'I never accept the view that war is inevitable' (Feiling, *Chamberlain*, p. 401). He wanted either to reassure his sister or to convince himself.

On Sunday 26 March Halifax discussed the Foreign Office proposal with Chamberlain, who 'approved in principle'.[1] His only real objection was that the plan to strengthen and clarify the Franco-Soviet Pact might 'lose us nearly as much sympathy as the association of [the] USSR in the Declaration itself would have done'.[2] He was also keen to maintain the distinction between the independence and the integrity of Poland and Rumania, presumably so as to leave room for possible revision of the *status quo*. He pointed out that a substantial German minority lived in the Polish Corridor, and that there were Hungarian, German, and Bulgarian minorities in Rumania.

It is thus conceivable, I suppose, that Herr Hitler might in these cases be able to raise a plea of 'self-determination' at least more plausible than that used in the case of Prague. No doubt this point has been taken into account by [the] FO and that is why the words 'defend independence of' have been used.

Since there is no evidence that the British did in fact press the French to strengthen the Franco-Soviet Pact, Chamberlain's objection must have been effective. Besides, the French themselves were just as reluctant.

It is clear that by this time, in fact as soon as his Four-Power Declaration scheme was shown to have failed, Chamberlain had virtually abandoned the initiative to Halifax and the Foreign Office. He kept a weather eye on the Foreign Secretary, who still consulted him closely, but there was no further major initiative from the Prime Minister. He became a sort of public-relations man for the Foreign Office, explaining their policy and justifying it to the public and to the politicians. There is no evidence of a further struggle against a British commitment on Chamberlain's part. In the heyday of Chamberlain's attempt to achieve a *rapprochement* with Germany, the Foreign Office had been responsible for keeping Britain's options open in case of failure. This was the central reason for Britain's unwillingness ever to allow Germany a free hand in eastern Europe. The Foreign Office strategy, executed with Chamberlain's express consent, had been to resist German expansion in central and southeastern Europe by economic means. Now the Foreign Office were

[1] Dilks, ed., *Cadogan Diaries*, 26 Mar. 1939, p. 164. Cadogan and R. A. Butler, Parliamentary Under-Secretary for Foreign Affairs, were also present at this important meeting.
[2] Minute by Chamberlain, 26 Mar. 1939, PREM 1/321.

attempting to exercise the options they had managed to keep open. It was natural enough that Chamberlain should allow the Foreign Office to get on with it. But this does require a revision of the commonly accepted view that although Halifax's influence increased decisively after 15 March 1939, Neville Chamberlain still exercised a virtual monopoly of decision-making at this time.[1]

On 27 March the Foreign Office plan for a conditional commitment to Poland and an unconditional guarantee of Rumania was put to a crucial meeting of the Cabinet Foreign Policy Committee, called for the first time since 8 February 1939.[2] Chamberlain preferred this forum to an emergency Cabinet meeting, which 'might have caused undue publicity'.[3] Emphasizing the need 'for urgent and immediate action', he began by telling the Committee about 'certain Conclusions which had been provisionally reached' at his meeting with Halifax the day before. The new Foreign Office proposals, he said, were designed to concentrate on Rumania, which seemed most likely to be the next victim of German aggression. He had taken the strategic arguments to heart: German control of Rumania 'would go far to neutralise what perhaps Germany most feared, an effective naval blockade'. A further consequence would be that Germany 'would be in a much stronger position than she is at present successfully to attack and over-run Poland. Poland herself would be wellnigh encircled and the moral effect on smaller States, like Greece and Bulgaria, in South-Eastern Europe, would be far reaching.' There had indeed been signs that morale was weakening. As Cadogan noted in his diary on 26 March, 'all the little States are weakening and showing funk—even Turkey'.[4]

Chamberlain thought that the British scheme would appeal to Poland in her own interests. There were, however, doubts as to whether Poland would in fact agree to all the conditions attached to the British offer of support, and in particular the two conditions that Poland must help 'if Great Britain or France were attacked by Germany, or if they went to war with Germany to resist German

---

[1] Middlemas, *Diplomacy of Illusion*, p. 447.
[2] Present were Chamberlain, Halifax, Sir John Simon (Chancellor of the Exchequer), Sir Samuel Hoare (Home Secretary), Lord Chatfield (Minister for Co-ordination of Defence), Sir Thomas Inskip (Dominions Secretary), W. S. Morrison (Chancellor of the Duchy of Lancaster), Oliver Stanley (President of the Board of Trade), R. A. Butler, Sir Horace Wilson, and Sir Alexander Cadogan.
[3] FPC Minutes, 27 Mar. 1939, CAB 27/624.
[4] Dilks, ed., *Cadogan Diaries*, 26 Mar. 1939, p. 163. See below, pp. 177–8.

aggression anywhere in Western Europe or Yugoslavia'.[1] Therefore, said Chamberlain, 'if Poland declined to enter a commitment of this kind then nevertheless we should be prepared to give her the unilateral assurance as regards the Eastern Front seeing that our object [is] to check and defeat Germany's attempt at world domination'.[2]

There is no record of the Sunday meeting at which all this was discussed,[3] but Halifax's remarks to the Cabinet two days later indicate that the doubts were his.[4] However, as he then explained, there would be no harm in throwing in the conditions, as Colonel Beck was unlikely to reach any decision before his arrival in London on 3 April.

What had caused this willingness to drop two out of the three conditions designed to secure reciprocal Polish assistance? It is probable that Halifax and Chamberlain had been informed of the strong views of the Polish Ambassador in Paris, Lukasiewicz, who, as we have seen, complained in no uncertain terms about the apparent levity of British foreign policy in a conversation on 24 March with William Bullitt, the American Ambassador.[5] The latter asked Kennedy, his colleague in London, to repeat Lukasiewicz's arguments to Chamberlain. Lukasiewicz later reported to Warsaw that on 26 March 'Ambassador Bullitt received in my presence a telephone call from Ambassador Kennedy regarding the conversation with Chamberlain'.[6] If the British were at all sensitive to American and to Polish opinion, which they were, they would have taken this warning to heart. In any case the idea of a conditional, bilateral pact with Poland was now crumbling, and Halifax was harking back to his earlier willingness to go to war with Germany regardless. This is clear from his remarks to the Foreign Policy Committee. He thought that

there was probably no way in which France and ourselves could prevent Poland and Roumania from being overrun. We were faced with the

[1] Halifax to Kennard and Hoare, 27 Mar. 1939, *DBFP* iv, no. 538.
[2] FPC Minutes, 27 Mar. 1939, CAB 27/624.
[3] Lord Butler writes that he has no record of the meeting in his diary. He is 'convinced that the idea of a guarantee to Poland was Halifax's, prompted by the Foreign Office and Cadogan. Neville Chamberlain agreed, but it was not his idea' (Lord Butler to author, 29 June 1973).
[4] Cab. Minutes, 29 Mar. 1939, CAB 23/98.
[5] See above, p. 133.
[6] Lukasiewicz to Beck, 29 Mar. 1939, in Jedrzejewicz, ed., *Diplomat in Paris*, p. 182.

dilemma of doing nothing, or entering into a devastating war. If we did nothing this in itself would mean a great accession to Germany's strength and a great loss to ourselves of sympathy and support in the United States, in the Balkan countries, and in other parts of the world. In those circumstances if we had to choose between two great evils he favoured our going to war.[1]

What Halifax was saying in his circumlocutory way was that the commitment to Poland could not be implemented. Instead, its purpose was to serve as a pretext for going to war with Germany. The only alternative was for Britain to abdicate as a Great Power. Furthermore, Germany was to be given no exit. For Halifax had taken the line with Poland that if she

> saw fit to make some voluntary agreement with Germany in regard to Danzig we should raise no objection. If, however, Poland was subjected to such pressure by Germany over Danzig as amounted to a threat to Poland's independence then we would regard the matter as one in which we were interested.[2]

But as Halifax very well knew, Colonel Beck was unlikely to yield to German pressure for an agreement over Danzig once Britain had strengthened his hand with a guarantee.

Cadogan was surprised at how readily the Committee accepted the Foreign Office proposals.[3] The only real friction was caused by concern about the role of Russia. Sir Samuel Hoare, the Home Secretary, wanted Russia in. Her omission 'would be regarded in many quarters as a considerable defeat for our policy. No one could accuse him of any predilections in favour of Soviet Russia, but he did attach very great importance to bringing in to the common front as many countries as possible.' Halifax explained that 'if we had to make a choice between Poland and Soviet Russia, it seemed clear that Poland would give the greater value. It was imperative that at the present juncture we must not risk offending Colonel Beck.' He conceded the importance of getting the Russians to supply material aid to the east European countries, but said that even the French 'thought that the Russians were very deceitful and unreliable, and would not in an emergency give much, if any, effective help. France seemed little interested in Russia, but attached

---

[1] FPC Minutes, 27 Mar. 1939, CAB 27/624.　　　[2] Ibid.
[3] Dilks, ed., *Cadogan Diaries*, 27 Mar. 1939, p. 164.

the most vital importance to the inclusion of Poland in the pact.'[1]

After 'further discussion', the Committee agreed to the Foreign Office proposals, and Cadogan went off to polish up the draft telegrams to the British representatives in Warsaw, Bucharest, and Paris. These were dispatched that night, with instructions to the first two capitals not to take action on them until French agreement had been confirmed.[2]

Nor was this quite the end of the affair. The next day, 28 March, the Chiefs of Staff were asked 'as a matter of urgency' to report on the military implications of the Anglo-French guarantee to Poland and Rumania.[3] They were not asked whether Russian help was more important from the strategic point of view than Polish help, but were simply told to assume 'that the USSR remain a friendly neutral to the extent of being willing to supply war material to Poland and Rumania'.[4] This was because they had already given their opinion that Russian help was essential and that on balance a Russian alliance, with Poland neutral, would be more valuable from the strategic point of view. In the meantime, however, the political assumption on which this opinion rested had been challenged by Chamberlain and Halifax, on expert advice. They believed that Russian help would not be forthcoming when it came to the point. It was therefore essential to concentrate first on Poland, a limitrophe power.

It would be a mistake to conclude that because the Chiefs of Staff were asked to consider this question as a whole only *after* the policy decisions had been taken that they had therefore not been consulted. Military opinion was not sought only in the form of Chiefs of Staff reports. British strategic planning was a continuing process and there was plenty of formal and informal contact between the Foreign Office, the Service Ministries, and the Chiefs of Staff.

---

[1] Colonel Fraser, the British Military Attaché in Paris, had reported in December 1938 that 'even prior to the crisis in September, the French had ceased to have any faith in military assistance from Russia. But at that time . . . Russia was regarded as a source from which these countries [Czechoslovakia and Rumania] could be provided with arms and munitions, and it was in this fact that, in their view, the chief value of the Franco-Russian Pact lay' (Fraser to Phipps, 22 Dec. 1938, enc. in C16018/36/17 (FO 432/5)).

[2] Halifax to Kennard and Hoare, 27 Mar. 1939, *DBFP* iv, no. 538.

[3] Ismay (Secretary to Committee of Imperial Defence) to F.O., and minute by W. Strang, 18 Apr. 1939, C5041/15/18 (FO 371/22969).

[4] 'Military Implications of an Anglo-French Guarantee of Poland and Rumania', draft report, n.d., COS 872 (CAB 53/47). The final report was dated 3 Apr. 1939.

A CONDITIONAL COMMITMENT

What the Chiefs of Staff were now being asked to do was to assess the implications of a political decision for Britain's strategic plans. This was an important question. Until now her war plans had been based on the assumption that Poland and Rumania would be neutral.[1] Now they were assumed to be allies.

The Chiefs of Staff fully confirmed the judgement about the importance of Poland—'the existence of an Eastern front for Germany depends on Poland being in the war'. But they issued a warning:

> We are not in a position to assess the deterrent effect of such a Pact upon Germany, but an important military implication is that if such a Pact were to encourage an intransigeant attitude on the part of Poland and Rumania it would thereby tend to precipitate a European war before our forces are in any way prepared for it, and such a war might be started by aggression against Danzig alone.[2]

Whether or not they were right to do so, Chamberlain and Halifax consciously assumed this responsibility.

On specific questions, the Chiefs of Staff believed that having Poland and Rumania as allies would not affect the situation at sea or in the air, but would definitely help on land. They had as good an opinion of the Polish army as the Military Attaché in Warsaw, but an extremely low opinion of the Rumanian army. They outlined various hypotheses about how the Germans would deploy their divisions, emphasizing the need to cover both the eastern and the western fronts, and concluded that

> In the opening phase of the war it is most improbable that Germany would undertake major offensives in both the West and the East.
>
> If she undertook a major offensive in the East there is little doubt that she could occupy Rumania and the Polish corridor. If she were to continue the offensive against Poland it would only be a matter of time (probably only a matter of months) before Poland was eliminated from the war.
>
> Even if Poland had been conquered, however, it might well be that the number of troops required in the East to hold down the conquered territory and safeguard it against possible attack from Russia would be little, if any, less than the number required to conquer Poland. She would moreover have suffered heavy casualties in the process.
>
> Similarly a German occupation of Rumania which is unlikely to take

[1] Memorandum by Chiefs of Staff: 'European Appreciation, 1939-40', 20 Feb. 1939, DP(P)44, CAB 16/183A.
[2] 'Military Implications of an Anglo-French Guarantee of Poland and Rumania', draft report, n.d., COS 872 (CAB 53/47).

very long, would, in conjunction with the provision for possible Russian attack on the Rumanian frontier . . . absorb a considerable number of divisions.

If Germany did not undertake a major offensive in the East, she would probably still have insufficient forces to attack the Maginot Line successfully. She would, however, probably be able to overrun Holland and perhaps a part of Belgium. This would, of course, have serious consequences for us as we have explained in previous Papers.[1]

The fate of Poland as outlined by the Chiefs of Staff was even more gloomy than this. They emphasized that Britain and France could give Poland no direct support in resisting a German invasion, and that Poland and Rumania would have to depend on the Soviet Union for their armaments, given the state of British and French production.

Despite the prediction about the length of time the Poles could resist Germany, the obvious conclusion to be drawn from this report was that Poland must be irretrievably committed to the British side. Should Hitler attack in the east and hold in the west, which was a more probable if not a certain scenario, this would give Britain and France a further few months to prepare for the onslaught, while holding up a number of German divisions in Poland. Furthermore the defeat of Poland would leave German troops confronting Soviet Russia, which meant the likelihood of a more durable eastern front. The value of Poland lay not in the capacity of her army to launch an offensive against Germany, which was virtually non-existent, but in her capacity to absorb German divisions. Above all she must not be allowed to supplement them by subordinating her foreign policy to Hitler's, or to allow them free reign in the west by maintaining an attitude of benevolent neutrality. It was the fear that Poland might do so that prompted the British finally to abandon the conditions they had attached to their promise of support.

[1] 'Military Implications of an Anglo-French Guarantee of Poland and Rumania', draft report, n.d., COS 872 (CAB 53/47).

8

BRITAIN, GERMANY, AND POLAND

On 27 March 1939 the British Government hoped for a mutual assistance pact between Britain, France, and Poland in support of Rumania and conducted their negotiations on this basis. Yet four days later, on 31 March, Neville Chamberlain announced the Government's decision to give Poland a unilateral and unconditional guarantee. Although described as an interim measure, the guarantee was offered without any previously obtained assurance from the Poles that they would either reciprocate or assist Rumania. In order to understand this shift in emphasis we must review the course of German-Polish relations after Munich and British reactions to them.

The Polish state, as we have seen, lived a precarious existence between Russia and Germany, since both harboured revisionist aims against her. Germany desired the return of territories lost as a result of the Treaty of Versailles, in particular the Free City of Danzig and the 'Polish Corridor' which separated Germany from East Prussia. Russia wanted back the tract of White Russian territory lost to Poland during the Polish expansionist war of 1920, the loss of which had been confirmed by the Treaty of Riga in 1921. The guiding principle of Polish foreign policy, laid down by the elder statesman Marshal Jozef Pilsudski and skilfully followed by Colonel Jozef Beck, the Foreign Minister, was the achievement of a balance between her two neighbours, so as not to antagonize either. To this end the Polish-Russian Treaty of Non-Aggression was signed in 1932, and the German-Polish Declaration of Non-Aggression in 1934. The balance became very precarious in September 1938, when Poland appeared to align herself with Germany in demanding and receiving the disputed coal-mining district of Teschen from Czechoslovakia.

After Munich, Hitler turned his attention to Germany's claims against Poland, although the Poles had in fact brought up the question themselves just three days before Chamberlain's visit to Bad

Godesberg on 22 September 1938. The Polish Ambassador in Berlin, Jozef Lipski, had then suggested to Hitler the possibility of concluding 'a direct Polish-German treaty to stabilize the position of the Free City' of Danzig.[1] Hitler waited to take up this question until his hand had been strengthened at Munich, but had no intention of forcing the issue in any way. He hoped by patient, though persistent, diplomatic pressure to get a settlement with Poland on his own terms. He wanted Poland to abandon her policy of equilibrium and to align herself once and for all with Germany, in what Ribbentrop called a 'general settlement' (*Gesamtlösung*).[2] As Hitler later told Carl Burckhardt, the League of Nations High Commissioner in Danzig, he wanted the Poles to 'conform completely to our foreign policy' ('ganz unserer Politik anschliessen').[3]

Ribbentrop broached the German proposals in an interview with Lipski on 24 October 1938:

1. The Free State of Danzig would revert to the German Reich.
2. An extra-territorial *Reichsautobahn* belonging to Germany and likewise an extra-territorial, multiple-track railroad would be laid through the Corridor.
3. Similarly, Poland would receive in the Danzig area an extra-territorial road or *Autobahn*, a railroad, and a free port.
4. Poland would receive a guarantee of a market for her goods in the Danzig area.
5. The two nations would recognize their common boundaries (guarantee) or each other's territories.
6. The German-Polish treaty would be extended 10 to 25 years.
7. Poland would accede to the Anti-Comintern Pact.
8. The two countries would add a consultation clause to their treaty.[4]

Ribbentrop also held out the hope, in case of a satisfactory settlement, of the fulfilment of one of Poland's principal aims, the Hungarian occupation of Sub-Carpathian Ukraine (Ruthenia) so as to give Poland and Hungary a common frontier. In Polish minds, the vacuum created in Ruthenia (the easternmost province of Czechoslovakia) by the growing movement for autonomy in Czechoslovakia

---

[1] Lipski to Beck, 20 Sept. 1938, *Documents and Materials Relating to the Eve of the Second World War* (Moscow, 1948), i, no. 23.

[2] Lipski to Beck, 25 Oct. 1938, Republic of Poland, Ministry for Foreign Affairs, *Official Documents Concerning Polish–German and Polish–Soviet Relations 1933–1939. The Polish White Book* (London, 1940), no. 44.

[3] Carl J. Burckhardt, *Meine Danziger Mission 1937–1939* (Zürich, 1960), p. 232.

[4] Record of Ribbentrop–Lipski Conversation, 24 Oct. 1938, *DGFP* v, no. 81.

BRITAIN, GERMANY, AND POLAND

offered dangerous opportunities for expansion by the Great Powers. The Poles justified their desire to the Germans, of course, in terms of a dam against Bolshevism.[1] In truth they were more worried by German ambitions, and especially the rumoured plan to unite all Ukrainians (including Polish and Russian Ukrainians) in a puppet Ukrainian state.[2]

Lipski told Ribbentrop that Poland would never allow Germany to incorporate Danzig. Colonel Beck confirmed this in no uncertain terms. He instructed Lipski to tell Ribbentrop that a German attempt to annex Danzig 'must inevitably lead to conflict'. He also wrote that he considered the Danzig question so vitally important that he was ready to 'have final conversations personally with the governing circles of the Reich'.[3] Beck hoped at the very least for a confirmation of Hitler's declaration of November 1937 that Danzig would never be the cause of conflict between Germany and Poland.[4]

Beck's talks with Hitler and Ribbentrop eventually took place at Berchtesgaden and Munich on 5 and 6 January 1939. Hitler explained that he wanted Danzig to 'come into the German community politically but remain with Poland economically'.[5] There was no intention

[1] Lipski to Beck, 20 Sept. 1938, *Documents and Materials*, i, no. 23.
[2] The British discounted the rumours of German designs on the Ukraine. Laurence Collier, head of the Foreign Office Northern Department, pointed out that (1) 'the Soviet Ukraine cannot be detached from the Soviet Union without a large-scale invasion from abroad'; (2) 'the Poles will fight the Germans rather than permit a German army to launch such an invasion from their territory, both since that must in the long run involve the loss of the Polish Ukraine and since in any case they would never allow German troops into their country'; but (3) 'they might, if subjected to sufficient pressure, be forced to remain neutral while the Germans launched their attack on the Soviet Ukraine through Roumania, and even perhaps, if sufficient inducements were combined with the pressure, to join in the attack themselves in the hope of securing some of the spoils'; though (4) 'the ultimate consequences to Poland are so obvious that it would require the very strongest pressure, coupled with the conviction that they could get no support from France, to make them amenable to any scheme of this sort' (Minute by Collier, 19 Jan. 1939, C528/15/18 (FO 371/22961)). This, thought Cadogan, pointed to the conclusion 'that Hitler, if he feels he must explode, will explode towards the West first' (Minute by Cadogan, 23 Jan. 1939, ibid.). Vansittart agreed that 'there are no ripe plums in the Ukraine' (Minute by Vansittart, 25 Jan. 1939, ibid.).
[3] Beck to Lipski, 31 Oct. 1938, *Polish White Book*, no. 45.
[4] Szembek, *Journal*, 7 Dec. 1938, p. 385. On 5 November 1937 Hitler had assured Lipski that (1) he did not intend to alter the Danzig Statute; (2) he did not intend ever to confront Poland with a *fait accompli* in Danzig; and (3) Polish rights would not be infringed (Memorandum by Ribbentrop, 6 Nov. 1937, *DGFP* v, no. 19. Also Lipski to Beck, 5 Nov. 1937, *Polish White Book*, no. 34).
[5] Record of Hitler–Beck Conversation, 5 Jan. 1939, *DGFP* v, no. 119.

of depriving Poland of access to Danzig, for the simple reason that the city could not survive without Polish trade. He assured Beck that although Danzig would sooner or later become part of Germany, 'no *fait accompli* would be engineered there'. At the same time Germany had to have freer access to East Prussia by means of an extra-territorial road and railway. Hitler was prepared in return to recognize and guarantee the Corridor, a step 'by no means easy' for him to take without widespread German criticism. Beck confined himself to outlining the need for an independent Polish foreign policy and went away to think about the Danzig problem, which seemed to him 'extremely difficult'.

The next day Ribbentrop repeated the German *desiderata*, offering the prospect of territorial gains at the expense of Russia if Poland would align herself definitely with Germany on the basis of the Anti-Comintern Pact. Beck again refused to be drawn, and recalled Marshal Pilsudski's dictum that Danzig represented a touchstone of German-Polish relations.[1]

Beck returned to Warsaw in a pessimistic frame of mind, according to Count Szembek, Under-Secretary at the Polish Foreign Ministry. He saw no viable solution to the Danzig impasse and resolved to tighten Polish relations with the western Powers, while stringing out the negotiations with Germany so as to avoid a direct confrontation.[2] No progress was made on the key issues when Ribbentrop returned to the charge in Warsaw on 26 January 1939, the fifth anniversary of the German-Polish Declaration of Non-Aggression.[3] Nevertheless the German tone continued to be friendly. This calm atmosphere was confirmed in Hitler's speech to the Reichstag on 30 January, and Lipski's interpretation was that Hitler believed he could achieve his aims 'by way of political and economic pressure, without having recourse to military action'.[4]

The German occupation of Bohemia and Moravia on 15 March, the annexation of Memel on 22 March, and the Treaty of Protection with Slovakia on 23 March upset the Polish position completely. The Poles now faced the German army on three fronts. Ribbentrop was not slow in pressing home the advantage. On 21 March he

[1] Record of Ribbentrop–Beck Conversation, 6 Jan. 1939, *DGFP* v, no. 120.
[2] Szembek, *Journal*, 10 Jan. 1939, pp. 407–8.
[3] Record of Ribbentrop–Beck Conversation, 26 Jan. 1939, *DGFP* v, no. 126.
[4] Lipski to Beck, 7 Feb. 1939, in Waclaw Jedrzejewicz, ed., *Diplomat in Berlin 1933–1939. Papers and Memoirs of Jozef Lipski, Ambassador of Poland* (New York, 1968), p. 491.

reiterated the German proposals in an interview with Lipski, intimating that Poland must soon reach the parting of the ways:

Poland must realize clearly that she could not take a middle course. Either Poland would remain a national State, working for a reasonable relationship with Germany and her Führer, or one day there would arise a Marxist Polish Government, which would then be absorbed by Bolshevist Russia.[1]

Lipski, pessimistic, reported that Germany had 'resolved to carry out her Eastern programme quickly, and so desires to have Poland's attitude clearly defined'.[2] However, Beck had no wish to define Poland's attitude in the sense desired by Germany. On 24 March he outlined future policy at a meeting of senior officials at the Polish Foreign Ministry. He defined Poland's vital interests:

Where is the line? It is our territory, but not only that. The line also involves the non-acceptance by our state, regarding the drastic spot that Danzig has always been, of any unilateral suggestion to be imposed on us. And, regardless of what Danzig is worth as an object (in my opinion it may perhaps be worth quite a lot, but this is of no concern at the moment), under the present circumstances it has become a symbol. This means that, if we join that category of eastern states that allow rules to be dictated to them, then I do not know where the matter will end. That is why it is wiser to go forward to meet the enemy than to wait for him at home.[3]

Lipski told Ribbentrop on 26 March that although Poland was prepared to further simplify the arrangements for German communication with East Prussia there could be no question of extraterritoriality. As for Danzig, he proposed a joint German-Polish guarantee of the Free City, since the League of Nations was no longer capable of fulfilling its own obligations in this respect.[4] He added that Poland had 'always considered Russia's access to European politics a dangerous thing'.[5]

Meanwhile the German annexation of Memel on 22 March had caused a palpably nervous reaction in Warsaw. The Government ordered mobilization measures and troop movements to cover Danzig. Ribbentrop now drew attention to these measures and warned Lipski that 'a violation of the sovereignty of Danzig territory

[1] Memorandum by Ribbentrop, 21 Mar. 1939, *DGFP* vi, no. 61.
[2] Lipski to Beck, 21 Mar. 1939, *Polish White Book*, no. 61.
[3] Memorandum on the Conference of Senior Officials with the Polish Minister for Foreign Affairs, 24 Mar. 1939, Jedrzejewicz, ed., *Diplomat in Berlin*, p. 503.
[4] For an elaboration of the League of Nations position see below, pp. 164-5.
[5] Beck to Lipski, 25 Mar. 1939, Jedrzejewicz, ed., *Diplomat in Berlin*, p. 507.

by Polish troops would be regarded by Germany in the same way as a violation of the Reich frontiers'.[1]

At this time Hitler was exercising a restraining hand on the Foreign Ministry and on Ribbentrop in particular. The latter's draft instructions of 24 March to Moltke, the German Ambassador in Warsaw, to follow up Ribbentrop's demands of 21 March, were cancelled on Hitler's orders.[2] The reason was that they 'presented the Poles with the option: friend or foe'.[3] His policy towards Poland at this juncture is clearly evident from his well-known directive to General von Brauchitsch, Commander-in-Chief of the army, on 25 March: 'The Führer *does not* wish to solve the Danzig question by force however. He does not wish to drive Poland into the arms of Britain by this.' He did, however, envisage satellite status for Poland and eventual irredentist gains at her expense.[4]

On 27 March Ribbentrop complained to Lipski about reports in the German press of anti-German demonstrations in Poland and repeated that he did not regard the Polish proposals as a basis for settlement. 'Relations between the two countries were therefore deteriorating sharply.'[5]

On 28 March Beck summoned Moltke in order to tell him, in response to Ribbentrop's similar statement to Lipski on 26 March, 'that if an attempt should be made by Germany to alter the status of the Free City unilaterally, Poland would regard this as a *casus belli*'.[6]

On 29 March the President of the Danzig Senate, Arthur Greiser, and the Director of its Foreign Affairs Department, Viktor Böttcher, called on Ernst von Weizsäcker, State Secretary in the German Foreign Ministry, to ask about the state of German-Polish discussions on Danzig. Greiser wanted to know what attitude to adopt in the future, and Weizsäcker advised him that there was

no cause to show the Polish Government a particularly accommodating

---

[1] Memorandum by Ribbentrop, 26 Mar. 1939, *DGFP* vi, no. 101. The German Armed Forces High Command (O.K.W.) took a less serious view of the Polish moves than the Army General Staff. In view of this uncertainty, Weizsäcker, State Secretary in the German Foreign Ministry, had advised Ribbentrop that it would be prudent to warn the Poles against nervous behaviour (Memorandum by Bismarck and minute by Weizsäcker, 25 Mar. 1939, ibid., no. 90).

[2] Ribbentrop to Lipski, draft, n.d., and minutes, ibid., no. 73.

[3] Weizsäcker to Moltke, 24 Mar. 1939, ibid., no. 88.

[4] Hitler to Brauchitsch, 25 Mar. 1939, ibid., no. 99.

[5] Record of Ribbentrop-Lipski Conversation, 27 Mar. 1939, ibid., no. 108.

[6] Moltke to Ribbentrop, 29 Mar. 1939, ibid., no. 118.

attitude in the treatment of Danzig-Polish questions . . . but that, on the other hand, I did not consider it advisable to provoke Poland in any way through Danzig. I thought it now possible to conduct a kind of policy of attrition towards Poland in order to make the Polish Government more disposed to the solution we aimed at for certain German-Polish questions, including also the Danzig question. Danzig should continue to behave just as during the last few weeks and months.[1]

This was how German-Polish relations stood when the British guarantee to Poland was announced on 31 March. The Germans had met with an unyielding opponent. Yet neither Hitler nor the German Foreign Ministry wished to force the issue. They prepared for a long siege. Neither the Poles nor the Germans advertised their respective positions. On the contrary both sides kept the most guarded secrecy about their discussions, because they wanted to avoid an open break. The Germans wanted to keep the negotiations going in their 'policy of attrition'; the Poles wanted to gain time for an eventual commitment from the British, whom they did not want to frighten away with the prospect of a German-Polish deadlock.

From October 1938 to March 1939 the British feared a German-Polish deal whereby Poland was either drawn into the German orbit or persuaded to adopt a policy of benevolent neutrality towards Germany. The danger of these eventualities was brought home during the Sudeten crisis, when Poland aligned herself with Germany in demanding the dismemberment of Czechoslovakia.[2] The clearest indication of such fears came from Sir Howard Kennard, British Ambassador in Warsaw, who wrote on 25 September 1938:

I hope you have not felt that my telegrams advocating, in effect, that Czechoslovakia should conciliate Poland by ceding the Teschen area have been overdone. I have felt obliged to suggest that this course should be earnestly considered, not from any *parti pris* in Poland's favour, but in view of the overriding importance of keeping this country from slipping on to the wrong side in the event of general hostilities.[3]

That did not mean that Poland's alignment in a European war was a

[1] Memorandum by Weizsäcker, 29 Mar. 1939, ibid., no. 124.
[2] The British Military Attaché in Paris, Colonel Fraser, wrote that 'the fact that Germany was able to denude the German-Polish frontier entirely of troops may be taken as evidence that, to say the least, a thorough understanding existed at that time between the German and Polish General Staffs' (Fraser to Phipps, 22 Dec. 1938, enc. in C16018/36/17 (FO 432/5)).
[3] Kennard to Sargent, 25 Sept. 1938, *DBFP* iii, no. 46.

foregone conclusion. Ten days later, when the tension had relaxed, Kennard wrote that in war Poland would have tried to remain neutral, but would in the last resort have come in on the ex-Allied side in deference to Polish public opinion. Only Russian intervention could have complicated this scenario.[1]

On 1 November Halifax wrote in his much quoted letter to Sir Eric Phipps that

> ... certain factors remain obscure. What is to be the role of Poland and of Soviet Russia? If the Poland of Beck, as I take to be the case, can never ally herself with Soviet Russia, and if France, having once burnt her fingers with Czechoslovakia, relaxes her alliance with Poland the latter can only fall more and more into the German orbit.[2]

This was not an eventuality the Foreign Secretary favoured, however,[3] especially as the Foreign Office were beginning to receive indications of a possible German attack on the West. It now became increasingly important to prevent a German-Polish *rapprochement* so as to keep open the possibility of Polish resistance to Germany in the east. There were plenty of rumours to suggest that the two sides were discussing Danzig and the Corridor, even the possibility of joint action against Russia. The most common interpretation of these German-Polish contacts was that Germany was to allow Poland a common border with Hungary (i.e. to allow Hungary to occupy Ruthenia) in return for concessions over Danzig and the Corridor.[4] Transit rights for Germany across the Corridor were mentioned and also the possibility of compensation for Poland in Russia and Lithuania.[5]

How the British reaction to German-Polish relations developed is well demonstrated by the complex diplomacy surrounding the Danzig question. At the Paris Peace Conference in 1919 both Poland and Germany claimed full sovereignty over Danzig, whose population was predominantly German but whose position at the mouth of the Vistula made the port a natural outlet for Polish trade. The Versailles Treaty imposed a compromise: Danzig became a Free City under the protection of the League of Nations, which was represented by a resident High Commissioner. Poland controlled the eco-

---

[1] Kennard to Halifax, 5 Oct. 1938, *DBFP* iii, no. 136.
[2] Halifax to Phipps, 1 Nov. 1938, ibid., no. 285.
[3] See above, pp. 43–4.
[4] Cienciala, *Poland and the Western Powers*, p. 178. Also *DBFP* iii, nos. 223 and 233. [5] Ibid., no. 298.

nomic life and the foreign relations of the city, while German autonomy was guaranteed by a Constitution providing for an elected Popular Assembly and Senate.

The rise of National Socialism resulted in a political struggle in Danzig and the elimination of all other parties. In 1935 the National Socialists attempted to modify the Constitution illegally in favour of the policy of Nazification (*Gleichschaltung*). After a clash between the Danzig Senate and the League of Nations Council the latter tacitly recognized the process of Nazification. By October 1938 the position of the League of Nations as protector of the Danzig Constitution was becoming untenable, and it was no longer capable of opposing such breaches as the enactment of the anti-Jewish Nuremberg Laws.

The British realized this and decided to recommend to the League Council that the High Commissioner should be withdrawn. They had the main responsibility for recommendations to the Council on Danzig as *rapporteur* to the Committee of Three, appointed by the Council to keep Danzig questions under review. Since Danzig had long since become a matter for direct German-Polish discussion, the British hoped that some sort of agreement might be reached. On 8 December 1938 Halifax instructed Sir Howard Kennard to elicit Polish views on the question.[1] Beck replied that he hoped the withdrawal of the High Commissioner could be postponed until after his negotiations on the matter with Germany, which he thought would be concluded in mid-January 1939.[2] This is what the Foreign Office had expected. They knew that the Poles wanted the League presence in Danzig to be maintained as a bargaining counter in their negotiations with Germany.[3] At the turn of the year Halifax was 'very conscious of the Polish point of view as regards the Danzig question, and . . . the last thing he wished to do was to precipitate matters and by doing so create embarrassment for Poland'.[4] He therefore accepted Beck's request to postpone the British recommendation for withdrawal of the High Commissioner, explaining to Phipps that

there was . . . to be remembered the possible undesirable effect of causing annoyance to Colonel Beck and the Polish Government on an issue of

---

[1] Halifax to Kennard, 8 Dec. 1938, *DBFP* iii, no. 411.
[2] Kennard to Halifax, 20 Dec. 1938, ibid., no. 437.
[3] Kennard to Halifax, 20 Nov. 1938, ibid., no. 319.
[4] Strang to Kennard, 31 Dec. 1938, ibid., no. 510.

which perhaps in no circumstances could we securely count on being able to influence the outcome, when we might in certain circumstances want Colonel Beck's assistance in a much graver situation.[1]

There were signs that Poland desired a *rapprochement* with the western Powers. Towards the end of December 1938, Kennard reported that Beck had suggested co-operation between the British and Polish navies. This was interesting,

insofar as it confirms my impression that these people are feeling distinctly nervous and are anxious to reinstate themselves in our good books so as not entirely to forfeit our sympathy and support in the event of any future trouble with Germany. It is also noteworthy that, as I have reported in a telegram about Danzig, it has been suggested that Beck would be willing to go to London to meet the Committee of Three if his negotiations with Germany are successful. I suspect that he would be very glad of the opportunity and such a visit might be useful so long as there was no likelihood of his being given a cold reception.[2]

R. L. Speaight of the Foreign Office Central Department noted that there was 'no doubt about M. Beck's anxiety and one can well believe that he would be glad to come to London. His visit in 1937 helped his prestige a lot, which is always an important consideration with the Polish M[inister for] F[oreign] A[ffairs].'[3] He did not understand Beck's suggestion for closer collaboration between the British and Polish navies. 'The Polish navy is after all quite insignificant, being powerless in opposition to Germany and only a small reinforcement in alliance with her. In any case Poland's future rôle is much too uncertain for us to want to look for closer collaboration at the moment with any branch of her armed forces.'

It was this uncertainty about Poland's future role that caused such intense speculation about the outcome of Beck's talks with Hitler at Berchtesgaden in early January 1939. Renewed German-Polish contact was given added significance in the light of Britain's major preoccupation at this time, the possibility of a German attack on Holland. On 11 January 1939 Kennard reported that under questioning Beck had been extremely evasive, but Strang concluded on the basis of Foreign Office information that 'the interview was amicable and on the whole reassuring for Poland; and that Herr

[1] Halifax to Phipps, 5 Jan. 1939, *DBFP* iii, no. 519.
[2] Kennard to Strang, 23 Dec. 1938, C27/27/55 (FO 371/23129).
[3] Minute by Speaight, 4 Jan. 1939, ibid.

Hitler was in one of his calm moods'.¹ These two assessments raised the possibility of a German-Polish deal to secure Germany's eastern front while Hitler attacked in the west:

> Germany cannot conduct a war on two fronts in present circumstances, and material conditions will make it easier for her to operate in the West than in the East. Furthermore, it is easier for Germany to secure her rear in the East during an operation in the West than to secure her rear in the West during an operation in the East. The attraction of Hungary and perhaps other States into the anti-Comintern Pact, and the attraction of Poland into the German orbit by promises in the colonial sphere, would give Germany an assurance of at least benevolent neutrality along her Eastern frontier.²

At the Foreign Policy Committee on 23 January 1939 Halifax was worried about the rumoured German attempt to draw Poland into alignment with the anti-Comintern Pact, especially in the context of the German threat to Holland which the Committee had been summoned to discuss. The Foreign Secretary thought that Danzig might be made a pretext for inviting Beck to visit London, in response to the latter's hint in December—'We might then learn something of what had taken place at Colonel Beck's recent interview with Herr Hitler.' The Committee agreed.³ The impression that Germany's object was to secure Polish neutrality before attacking the West was supported by evidence from Berlin⁴ and Warsaw. Kennard linked this aim with Ribbentrop's visit to Warsaw on 26 January, significantly the fifth anniversary of the German-Polish Pact.⁵ R. L. Speaight deplored the lack of hard information but noted that the chief purport of the talks 'was that Poland should take no action against Germany provided Germany's next adventure did not affect her territory'.⁶

The British soon received more reassuring news, however, and their suspicions, which had been encouraged by Beck's evasiveness, receded along with the immediacy of the threat to the West. On 22 February Kennard reported that 'both I and my French colleague see a distinct *revirement* in official opinion here in favour of France and ourselves ... [and] there is a general feeling that Colonel Beck

---

¹ Minute by Strang, 17 Jan. 1939, *DBFP* iii, no. 541.
² Ibid.
³ FPC Minutes, 23 Jan. 1939, CAB 27/624.
⁴ Ogilvie-Forbes to Halifax, 26 Jan. 1939, *DBFP* iv, no. 20.
⁵ Kennard to Halifax, 27 Jan. 1939, ibid., no. 31.
⁶ Minute by Speaight, C1101/54/18 (FO 371/23015).

is getting back on to the fence again'.¹ Roger Makins of the Foreign Office Central Department wrote that

> it is clearly to our interest to get Colonel Beck firmly into the saddle on the fence again with if possible a bias to our side. The simplest way of doing this is to convince him both of our desire and our will to resist German and Italian pressure. If he leaves London convinced of these points his visit will have been worthwhile. Anything we can do to help the Poles e.g. in connexion with Danzig, commercial credits or Jews will be helpful but subsidiary to this main point.²

During February the Foreign Office noted with satisfaction the increasingly anti-German mood of the Poles, prompted more by minor irritants than by momentous issues.³ On 25 February Kennard reported that Polish persecution of the German minority had intensified. Speaight minuted that it was 'difficult to know to what extent these anti-German manifestations are directly encouraged by the Government. I doubt if M. Beck, for one, is very happy about them. Indeed they must be regarded in some degree as a protest against his Germanophile tendencies.'⁴ British suspicions were never far below the surface.

At the same time Beck was reported to be saying that 'Polish and British aims in Northern Europe seem to more or less coincide',⁵ and his visit to London was fixed for 3 April.⁶ On 7 March Kennard reported that anti-German feeling was stronger than ever, but that Beck

> is undoubtedly in rather a hole. His efforts to get back on the fence, which are very welcome to public opinion here, expose him to severe German criticism and suspicions. He knows full well that Danzig is his Achilles' heel and that at any moment Germany may put on the screw with painful or even disastrous results.⁷

---

[1] Kennard to Sargent, 22 Feb. 1939, *DBFP* iv, no. 139.
[2] Minute by Makins, 22 Feb. 1939, C2358/1321/55 (FO 371/23148).
[3] The smallest pretext was often made the occasion for manifestations of nationalist feeling. It was Polish postage stamps in November 1938 and students' pranks in January and February 1939, both in Danzig. The latter incidents led to widespread student rioting in Poland, with demonstrations in Warsaw against the German Embassy (Jedrzejewicz, ed., *Diplomat in Berlin*, pp. 475-6, and p. 495).
[4] Minute by Speaight, 7 Mar. 1939, C2666/54/18 (FO 371/23015).
[5] Kennard to Halifax, 25 Feb. 1939, *DBFP* iv, no. 148.
[6] Kennard to Halifax, 4 Mar. 1939, ibid., no. 175.
[7] Kennard to Cadogan, 7 Mar. 1939, ibid., no. 187.

Should Germany decide to do so, Kennard had learned from his German colleague in Warsaw, von Moltke, she was likely to insist on the return of Danzig to the Reich and on an extra-territorial strip across the Corridor. But von Moltke had also assured him that no negotiations were in progress and that they were unlikely to begin 'for some months to come'.[1] The Foreign Office Central Department, noting the muted German reaction to clashes between German and Polish students, concluded that the Germans 'quite clearly do not want to precipitate the Danzig question'.[2]

At the time of the German occupation of Bohemia and Moravia, the British had a fairly accurate picture of the situation facing the Poles, although they had no exact details and they were apparently ignorant of the continuing contacts between Germany and Poland. As the crisis developed, Polish fears were further clarified: 'What Poland would dislike would be a Slovakia nominally independent but in fact dominated by Germany.'[3] The Polish Government revealed their panic in the almost indecent haste with which they recognized Slovakia as an independent state and appointed a diplomatic representative, both on 15 March.[4] At the same time the old idea of a Hungarian occupation of Ruthenia to give Poland and Hungary a common border seemed to lose its value. As the Polish Vice-Minister for Foreign Affairs, Arciszewski, admitted to Kennard on 15 March, 'even if the Reich agreed to it Hungary would probably fall so far under German influence that the common frontier would form no barrier to Germany's further penetration eastward'.[5]

Beck now openly declared his interest in securing help from the West, asking what the French would do in case of a German attack on Danzig. The French Prime Minister, Daladier, replied that French help in this case would be contingent on a Polish commitment to Rumania.[6] Halifax, as we have seen, was less cautious. Although on 14 March he and his Foreign Office advisers had agreed to the contrary, by 19 March he had decided that Britain would have to fight for Danzig, which had now become the object

[1] Kennard to Halifax, 24 Feb. 1939, ibid., no. 144.
[2] Minute by Makins, 3 Mar. 1939, C2596/54/18 (FO 371/23015).
[3] Kennard to Halifax, 11 Mar. 1939, *DBFP* iv, no. 207.
[4] Kennard to Halifax, 15 Mar. 1939, ibid., no. 269.
[5] Ibid. The Polish newspaper *Slovo* now described the common frontier with Hungary as 'a barbed-wire fence put up to stop an elephant' (*The Times*, 18 Mar. 1939, p. 11).
[6] Phipps to Halifax, 18 Mar. 1939, *DBFP* iv, no. 402. See above, pp. 134–5.

of rumours from many sources. As early as 15 March the British representative in Danzig, Gerald Shepherd, reported the League High Commissioner's view 'that extremely grave developments may take place in Danzig in the almost immediate future. He apprehends occupation of Free City during the coming weekend by troops from East Prussia.'[1] However, Kennard soon reported from Warsaw that the Polish Government had no information 'of an alarming character' about the situation in Danzig, which he got Beck to confirm. Beck also said that Poland would fight in case of a German occupation of the city.[2] Thus the rumours of a German attack on Danzig did not begin, as is often supposed, a day or so before the guarantee to Poland was announced on 31 March. They did not, therefore, precipitate the announcement. In any case they were never confirmed. But they left the British apprehensive, and together with the realization that Britain would have to pay a price for Polish help in maintaining the *status quo* elsewhere in Europe, they prompted Halifax to make up his mind that Britain would have to fight for the Free City after all. On 19 March he told the Russian Ambassador, Ivan Maisky, that if Beck 'found it possible to reach a settlement with the German Government in regard to Danzig, well and good; if, however, out of the Danzig question emerged a threat to Polish independence, that would at once, in my view, constitute a question of interest to us all'.[3] He repeated this to the Polish Ambassador, Count Raczynski, on 21 March.[4]

Tension mounted steadily and was given added impetus by the German annexation of Memel on 22 March. From then on the pace quickened. In addition to numerous further reports of an imminent German attack on Danzig, together with Polish troop movements in the area, there were reports suggesting that negotiations were taking place between Germany and Poland. The British knew that Germany had only recently proposed Poland's accession to the anti-Comintern Pact,[5] and that German-Polish discussions on a settlement must come soon.[6] Kennard learned from Moltke that 'the Danzig question was in continual discussion and efforts were being made to bridge the gap between extreme German demands [which

[1] Shepherd to Halifax, 15 Mar. 1939, *DBFP* iv, no. 293.
[2] Kennard to Halifax, 17 Mar. 1939, ibid., no. 391 and n. 1.
[3] Halifax to Seeds, 19 Mar. 1939, ibid., no. 432.
[4] Halifax to Kennard, 21 Mar. 1939, ibid., no. 471.
[5] Ogilvie-Forbes to Halifax, 25 Mar. 1939, ibid., no. 520.
[6] Kennard to Halifax, 25 Mar. 1939, ibid., nos. 523 and 524.

Kennard had reported on 24 February][1] and Polish objections'.[2] On 25 March the French Ambassador in London, Charles Corbin, informed Sir Alexander Cadogan that his Government thought negotiations over Danzig were under way between Germany and Poland.[3] Kennard tried to confirm this in Warsaw, but without success.[4] Confirmation was finally received from Sir George Ogilvie-Forbes, British Chargé d'Affaires in Berlin, who reported on 28 March that the 'Polish Ambassador confirms that Danzig question is at present [under] discussion mainly I understand in Warsaw'.[5] British and French speculation about the progress and possible outcome of these talks mounted feverishly, prompting Halifax to comment to Corbin that 'the more one pondered the situation, the more evident it became how key a position that of Poland was'.[6] Halifax now wanted Polish adherence to an anti-German coalition at all costs. Yet he had grave doubts as to whether this aim could be achieved after all.

What troubled the British was the secrecy surrounding Polish intentions. Surely if Beck were really interested in a commitment from Britain he would exaggerate rather than play down the threat to Danzig, or at least keep the British informed about the German demands. As R. L. Speaight had remarked following Beck's talks with Hitler in January 1939:

> The very fact of M. Beck's more than usually marked evasiveness may indeed be taken as a further indication that he has gone further than he wished to admit in yielding to German pressure. If no such demands had been made of him ... there would have been no point in making a secret of the discussions; while if he had stood up to the German demands, he would presumably have been anxious to enlist sympathy and support from H.M. Government.[7]

On 29 March Kennard reported that Arciszewski, Polish Vice-Minister for Foreign Affairs, had confirmed to him that the Germans had communicated their requirements to Lipski in Berlin 'within the past fortnight'. They wanted a change in the status of

---

[1] Kennard to Halifax, 24 Feb. 1939, ibid., no. 144.
[2] Kennard to Halifax, 27 Mar. 1939, ibid., no. 534.
[3] Halifax to Campbell (Paris), 27 Mar. 1939, ibid., no. 540.
[4] Kennard to Halifax, 28 Mar. 1939, ibid., no. 547.
[5] Ogilvie-Forbes to Halifax, 28 Mar. 1939, ibid., no. 550.
[6] Halifax to Phipps, 28 Mar. 1939, ibid., no. 553.
[7] Minute by Speaight, 13 Jan. 1939, C403/54/18 (FO 371/23015).

Danzig, a motor road across the Corridor, and Poland's adherence to the Anti-Comintern Pact.[1] Speaight commented significantly:

> Mr. Arciszewski is scarcely less slippery than his chief. On March 28th he inferred that Berlin had put forward no definite *desiderata*. He now admits that three very positive *desiderata* have been communicated within the last fortnight. M. Beck is evidently still on his fence.[2]

The British feared that Poland might yet slip from their net. They thought that the Poles might be preparing to make a deal with the Germans, not, as the French purported to believe, with a view to an alliance, but with a view to benevolent neutrality.[3] The possibility existed that Poland would either willingly or under threat of force accede to German demands and therefore be lost to the anti-German coalition that Britain was trying to pull together. Although there was just as much reason to believe that Poland would forcibly resist a German *coup* in Danzig, Roger Makins concluded on 29 March that

> the latest information indicates that the Polish Ministry of Foreign Affairs at all events are prepared to go a very long way to meet the German demands. In principle a German-Polish deal over Danzig would suit us well enough, as Danzig is by no means a good casus belli, and we can hardly support Poland unless we support Polish rights in Danzig, if she insists on maintaining those rights.
>
> I should be surprised, however, if the Germans agreed to accept less than 99% of her demands without a quid pro quo, which would probably consist of a guarantee of neutrality by Poland. This is the sort of bargain

---

[1] Kennard to Halifax, 29 Mar. 1939, *DBFP* iv, no. 564.
[2] Minute by Speaight, 30 Mar. 1939, C4364/54/18 (FO 371/23015).
[3] Aléxis Léger, head of the French Foreign Ministry, informed a member of the British Embassy staff in Paris on 18 March that he knew 'from a source very secret but absolutely sure and authoritative' that the real purpose of Beck's visit to London was to ask for an alliance, which he knew was unacceptable. 'He would then return to Poland and report his request and its rejection . . . say that there had been two alternatives for Poland, viz. to lean on Great Britain or Germany, and that now it was clear that she must lean on Germany. . . . [Beck] wanted to get off the difficulties of the moment even at the cost of being the vassal (perhaps the chief vassal) of the new Napoleon' (Phipps to Halifax, 18 Mar. 1939, *DBFP* iv, no. 405). The Foreign Office were less cynical at the time, although their suspicions were encouraged by these sort of insinuations from the French, whose goal was clearly to get a commitment from Britain. Frank Roberts of the Central Department noted with the concurrence of his seniors that 'the French always think the worst of Colonel Beck. We shall soon know his proposals, but I doubt very much whether his plans will be so sinister as is suggested here' (Minute by Roberts, 21 Mar. 1939, C3455/3356/18 (FO 371/23060)).

which might possibly appeal to Colonel Beck, and the situation will need most careful watching.[1]

He later added that such a 'corrupt bargain would in the long run be highly disadvantageous to us: it would shake Polish morale, increase their vulnerability to German penetration, and so defeat the policy of forming a bloc against German expansion'.[2]

The British were now in a dilemma: they could not assure themselves of Poland's committing herself against Germany without committing themselves to what they knew to be a highly dangerous and unstable situation in Danzig. In choosing to do so, they accepted the consequences. It is a well-established legal principle that men must be presumed to intend the consequences of their actions and therefore cannot evade responsibility for them. By encouraging the Poles to reject German terms for a settlement of Danzig, the British increased the likelihood that Hitler would resort to force in order to break the deadlock. They allied themselves, in the words of the Rumanian Foreign Minister, Gafencu, 'not to peace, but to continental war'.[3]

[1] Minute by Makins, 29 Mar. 1939, C4859/54/18 (FO 371/23016).
[2] Minute by Makins, 30 Mar. 1939, C4860/54/18 (ibid.).
[3] Quoted in Gilbert and Gott, *The Appeasers*, p. 236.

9

THE UNCONDITIONAL GUARANTEE

WE have seen that the idea of unconditional intervention on behalf of Poland and Rumania was present in Halifax's mind as early as 21 March 1939,[1] and that despite Bonnet's success in persuading the Foreign Secretary to attach conditions to British support, Halifax accepted the possibility that at least some of those conditions would have to be removed if need be. Chamberlain had explained this to the Foreign Policy Committee on 27 March,[2] and at 11 a.m. on 29 March Halifax repeated it to the full Cabinet. He explained that under the present arrangement Poland was being asked

> to enter into a reciprocal arrangement by which (in consideration of Great Britain and France undertaking to come to Poland's help) if Great Britain or France were attacked by Germany, or, if they went to war with Germany to resist German aggression elsewhere in Western Europe or Yugo-Slavia, Poland would come to their aid. [Halifax] said that he had felt some doubt whether this was not asking too much of Poland. He thought, however, that there would be no harm in including the proposal in the telegram to Warsaw as he had reached the conclusion that Colonel Beck was unlikely to reach any definite decision on it before he visited this country at the beginning of the ensuing week.[3]

Halifax was apparently resigned to waiting for Beck's visit on 3 April. However, various pressures were building up which tended to force the pace.

Informed opinion continued to call for action, and fretted at the apparent lack of progress in the negotiations. The press got hold of the idea that the British Government were prepared to await Colonel Beck's arrival. The *Observer*'s Diplomatic Correspondent commented on 26 March that 'the ironic situation was reached yesterday that the discussion of the proposal for immediate action is postponed for ten days'.[4] On 29 and 30 March the press was full of rumours

---

[1] See above, pp. 135–6. [2] See above, pp. 151–2.
[3] Cab. Minutes, 29 Mar. 1939, CAB 23/98.
[4] *Observer*, Diplomatic Correspondent, 26 Mar. 1939, p. 17.

THE UNCONDITIONAL GUARANTEE 175

about an imminent German attack on Danzig, and stressed the importance of Poland as opposed to Russia in building an anti-German coalition.¹ There is no doubt that the press was in a belligerent mood. It is probable that Halifax was receptive to it, even though he often proclaimed his immunity from public opinion.²

Perhaps more decisive in its influence was opinion within the Conservative Party and in particular that of the 'Eden group'.³ After the Prague *coup* the group's attitude towards the Government was that 'we must fight if they surrender and support if they fight'.⁴ By 24 March, however, Eden was convinced, according to Nicolson, that the group

> should come out (violently if need be) for a three Party Government and the organization of our industry, wealth and manpower on a war footing. He [Eden] is prepared to come out on that in the Foreign Affairs debate [scheduled for 3 April as a result of demands by the Labour Opposition] but will not do so until he has seen Halifax.⁵

We do not know what passed between Eden and Halifax during their meetings at this time, other than that the general subject of discussion was the need for an all-party Government. Halifax had favoured some such step ever since Munich, but met with resistance from Chamberlain.⁶ It is likely that Halifax gave Eden definite encouragement, because on 25 March Halifax told his colleagues at the Foreign Office that in view of 'the difficulty of conducting delicate and swift diplomacy with a parliamentary government . . . it all really now pointed to the need for an All-Party Government'.⁷

¹ Namier, *Diplomatic Prelude*, p. 105.
² Oliver Harvey recorded that Halifax 'emphasized the great value of being unconcerned and unaffected by public opinion; he quoted instances of his own experience of opinion at home over his Indian reforms and how they had taught him how quickly it changed' (*Harvey Diaries*, 14 Jan. 1939, p. 243).
³ See above, p. 101 n.
⁴ Nicolson Papers, Diary, 20 Mar. 1939.
⁵ Ibid., 24 Mar. 1939.
⁶ Halifax, *Fullness of Days*, pp. 202–3.
⁷ *Harvey Diaries*, 25 Mar. 1939, p. 268. Next day Harvey, who was close to Eden, submitted a memorandum on the subject to Halifax. He outlined the advantages of an all-party Government:

'a. foreign policy—easier to conduct swiftly and confidentially,
b. home policy—conscription or national compulsory register, labour restrictions, diluting of labour, overtime, pooling of trade secrets, "mobilisation of industry" all become possible,
c. psychological effect at home and abroad.'

The trouble was that Labour refused to serve under Chamberlain, 'who in the past has never taken the least trouble to reconcile them but has only embittered

In any case on 27 March the Eden Group decided to table a motion in the House of Commons calling for a truly national government. Harold Nicolson, a member of the group, recorded his impatience:

> PM makes a statement about Rumania. . . . He has really nothing to report and meanwhile a fortnight has passed since the Ides of March and Germany is now threatening Poland. Grave anxiety in the House coupled with the feeling that Chamberlain is losing the confidence of the country.
>
> A meeting [of the Eden Group] to discuss the situation. Duff Cooper, Amery, Anthony Eden, Wolmer, Harold Macmillan etc. etc. There are two schools of thought. Those who want a coalition Govt. and those who want conscription. We are not quite sure which is the cart and which the horse. The opposition (a) love the new foreign policy and friendship with Russia (b) long to get rid of Chamberlain (c) would accept some form of national service if they could get a. and b. The Conservatives (a) long for conscription (b) don't want to sacrifice Chamberlain (c) rather dislike the foreign policy. We decide to put down a motion urging a national govt. for the purpose of being 'entrusted with full powers over the nation's industry, wealth and man-power in order to enable this country to put forward its maximum military effort in the shortest possible time. . . .' Amery does not want to sign. Duff promises to get Winston [Churchill] to join us. This will burst on the world tomorrow night.[1]

It is quite possible that Halifax connived at this increase in parliamentary pressure engineered by Eden and possible also that Chamberlain was aware of the fact. For the reaction of the Whip's Office was to interpret the motion as an attempt to create a split between Halifax and Chamberlain, an interpretation which would compel Halifax to confirm his loyalty to the Prime Minister. Eden disabused David Margesson, the Chief Whip, on this score, saying that 'the last thing we had in mind was to attack Chamberlain. That it never entered our heads to create a split between Chamberlain and Halifax. And that the fact that our resolution was so interpreted shows what a rotten state the Conservative Party must be in.'[2]

Halifax also felt pressure, both from the Parliamentary Opposition

---

party divisions and gone out of his way to taunt them'. Nor would Chamberlain consent to bring in Churchill and Eden, 'except across his dead body. He believes they would be tiresome to him (and I am bound to say I think they would).' Harvey now favoured Halifax as Prime Minister: 'If an all-party government could be formed under your leadership it would be acceptable to all' (Harvey to Halifax, 26 Mar. 1939, *Harvey Diaries*, pp. 268–70).

[1] Nicolson Papers, Diary, 27 Mar. 1939.
[2] Ibid., 29 Mar. 1939.

and from within the Cabinet, for the inclusion of Russia in the British scheme. Once more it was Sir Samuel Hoare, the Home Secretary, who returned to this awkward question at the Cabinet on 29 March. He wanted a definite arrangement to secure her support, and wondered why the French had made no move to strengthen the Franco-Soviet Pact. Walter Elliott, the Minister of Health, wanted an Anglo-Russian alliance.[1] Ivan Maisky, the Russian Ambassador, who had not yet been officially informed even that the idea of a Four-Power Declaration had been dropped, wanted to know what the Prime Minister meant by his statement of 28 March that the British Government were proposing to go 'a great deal further than consultation'.[2] He was at last informed about the new plan.[3]

Meanwhile morale in the Balkan countries, whom Britain wanted to impress with Polish determination, was steadily weakening. The Foreign Office were particularly worried about Greece and Turkey. In their 'European Appreciation 1939–40', setting out British strategy in case of war, the Chiefs of Staff wrote that they attached 'the highest importance to the military advantages to be derived from having Turkey and Greece as our allies in war against Germany and Italy'.[4] The Turks had been gratified by British financial aid in 1938, but the invasion of Bohemia and Moravia, and especially the German-Rumanian Trade Treaty caused them to despair. As the British Ambassador, Sir Hughe Knatchbull-Hugessen, reported on 25 March 1939, 'it is felt that the Balkans are now completely open to further penetration on the same lines'.[5] Meanwhile the lack of reaction from the West had 'created the impression that His Majesty's Government and France have failed and are retreating before the present German threat'. The Germans were asking the Turks for their neutrality and the Turkish Foreign Minister, Şükrü Saracoğlu, warned that

it would be unreasonable to expect Turkey of her own accord to resist this

---

[1] Cab. Minutes, 29 Mar. 1939, CAB 23/98.
[2] 345 HC Deb., 5 s., col. 1884; Halifax to Seeds, 29 Mar. 1939, *DBFP* iv, no. 565.
[3] Which incidentally he thought 'would be a revolutionary change in British policy and might have far reaching results. It would increase enormously the confidence of other countries and might have a very great effect' (Halifax to Seeds, 29 Mar. 1939, *DBFP* iv, no. 565). Cf. Maisky's retrospective analysis in his *Who Helped Hitler?*, pp. 112–15.
[4] Memorandum by Chiefs of Staff: 'European Appreciation 1939–40', 20 Feb. 1939, DP(P)44, CAB 16/183A, p. 64.
[5] Knatchbull-Hugessen to Halifax, 25 Mar. 1939, C4050/3356/18 (FO 371/23061).

pressure unless she was certain of support from the West. [The] Minister for Foreign Affairs felt it was absolutely necessary for France and Great Britain to make a firm stand and to define their attitude clearly if further German threats in this part of the world were to be withstood. Otherwise the impression would be created that the Western Powers were washing their hands of all Eastern Europe as far as the Bosphorus.[1]

Knatchbull-Hugessen thought that 'this is the critical moment with Turkey'.[2]

At the same time General Metaxas of Greece was reportedly threatening to remain neutral in a European war unless a guarantee were forthcoming from Britain.[3] Sir Orme Sargent and Sir Lancelot Oliphant wanted an immediate alliance with both Greece and Turkey.[4] On 29 March Halifax was so worried that he told the Cabinet that there 'might be a question of issuing immediate guarantees to Greece and Turkey in an emergency'.[5]

On 17 March the Chiefs of Staff had been asked to report on the desirability of an alliance with Greece and Turkey. They advised that the first essential was a secure Mediterranean, and hence a friendly or at least neutral Italy. An alliance with Greece and Turkey 'might render Italian hostility inevitable'. On the other hand it was imperative 'to make *absolutely certain* that [Turkey] would be our ally in any war in which Italy was hostile'. As a British ally Turkey could close the Black Sea to Italian shipping, and Italian possessions in the Dodecanese would become 'commitments for defence' rather than 'vantage points for attack'. Britain could also use Turkish air and naval bases. The Chiefs of Staff passed the buck to the Foreign Office. If the Foreign Office thought that Turkey would be with Britain in any case, then there was nothing to gain from an alliance with her as long as there was any hope of detaching Italy from the Axis. If on the other hand Turkey was not completely reliable, 'then we attach more importance to making certain of the friendship of Turkey than to the consequent risk of alienating Italy'. The Chiefs of Staff revised their earlier assessment of Greece. She would be more of a liability than an asset as an ally, since

[1] Knatchbull-Hugessen to Halifax, 25 Mar. 1939, C4050/3356/18 (FO 371/23061).
[2] Knatchbull-Hugessen to Halifax, 25 Mar. 1939, C4051/3356/18 (ibid.).
[3] Rendel (Sofia) to Halifax, 25 Mar. 1939, C4504/3356/18 (FO 371/23062).
[4] Minute by Oliphant, 30 Mar. 1939, C4472/3356/18 (ibid.).
[5] Cab. Minutes, 29 Mar. 1939, CAB 23/98.

THE UNCONDITIONAL GUARANTEE

Britain would be committed to defending her long northern frontier. Therefore they preferred benevolent neutrality.[1]

Far Eastern developments also argued for immediate action of some sort. The British had known for some time that Germany and Italy were pushing for Japanese agreement to convert the anti-Comintern Pact into a mutual defence pact. The Japanese had always refused to contemplate making such an alliance applicable to anything more than Russian aggression, whereas the Axis partners wanted Japanese assistance in case of trouble with Britain and France as well.[2] It was the more cautious elements in Tokyo, and especially the Naval Staff, who opposed an alignment against the Anglo-Saxons.[3]

But in March 1939 the increasingly active diplomatic contacts between Tokyo and Berlin raised the fear that a military pact was imminent. On 27 March the War Office reported that an important decision was being discussed in Tokyo, probably bearing on relations with Germany. The German invasion of Bohemia and Moravia had strengthened the position of the pro-German elements, particularly the army, although 'there is still strong opposition to European entanglements'.[4] On 29 March Japan annexed the Spratley Islands, a sequel to her occupation in February of Hainan Island. Both points were strategically important. Hainan Island, off the South China Coast, provided a base for air attacks against Indochina and against the route from Singapore to Hong Kong. The Spratley Islands lay in the South China Sea between Borneo and Indochina, only 750 miles from Singapore. The Foreign Office suspected that such attacks had been 'undertaken at the instigation of the Germans and Italians, or anyhow in pursuance of some plan concerted with

[1] COS Sub-Committee, Draft Report, 'Alliance with Turkey and Greece', 31 Mar. 1939, CAB 53/47.

[2] For the complex negotiations between Germany, Italy, and Japan in 1938–9 see Mario Toscano, *The Origins of the Pact of Steel* (2nd edn., Baltimore, Md., 1967), chapters 1–3.

[3] Akira Iriye has put the Japanese dilemma very clearly: 'both army and navy turned to Germany as a way out of the predicament confronting Japan: if a German alliance could restrain the Soviet Union, Japan would be enabled to concentrate on the war in China. . . . Whereas the army was willing to purchase the German alliance by committing Japan to fight against Britain, however, the navy refused to go along, until conditions changed drastically in 1940' (Akira Iriye, 'Japan's Foreign Policies between World Wars', in E. M. Robertson, ed., *The Origins of the Second World War*, p. 268).

[4] Summary of military information no. 6 (New Series) for 48 hours ending 1200 hrs. 27 Mar. 1939, War Office, C4234/15/18 (FO 371/22967).

them'. Such a plan could be designed to force the dispatch of the British and French fleets to the Far East and so create an ideal opportunity for an Axis attack in Europe.[1] Halifax, whose long struggle with the Treasury for the establishment of a £10 million Chinese Currency Stabilization Fund ended successfully with its approval by the Cabinet on 22 February 1939, now asked the Cabinet to approve further measures for exerting economic pressure on Japan.[2]

On 30 March Sir Robert Craigie, the British Ambassador in Tokyo, gained the 'strong impression' during an interview with the Japanese Foreign Minister, Arita, that

> the Japanese Government have now decided—or virtually decided—to convert [the] Anti-Comintern Pact into an alliance against the U.S.S.R. I also learn from a reliable source that this project, which at one moment seemed to have received its *coup de grâce*, has been resuscitated by the effect on the army of 'irresistible' power displayed by Germany in Czecho-Slovakian *coup*.[3]

Craigie warned Arita not to commit his country 'to entanglements which he might live bitterly to regret—entanglements with countries whose political and economic weaknesses . . . were daily becoming more obvious to the whole world'. What better way to strengthen the hand of those in Japan who opposed the stronger connection with Germany than to increase the likelihood of war in Europe?

But the determining factors were closer to home. On 29 March Halifax read a fairly lengthy memorandum by a Polish friend of his Private Secretary, Oliver Harvey. Its influence was possibly crucial. It was written by Jan Ciechanowski, who had been Polish Minister

---

[1] Memorandum by Halifax: 'Situation in the Far East', and accompanying FO Memorandum, 30 Mar. 1939, CP 76(39), CAB 24/284. There is no evidence in the German documents that such a plan existed, nor, in view of their extremely cautious attitude towards European entanglements, were the Japanese likely to have responded to one.

[2] Ibid. The stabilization fund was another result of the Foreign Office thesis that Britain's economic strength should be used as a weapon in support of her foreign policy aims. In view of her military weakness, 'the best hope for the preservation of British influence and interests in China lies in a prolongation of the [Sino-Japanese] hostilities until Japan is exhausted'. The stabilization fund 'would enable China to maintain the currency and prolong the war for another year while continuing the service of her existing foreign debts' (Cab. Memorandum by Halifax: 'Assistance to China', 1 July 1938, CP 152 (38), CAB 24/277). The Cabinet had not been prepared to authorize the step in July 1938, when it was first proposed, and wanted the United States to act in conjunction with Britain (Cab. Minutes, 6 July 1938, CAB 23/94).

[3] Craigie to Halifax, 30 Mar. 1939, *DBFP* viii, no. 586.

in Washington, was later to represent the Polish Government in exile in London, and at this period divided his time between Paris and his estates in Poland. He had resigned from the Polish Diplomatic Service 'over differences with Marshal Pilsudski about the internal regime in Poland', and 'keeps in close touch with events'.[1] Ciechanowski's memorandum, 'On the possibility of saving peace by an immediate Franco-British declaration of military assistance to Poland in case of German aggression', was presumably written in a private capacity, although in view of his official links this is not certain. His argument was that Hitler's occupation of Bohemia and Moravia, his annexation of Memel, his 'so-called treaties' with Lithuania, Rumania, and Slovakia, together with Hungary's annexation of Ruthenia, had 'once more greatly altered the map of Europe and . . . seriously affected her balance of power'.[2] Meanwhile

> the hesitant efforts on the part of the Western Powers to dam Hitler's probable next expansionist moves by hurriedly erecting a military front composed of Great Britain, France, Soviet Russia and possibly Poland, are too dilatory and undecided to impress Hitler and may, on the contrary, provoke him to speed up his further activity.[3]

Ciechanowski next described the threatened position of Poland, 'the only remaining independent State in Central Europe', and pointed out that Poland could not join an anti-German coalition before she was directly menaced 'without giving Hitler a welcome pretext for attacking her'. Ciechanowski's solution, and one to which Halifax was already receptive, was for Britain and France

> jointly to declare without any further delay that they will definitely oppose any German aggression against Poland, and will support her should she be forced to defend herself. In making such a declaration, it would probably be wiser not to make Soviet Russia a party to it for the time being, until Poland made a definite request to this effect. If such a joint Franco-British declaration of support for Poland in case of any attack by Germany is to be a deterrent for Hitler, it is essential that it should be made immediately and unequivocally before Hitler's next move.

Here for the first time was the explicitly stated idea of an immediate, unilateral, and unconditional declaration of support for Poland.

[1] Minute by Harvey, 29 Mar. 1939, C4276/54/18 (FO 371/23015).
[2] Memorandum by Ciechanowski: 'On the possibility of saving peace . . .' ibid.
[3] Ibid. The word 'hesitant' was underlined by Halifax in his characteristic red ink.

Halifax read the memorandum at a crucial time. Whether its influence was decisive or merely reinforced Halifax's previous conviction, the Foreign Secretary was certainly impatient enough now to seek Chamberlain's approval for such a step.

An ideal opportunity was presented by a further important event that took place on 29 March, a report by the junior Berlin correspondent of the *News Chronicle*, Ian Colvin, that Poland was under threat of imminent attack by Germany. The sudden change in the Government's tactics that led to the announcement of the guarantee to Poland on 31 March has been widely ascribed, not least by himself, to the twenty-six-year-old correspondent, but his real influence was less than is generally supposed. In fact he appears to have been used by Halifax to impress both Chamberlain and his Cabinet colleagues.

Colvin is an enigmatic character who maintained contact with the British Embassy in Berlin, particularly with Sir George Ogilvie-Forbes, the head of Chancery, and with the Military Attaché, Colonel F. N. Mason-MacFarlane. He was used as an intermediary by the German opposition to Hitler in September 1938, and was probably one of Vansittart's network of informants.[1] He may have done all this in some official capacity or, as is more likely, out of journalistic flair on the basis of some well-placed contacts. Frank Roberts of the Foreign Office Central Department described Colvin's accounts as 'sometimes highly-coloured and imaginative'.[2] The Foreign Office were not surprised when the German Government threatened not to renew his visa past 31 March 1939, for submitting tendentious reports to the *News Chronicle*.[3]

---

[1] He has written biographies of Admiral Canaris, Chief of German Intelligence (*Chief of Intelligence*, London, 1951), and of Vansittart, who was a major source of Foreign Office intelligence, although much of it appears to have been discounted (*Vansittart in Office. An historical survey of the origins of the second world war based on the papers of Sir Robert Vansittart* (London, 1965)).

[2] Minute by Roberts, 14 Apr. 1939, C5032/54/18 (FO 371/23016).

[3] Foreign Office files on the subject of Anglo-German relations in the first quarter of 1939 are full of references to complaints by the German Government about the *News Chronicle*, the most virulently anti-German newspaper in Britain. On 2 January H. G. Wells contributed an article in which he described Hitler as a certifiable lunatic and suggested that it would be a patriotic act if he were to be put away. The German Ambassador, Dirksen, complained to Halifax, who probably took great delight in riposting that 'so long as action continued to be taken in Germany that so greatly shocked world opinion, criticism directed at the person who was held principally responsible was inevitable'. Nor was Dirksen mollified by the observation that Wells had made equally derogatory remarks about the King and Queen of England (Halifax to Ogilvie-Forbes, 5 Jan. 1939, *DBFP* iii, no. 518). On 17 February the State Secretary in the German Foreign

By his own account Colvin heard in January 1939 that

a victualling contractor to the German army had then received instructions to provide the same amount of rations as he had supplied in September 1938, and to have them ready by March 28th, 1939. They were to be delivered to forward dumps in an area of Pomerania that formed a rough wedge pointing towards the railway junction of Bromberg in the Polish Corridor.[1]

On 27 March Colvin related this to Mason-MacFarlane at the Embassy and connected it with newspaper reports of incidents involving the German minority at Bromberg, which all suggested to him a German move in that direction:

Mason-MacFarlane agreed that a rapid move to cut the Polish corridor might be intended, though he had no positive information. He advised me to take my information to London myself. To both of us it seemed that written reports were largely discounted in London, if indeed they were read at all.[2]

On 28 March Colvin flew to London and saw the head of the Foreign Office News Department, Sir Reginald Leeper, who arranged for him to see Cadogan and Halifax the next day.

On 29 March Colvin told his story about the victualling contractor to Halifax. His second main point was to stress the role of the German opposition to Hitler, whose plot to remove the Führer from power in September 1938 had been undermined by Chamberlain's initiative in settling the Sudeten crisis without threatening war. Colvin emphasized that a firm line was required now.

Halifax arranged for Colvin to see the Prime Minister that evening.

Ministry, Baron Weizsäcker, informed the British Ambassador, Sir Nevile Henderson, that his Government 'did not desire a representative of the "News Chronicle" at all in Germany and had decided not to renew the residence permits of Mr. Harrison and Mr. Colvin, his assistant' (Minute by Roberts, registered 21 Mar. 1939, C3568/16/18 (FO 371/22988)). The F.O. invoked a Gentleman's Agreement which forbade the expulsion of journalists for any but personal reasons, and threatened to retaliate. They eventually worked out a deal whereby Colvin was allowed to stay but Harrison had to leave. But the F.O. thought most journalists a nuisance: ' "The Times" and "Reuter" representatives are often useful scouts and touts for the Embassy, but the remaining correspondents are a liability rather than an asset. They never obtain any news worth having. They waste the time of the Staff and often cause embarrassment by sending silly messages' (Minute by Kirkpatrick, 23 Feb. 1939, C2109/16/18 (ibid.)).

[1] Colvin, *Vansittart in Office*, p. 298. [2] Ibid., p. 299.

They assembled at the House of Commons together with Cadogan, Leeper, and Chamberlain's Parliamentary Private Secretary, Lord Dunglass, and another person Colvin took to be head of the Secret Intelligence Service. Colvin repeated his story. Chamberlain was sceptical about the German opposition: 'What have these people to offer us?' Colvin did not know but promised to find out, although when he returned to Berlin he was advised not to do so.[1] After the meeting Halifax remained behind with the Prime Minister, and later reported to Cadogan that Chamberlain had 'agreed to the idea of an *immediate* declaration of support for Poland, to counter a quick putsch by Hitler'.[2] Chamberlain wrote to his sister that 'we then and there decided' that Poland should be guaranteed.[3]

There is little doubt that Colvin was used by the Foreign Office to force the pace, and that the reason they did so was to put an end to the uncertainty they felt about both German and Polish intentions. In the first place it was unprecedented that a journalist coming to London with very stale information should be given an audience not only with the Foreign Secretary but also with the Prime Minister. That Colvin's information about the victualling contractor was already known does not, of course, attenuate its importance. It may have increased it.[4] But it is worth recording that on 3 March Colonel Mason-MacFarlane had himself reported that 'the only information that I have indicating preparations against Poland is a report that Army supplies (food stuffs) are being collected in Eastern Pomerania, and that a contractor concerned has been told to get his job finished by March 28th'.[5] The Secret Intelligence Service received 'various reports in mid-March' about German military preparations to be concluded by 28 March for an attack on Poland, noting that 'this is

[1] Colvin, *Vansittart in Office*, pp. 303–10.
[2] Dilks, ed., *Cadogan Diaries*, 29 Mar. 1939, p. 165.
[3] Chamberlain to Hilda Chamberlain, 3 Apr. 1939, Cambridge University Library, Templewood Papers, T.P. XIX (C) 12.
[4] The Foreign Office encouraged British diplomatic missions to report all information, including rumours, and not to censor gossip 'which they often think not worth reporting'. As Strang wrote to Ogilvie-Forbes in December 1938, 'I think that at the present time, when such grave issues are at stake, it is perhaps better to report too much than too little. As you know, we get a great deal of information from other sources, and it may sometimes happen that an apparently insignificant piece of information which the Embassy may be in a position to supply fits into its place in the picture' (Strang to Ogilvie-Forbes, 31 Dec. 1938, C143/15/18 (FO 371/22961)).
[5] Minute by Mason-MacFarlane, 3 Mar. 1939, enc. in A. Holman (Berlin) to Strang, 3 Mar. 1939, C2882/13/18 (FO 371/22958).

THE UNCONDITIONAL GUARANTEE   185

the only case in which they [the S.I.S.] have been able to substantiate rumours of definite dates fixed for action'.[1]

Furthermore there were others warning the Foreign Office about a threatened German attack on Poland. On 28 March Herschel Johnson, First Secretary at the American Embassy in London, informed Sir Orme Sargent that Biddle, the American Ambassador in Warsaw, had just reported that

> Hitler considers Ribbentrop deserves great credit for the Memel *coup* and that, on the strength of this, Ribbentrop is now pressing for immediate action against Poland, pointing out that Great Britain and France will fail to support Poland and that this failure would serve to alienate American opinion from France and Great Britain.[2]

What did the Foreign Office think of all these reports? They recognized that their information was 'somewhat conflicting'. On the one hand the possibility of an attack on Poland definitely existed; on the other hand there were equally weighty reports suggesting that Hitler 'required Beck provisionally', that he was 'anxious to avoid conflict with Poland' and that it was 'unlikely that he would adopt a dynamic solution as in the case of Czecho-Slovakia'.[3]

'The conclusion to be drawn', wrote Ivone Kirkpatrick of the Central Department,

> is the usual one in so far as Hitler's plans are concerned. We know that his ultimate aim is to eliminate or neutralise Poland and Roumania. Which of these two aims will be realised first is a matter for speculation. We also know that Germany is putting herself into a position in which she will be

---

[1] Minute by Roberts and Jebb, 24 Apr. 1939, C6143/15/18 (FO 371/22971). This was a summary, prepared on Halifax's instructions, of secret information about dates set for military action by the Axis which the Foreign Office had received before the guarantee to Poland. Noting the large number of conflicting and misleading reports, Cadogan observed that 'it is important to draw the right lesson from this, which is *not* to ignore all the reports that we got, but to remember that there are doubtless plans ready in Germany for every kind of enormity. What we can hardly ever tell—what probably no one, except Hitler, in Germany knows—is *which* will be decided on and *when* it will be put into execution. Apart from that, it is undoubtedly part of the German policy to plant stories on us through spotted agents of our own, in order to keep our nerves on edge and to distract us' (Minute by Cadogan, 25 Apr. 1939, ibid.). Vansittart pointed out that all his own sources of information had been right (Minute by Vansittart, ibid.).

[2] Halifax to Kennard and Ogilvie-Forbes, 30 Mar. 1939, *DBFP* iv, no. 571, and minute by Sargent, 29 Mar. 1939, C4505/54/18 (FO 371/23105).

[3] Memorandum by Kirkpatrick: 'The Possibility of a German Attack on Poland', 30 Mar. 1939, C4621/15/18 (FO 371/22968).

able to attack either Poland or Roumania. The final decision may, as in the past, be precipitated by events which Hitler can neither foresee nor control. It is possible that the recent attitude of Poland, which the Germans regard as truculent, may precipitate an early German-Polish crisis. In this connexion the attitude of the German press is illuminating. Yet it would be a mistake to assume that because the German press is attacking Poland Hitler is committed to an early act of aggression. In the case of Czecho-Slovakia the first press attacks last year were used merely to prepare public opinion and did not denote an immediate invasion of Czecho-Slovakia.[1]

Sir Orme Sargent thought that the German press campaign might be 'intended to influence any negotiations between the German and Polish Governments over Danzig and/or to intimidate Col. Beck before his visit to London, so as to ensure that he does not commit himself too far to His Majesty's Government'.[2] Cadogan thought it could be designed 'to direct our attention from what may be his main aim—Roumania'.[3]

Although both Cadogan and Harvey noted that Halifax seemed impressed by Colvin's report, he was probably far more impressed with its potential as a means of persuading the Cabinet to support the idea of an immediate and unconditional guarantee for Poland. Certainly Cadogan was unconvinced: 'I am getting used to these stories.'[4] The story itself was nothing new—it was merely a piece in the puzzle, and a duplicate piece at that. R. A. Butler, Parliamentary Under-Secretary for Foreign Affairs, noted in his diary shortly thereafter that in his determination to shift away from the policy of 'appeasement', Halifax was none too scrupulous about the methods he used:

Sometimes he has moved the Cabinet by the use of what appeared at first sight to be rumours. For instance, the Berlin correspondent of the *News Chronicle* was used to impress the Cabinet with the possibility of the invasion of Poland. But whatever the methods it is clear that Halifax is determined to set up a force counter to Germany and that he is going ahead single mindedly.[5]

There is one aspect of Colvin's report that possibly did impress

[1] Memorandum by Kirkpatrick: 'The Possibility of a German Attack on Poland', 30 Mar. 1939, C4621/15/18 (FO 371/22968).
[2] Minute by Sargent, 30 Mar. 1939, ibid.
[3] Minute by Cadogan, 30 Mar. 1939, ibid.
[4] Dilks, ed., *Cadogan Diaries*, p. 165.
[5] Butler, *The Art of the Possible*, p. 77.

THE UNCONDITIONAL GUARANTEE 187

Halifax. During their interview Colvin apparently emphasized the views of the British Military Attaché in Berlin, Colonel F. N. Mason-MacFarlane, who had suggested the journalist's trip to London in the first place. Colvin even quoted verbatim from a dispatch that Mason-MacFarlane was sending over that day.[1] This suggests the possibility that Colvin was used not only by Halifax in his effort to sway the Cabinet, but also by Mason-MacFarlane in his efforts to sway Halifax. By using an unconventional channel the Military Attaché hoped to heighten the impact of his views. These were nothing if not forceful, and corresponded with the traditional British doctrine of the balance of power. This in addition to the fact that he was the man on the spot made him a source of some influence in the Foreign Office, an influence which has been largely overlooked. Ivone Kirkpatrick, who had been a colleague of his, judged that 'Colonel MacFarlane is well informed and level-headed, and his views are entitled to respect'.[2]

We have already seen how Mason-MacFarlane's views on the importance of facing Germany with a hostile power on her eastern front influenced the formulation of the second British policy initiative.[3] He now returned to the charge with a long memorandum on the German military situation, which according to the Chargé d'Affaires in Berlin, Ogilvie-Forbes, ranged 'far outside his ambit' and raised issues appropriate for Cabinet consideration. Its purport was 'that we should go to war within the next month'.[4]

First he repeated his old argument that an eastern front was essential to prevent German control of the economic resources of central and south-eastern Europe. Such control would negate the effects of Britain's only real strategic weapon—blockade. But the chances of establishing any sort of front farther west than the frontiers of Russia, Turkey, and Greece were 'receding daily'.

> How can we establish the front we desire, and by which alone we seem likely to be able to avoid the possibility of disaster in three or four years time? By making it clear to all concerned—secretly and without advertising Russia's share in the arrangement—that from the military point of view Germany is now not capable of tackling a major war in which she would have to fight for and hold the economic areas possession of which is

[1] Cab. Minutes, 30 Mar. 1939, CAB 23/98.
[2] Minute by Kirkpatrick, 27 Jan. 1939, C1143/15/18 (FO 371/22962).
[3] See above, pp. 148–9.
[4] Ogilvie-Forbes to Strang, 29 Mar. 1939, *DBFP* iv, Appendix V, p. 623.

essential to her if she is to be able to resist blockade for more than a few months. We must make it clear that any further aggression on Germany's part—whether by force of arms or merely in the shape of economic pressure supported by menace—will immediately entail armed intervention by France and ourselves.[1]

Mason-MacFarlane urged that progress in rearmament should be stressed in order to make this policy credible. He then enumerated the weaknesses of the German army, warning that they would not last, and advocated a preventive war with the object of increasing Germany's difficulties and hence discontent and opposition to Hitler:

> It is true that grave elements of discontent within the country exist. But to produce the organized resistance to the Party or dissension within its ranks which can alone produce disruption, something more than a continuation or even an appreciable increase in the present perfectly bearable 'hardships' and inconveniences under which the German people suffer is required. War, and war now with a 'near' eastern front, would hit them hard and quickly and might well produce the hoped-for results. Without war, and with increasing benefits from Germany's eastern neighbours, these results may never be achieved.[2]

Kirkpatrick noted on 30 March that Britain obviously could not force a war on Germany, but that Mason-MacFarlane's recommendation for the eastern front had been adopted.[3] Cadogan minuted on 31 March: 'I hope the Military Attaché will approve our action today. I gather so.'[4]

It is difficult to say exactly how seriously Halifax and his advisers took the argument about internal resistance to Hitler. He probably thought of it in terms of a gamble with very long odds. The British distinguished within Germany two broad categories of potentially effective opposition to Hitler and the extremist Nazis. The first consisted mainly of Government administrators, and particularly those in charge of the economy. These apparently believed that Hitler's rearmament policy was placing an intolerable strain on the economy, and disliked the fact that essential resources were being diverted into non-productive activities. The epitome of this type was Dr. Hjalmar

---

[1] Memorandum by Mason-MacFarlane, 28 Mar. 1939, *DBFP* iv, Appendix V, p. 625.   [2] Ibid., p. 627.
[3] Minute by Kirkpatrick, 30 Mar. 1939, C4760/13/18 (FO 371/22958).
[4] Minute by Cadogan, 31 Mar. 1939, ibid.

Schacht, President of the Reichsbank until dismissed by Hitler in January 1939 for opposing the further expansion of Reichsbank credit.¹ The British interpreted this as a set-back for the German 'moderates', which indeed it was. Henceforth the British pinned their hopes for moderation increasingly on Hermann Göring, Germany's 'economic dictator' in charge of executing the Four-Year Plan. On 3 January 1939 Sir George Ogilvie-Forbes, the Chargé d'Affaires in Berlin, urged the British Government to exert 'all our efforts to cultivate and maintain good relations with Field Marshal Göring and the moderate Nazis with a view to their exercising a restraining influence on the extremists, such as Ribbentrop, Goebbels and Himmler, who at present have the ear of Hitler'.² Sir Orme Sargent thought that 'although it might be unwise for us to give the impression that we are running after Field-Marshal Göring, I would certainly be in favour of responding to any advances which he might make to us at any time'.³ One such response resulted in Frank Ashton-Gwatkin's fruitless visit to Berlin in February 1939.⁴

The second category of dissidents, although there was never a clear line of demarcation, was the group of 'nationalist Conservatives' identified particularly with the army leadership. Many were civilians, including the reputed central figure of opposition to the Nazi regime, Carl Goerderler, formerly Mayor of Leipzig. The army resented Hitler and his jealous entourage, and never forgave them for their treatment of General von Fritsch.⁵ Furthermore they believed that Hitler was leading Germany into a war which she could not win. In August 1938 the Foreign Office learned that a high-placed group of officers in the Counter-Intelligence Section of the Armed Forces High-Command (O.K.W.) was planning to overthrow Hitler should Britain threaten war over Czechoslovakia. Their agents came to

¹ Memorandum by G. H. S. Pinsent: 'The Implications of Dr. Schacht's Dismissal', 1 Feb. 1939, C2015/8/18 (FO 371/22950); Hjalmar Schacht, *Account Settled*, trans. Edward Fitzgerald (London, 1949), pp. 133-7.
² Ogilvie-Forbes to Halifax, 3 Jan. 1939, *DBFP* iii, no. 515.
³ Minute by Sargent, 12 Jan. 1939, C173/15/18 (FO 371/22960).
⁴ See above, p. 81.
⁵ In January 1938 Field-Marshal von Blomberg, Minister of War, married a typist in the War Ministry who was later alleged to have been a prostitute. The German officer corps demanded his resignation, and General von Fritsch would have succeeded him had it not been for the jealousy of Himmler, Heydrich, and Göring, who trumped up a record of homosexuality. Although Hitler was apparently not behind these machinations, he took the opportunity to assume the Supreme Command of the Armed Forces (Robert J. O'Neill, *The German Army and the Nazi Party, 1933-1939* (London, 1966), Chapter 11).

London but pleaded in vain.[1] Chamberlain wrote of one of them that 'he reminds me of one of the Jacobites at the Court of France in King William's time'.[2] The trouble was that the foreign-policy aims of this group differed little in substance from Hitler's, although they may have been pursued with less impatience. In December 1938 Carl Goerderler promised to instigate a military *coup* if Britain and France would only break off diplomatic relations with Germany. The opposition would then form a 'moderate' Government and negotiate with Britain on the basis of Goerderler's programme, which Cadogan thought 'too much like "Mein Kampf"'.[3] Cadogan nevertheless consulted both Admiral Sinclair, head of the Secret Intelligence Service, who was 'very sceptical', and Neville Chamberlain. 'He would have none of it: and I think he's right. These people must do their own job.'[4]

On 3 January 1939 Sir George Ogilvie-Forbes sounded a 'note of warning':

I have heard from various sources that the impression is still current in authoritative circles in London that in a war with Germany we would hold a trump-card which might turn the scale, namely, the power to provoke internal revolt. With the greatest respect, I submit that this is a dangerous fallacy. If and when Hitler decides that a war with Britain is necessary, the Germans, extremists and moderates, will, with their characteristic discipline, follow him to a man, and any would-be opposition will be promptly and ruthlessly dealt with by the S.S. It will be a long time, and only after much reciprocal destruction, that opposition will show its head with effect. This, indeed, is not a trump-card which we hold already; it is at best a trump-card which might turn up.[5]

[1] 'Unofficial German Approaches, August–September 1938', *DBFP* ii, Appendix IV.
[2] Chamberlain to Halifax, 19 Aug. 1938, ibid., Appendix IV (ii).
[3] Dilks, ed., *Cadogan Diaries*, 10 Dec. 1938, p. 128. Goerderler's programme is significant: 'We are asked to "liquidate" the [Danzig] Corridor; to give Germany a block of colonial territory, to be administered "according to the principles of International Law"; to give Germany an interest-free loan of £400 to £500 million. In return we get a promise that Germany will return to a free exchange system; an assurance that Germany "aims" at no hegemony in S.E. Europe; a German guarantee of the status quo in the Mediterranean; a German promise to co-operate in the Far East. . . . We are expected to deliver the goods and Germany gives us I.O.U.s' (quoted ibid., pp. 128–9). Cf. *Harvey Diaries*, 11 Dec. 1938, p. 227. For an interesting discussion see Hermann Graml, 'Resistance Thinking on Foreign Policy', in Hermann Graml *et al.*, *The German Resistance to Hitler* (Berkeley, 1970).
[4] Dilks, ed., *Cadogan Diaries*, 11 Dec. 1938, p. 129.
[5] Ogilvie-Forbes to Halifax, 3 Jan. 1939, *DBFP* iii, no. 515.

THE UNCONDITIONAL GUARANTEE

Cadogan took the point, but observed that it 'should not deter us from doing everything we possibly can to encourage dissidents in Germany'.[1] This more positive attitude towards the German dissidents derived from the fact that the German extremists seemed to be getting more extreme. As Gladwyn Jebb, Cadogan's Private Secretary, noted on 19 January 1939:

> the extremist leaders are advocating a course which is likely to lead to a general war in the spring, and ... this is opposed not only by important people in the Army, the industrial world, and so on, but even by the moderates in the ranks of the party itself.[2]

One of the foremost advocates of the argument that a firm line by Britain would encourage the opposition to Hitler was Vansittart, whose stock went up after the invasion of Bohemia and Moravia, and whose advice began to carry more weight with Halifax.[3] On 27 March 1939 he showed Halifax a letter from a German friend admonishing Britain for her inaction, which 'threatens to make the German Moderates feel that further resistance is almost hopeless'. The writer warned that 'if you do not wish entirely to lose support in Germany ... you must employ such methods as will now involve full commitments'. He stressed the feeling in the army against the risk of a two-front war:

> Unless one absolutely necessary pre-condition to a German offensive in Western Europe, namely, the security of Germany's eastern flank, is assured, the German General Staff will certainly oppose with all its might and main any big scale operation against the Western Powers (remember the slogan of the famous General von Seeckt: 'Haltet mir den Rücken frei'—'keep my rearguard secure and invulnerable').[4]

These arguments were now being voiced by Colonel Mason-MacFarlane as well, and if Halifax believed at all in the likelihood of deterring Germany at this point, the process, he thought, would operate not on Hitler or on the extremists but on the 'moderates' and especially the army. At least, this was how he justified his new plan for an unconditional, unilateral declaration of support for Poland

---

[1] Minute by Cadogan, 16 Jan. 1939, C173/15/18 (FO 371/22960).
[2] Memorandum by Jebb: 'Summary of Information from Secret Sources', 19 Jan. 1939, FP(36)74, CAB 27/627.
[3] Cadogan conceded on 26 March 1939: 'I must say it is turning out—at present—as Van predicted and as I never believed it would' (Dilks, ed., *Cadogan Diaries*, p. 163).
[4] Minute by Vansittart and enc., 27 Mar. 1939, C4495/15/18 (FO 371/22968).

to his colleagues in the Cabinet, who met in emergency session at 11 a.m. on 30 March 1939.

Halifax related the message from Biddle in Warsaw and the substance of Colvin's report. He recognized that all this was 'uncertain evidence' but disliked the thought that Hitler 'might act before our major arrangements had been concluded'.[1] By openly declaring Britain's intention to support Poland if attacked by Germany, Halifax said he hoped to achieve two things:

> First, the knowledge that we should take such action might cause the plan to be suspended and would thus react to the discredit of Herr Hitler in Army circles; secondly, when our statement became known it would help to educate public opinion in Germany as to the likelihood that Herr Hitler's present course of action would result in Germany becoming engaged in war on two fronts.

Halifax acknowledged several objections to his proposal. First, 'we gave Colonel Beck what he wanted without obtaining any reciprocal undertaking from him'. Second, 'there was some risk of upsetting the prospects of direct agreement between Germany and Poland. Negotiations were in progress but we did not know how they were proceeding.' Third, such a declaration would be very provocative to Germany, although he himself 'had no particular objection to a provocative statement, provided that it did not land us in an unpleasant situation'. Fourth, Rumania was left out. Fifth, the declaration was 'rather heroic action to take, on the meagre information available'. Sixth, it was undesirable to upset Franco-Italian negotiations which were now under way. Seventh, it was undesirable to upset the Franco-British approaches to Warsaw and Bucharest, which had been authorized the night before (29 March), setting in motion the negotiations for the second British initiative, the Anglo-French guarantee of a Polish-Rumanian Pact.

In view of all these objections, Halifax proposed to have a draft declaration (drawn up the night before by Halifax, Cadogan, and Butler) agreed between Britain and France and concerted with the leaders of the Opposition. The Dominions would also be informed about it. 'It would then be possible for this draft statement to be published at a moment's notice, if the situation should require it, in consultation with the French Government.'

The Cabinet wanted to know what sort of situation would require

---

[1] Cab. Minutes, 30 Mar. 1939, CAB 23/98.

its publication, and whether such a situation was really imminent. Halifax could not say for sure. He believed that 'plans had been prepared by Germany for a number of adventures, including an attack on Poland. The real question was which adventure Germany proposed to undertake next and at what date.' In any case, he continued,

he did not think that what he was now proposing represented any material departure from the policy which had been approved by the Cabinet on the previous day. Policy was to resist Germany's attempts at domination. If Poland was the next object of aggression, we must face the situation at once, and the best means of stopping German aggression was almost certainly to make clear that we should resist it by force.[1]

Support for this view came from Lord Chatfield, Minister for Coordination of Defence, who reported the opinion of the Chiefs of Staff that 'if Germany were to attack Poland, the right course would be that we should declare war on Germany'. It is not at all clear where he got this. As we have seen, on 18 March the Chiefs of Staff had advised against challenging Germany, and on 28 March they had stressed Britain's inability in practice to intervene in eastern Europe. However, Chamberlain apparently refused to allow their objections to be circulated in writing to Cabinet Ministers (who did not automatically receive Chiefs of Staff papers) because they amounted to a 'criticism of his policy'.[2] Once again the Cabinet was being none too scrupulously 'persuaded' to follow the Halifax lead. On the other hand it is not permissible to conclude that the Government were under the illusion that the guarantee could be implemented.[3] As Chatfield admitted, 'it would be impossible to prevent Poland from being overrun . . . within two or three months'.

The Lord Chancellor, Lord Maugham, pointed out that recent telegrams gave the impression that the danger was limited to Danzig. He agreed that Britain must not allow Germany to undermine Polish independence, but thought that 'we should not encourage Poland to go to war with Germany about Danzig'. Any public declaration would be 'construed as an attempt by us to prevent the Germans from trying to absorb Danzig'. Sir John Simon, the Chancellor of the Exchequer, evidently held the same view. Chamberlain agreed that it was important not to commit Britain 'on some point which did not

---
[1] Ibid. [2] Liddell Hart, *Memoirs*, ii. 221.
[3] B. H. Liddell Hart, *History of the Second World War* (London, 1970), p. 11.

affect the independence of Poland', but Danzig was important: 'If the Poles regarded the Danzig issue as constituting a threat to their independence, and were prepared to resist by force, then we should have to come to their help.'

The Cabinet's apprehension was not restricted to the possibility of a sudden German attack on Poland, whether at Danzig or anywhere else. But the fact that they took account of such a possibility was not surprising. Harold Nicolson recorded in his diary on 30 March that 'the lobbies are buzzing with anxiety. The only difference of opinion seems to be whether the German ultimatum to Poland is a 24 or a 48 hour ultimatum. . . . Never have I seen the lobbies in such a state of excitement and flurry. All v. foolish.'[1] Furthermore the Foreign Office had some hard information about a possible German attack, as we have seen.

But the second possibility, and one which the Cabinet took more seriously, was that the Poles might be tempted or cajoled, in Mason-MacFarlane's words, to 'let us down and bow to the bully at the gate'.[2] Chamberlain said that he was

uneasy at the fact that our Ambassador in Warsaw could obtain no information as to the progress of the negotiations between Germany and Poland. One possible, but very distasteful, explanation of this was that Polish negotiators were, in fact, giving way to Germany. . . . It was of the utmost importance to take all possible steps to ascertain what was happening in these negotiations.[3]

Sir John Simon agreed that

the real difficulty before the Cabinet was to know what was behind Polish policy. The German method was all too familiar. They might threaten to lay Warsaw in ruins in a few days with their air force. It was difficult to know what line Poland would take if faced with a threat of this kind.

Walter Elliott, Minister of Health, agreed. Since the Chiefs of Staff advised that 'it was better to fight with Poland as an ally than without her . . . we ought to take steps to ensure that Poland did resist German aggression. There were pro-German and pro-French parties in Polish opinion, and we should do our best to strengthen the latter.' Lord Chatfield pointed out that in view of the uncertainty of the

[1] Nicolson Papers, Diary, 30 Mar. 1939.
[2] Memorandum by Mason-MacFarlane, 28 Mar. 1939, *DBFP* iv, Appendix V, 627.
[3] Cab. Minutes, 30 Mar. 1939, CAB 23/98.

situation it was rather pointless merely to have a draft statement ready for publication—it would be better to issue one early so as to give 'more timely warning'. His colleagues agreed, and it was suggested that this could best be accomplished by rigging a Parliamentary Question and Answer the following day, 31 March. Chamberlain thought it would be necessary to consult the French and Polish Governments first, and suggested that the pretext for the statement should be the 'various rumours which were circulating as to a possible German *coup* against Poland'.

At this point Lord Chatfield produced a memorandum which he had just received from the Chiefs of Staff, based on their discussion that morning with the Deputy Director of Military Intelligence at the War Office. Regarding German troop dispositions opposite Poland,

the significant feature is the concentration of German troops opposite Silesia (coal and iron districts). In the North there are four to five divisions on either side of the corridor. This is practically normal.

The D.D.M.I. interprets the concentration opposite Silesia, not as an intention to invade Poland from the south west, *but as forming an effective threat in any negotiations with Poland. There is in fact no evidence that either the Germans or the Italians intend to make any major move* but they are employing the same technique as they adopted when they started the Dutch hare running with such success in February by spreading rumours . . .[1]

The Chiefs of Staff thought that if the Cabinet decided to go ahead with the announcement, certain conditions should apply. The guarantee should operate only if there were a definite act of aggression against Polish territory (this excluded Danzig) which the Poles resisted, and if they appealed for help. Furthermore, Poland must make a reciprocal commitment ('Otherwise there would be no two front war for Germany'), Rumanian resources must somehow be denied to Germany in the event of war, and France must be fully committed with Britain.

The memorandum provided further evidence that, despite the rumours, there existed no major German threat to Poland. Instead the Germans appeared to be pressuring the Poles into agreeing to some sort of solution to the Danzig problem. This was precisely what the Foreign Office, Halifax, Chamberlain, and the Cabinet now wanted to prevent, because they feared that such an agreement might be reached on the basis of Polish neutrality in return for German acceptance of 'less than 99% of her demands', as Roger Makins put

[1] Cab. Minutes, 30 Mar. 1939, Annex B, CAB 23/98. Author's emphasis.

it.¹ This is why the British, to ensure a German-Polish deadlock, were prepared to issue the Poles with a 'blank cheque'; why Chamberlain had rejected Lord Maugham's plea not to encourage Poland to go to war with Germany over Danzig; and why Halifax was ready to disregard both his earlier conditions and the objections to his proposal which he had just enumerated. The British were in a dilemma: even if they did not wish to fight for Danzig, they were forced to do so if they wanted to be sure of Poland. The British fully realized the consequences of what they were doing. Nobody believed that a guarantee reduced the risk of war. As the Chiefs of Staff had clearly warned on 28 March: 'if such a Pact were to encourage an intransigeant attitude on the part of Poland and Rumania it would thereby tend to precipitate a European war before our forces are in any way prepared for it'.² This was also Lord Maugham's objection, but he was overruled. Thus the very action that Britain took to improve her international position in March 1939 increased the risk of conflict. A further paradox was that it was Britain's weakness that dictated this course. Had she been in as strong a position as in 1914, she could have remained aloof.

As we have seen, the German Government were not attempting at this juncture to force the issue of their demands on Poland, and there is no evidence that Beck was in fact ready to buy a breathing space for his country in return for neutrality. He was well aware that his only hope lay in the power of the West to defeat Germany, and that any respite would probably be short-lived. On the other hand he feared that if he informed Britain and France of his refusal to accept Germany's demands, they might decide that an advance commitment to Poland was unnecessary. The British misread the situation. Yet even had they read it correctly, there is little doubt that Chamberlain and Halifax, together with the majority of the Cabinet, were ready to challenge Germany.

It is significant that their chosen method was designed to result in somebody else's war first. For the British were still conscious of their weakness. As Halifax told his Private Secretary a few days later, he 'wanted to gain time because every month gave us 600 more aeroplanes'.³ What better way to gain time, given that war was con-

---

¹ Minute by Makins, 29 Mar. 1939, C4859/54/18 (FO 371/23016). See above, pp. 172–3.
² 'Military Implications of an Anglo-French Guarantee of Poland and Rumania', draft report, n.d., COS 872, CAB 53/47. See above, p. 155.
³ *Harvey Diaries*, p. 278.

sidered inevitable, than to direct the German military machine against the Poles? The Chiefs of Staff had estimated that Poland could resist for 'a matter of months'.[1] That meant more aeroplanes. It would also give Britain's main strategic weapon time to take effect. As the Chiefs of Staff had written in September 1938, 'it must be realised that no blockade can take effect immediately, and the whole system ... can only be developed to its full capacity after some months'.[2]

The Cabinet approved the new course: to make a declaration of support for Poland in a Government answer to a Parliamentary Question next day. Explanatory telegrams were sent off to Paris and Warsaw. The Foreign Office wanted French approval for the declaration, but merely 'presumed it would be in accord with the Polish Government's wishes'.[3] This formulation was the result of controversy in the Foreign Office and in the Cabinet. Vansittart, as suspicious of Colonel Beck and his motives as was his friend and correspondent at the French Foreign Ministry, Aléxis Léger, did not want to give the Poles a chance to disagree with the declaration. Cadogan disliked this approach,[4] but Halifax agreed with Vansittart. On the other hand the Secretary of State for India, Lord Zetland, did not see how the declaration could be made without a prior request from Poland.[5]

That distrust of Colonel Beck was mounting in the Foreign Office is evident from a telegram dispatched to Sir Howard Kennard in Warsaw on 29 March asking him: 'In view of reasons which we have for lack of confidence in M. Beck, would you think it desirable to make a communication [about the proposal for a conditional Anglo-French guarantee of a Polish-Rumanian Pact] also to some other personality, such as the President or the Marshal?'[6] In the event Kennard asked the French Ambassador, Léon Noël, to do this for him.[7]

On the afternoon of 30 March the Cabinet Foreign Policy Committee met to consider the draft statement of unconditional support

[1] See above, p. 155.
[2] Memorandum by Newall, Chief of the Air Staff, 23 Sept. 1938, H/XIX/17 (FO 800/318).
[3] Halifax to Kennard, 30 Mar. 1939, *DBFP* iv, no. 568.
[4] Dilks, ed., *Cadogan Diaries*, 30 Mar. 1939, p. 165.
[5] Cab. Minutes, 30 Mar. 1939, CAB 23/98.
[6] Halifax to Kennard, 29 Mar. 1939, *DBFP* iv, no. 563. The reference was to President Moscicki and to Marshal Smigly-Rydz, the Defence Minister, who were considered more reliable than Beck.
[7] Kennard to Halifax, 30 Mar. 1939, ibid., no. 575.

for Poland. Halifax admitted that if France or Poland raised any objections, 'its publication would require further consideration', but advised his colleagues not to wait 'for confirmation of the rumours of an imminent German attack on Poland'. The reason was that such confirmation was extremely unlikely. As the Chiefs of Staff had pointed out that morning, and as Sir Horace Wilson now reminded the Foreign Policy Committee, there was 'little, if any, sign of the concentration of German troops against the Polish frontier'. Chamberlain agreed that the available information 'did not support the theory that Germany was contemplating an immediate military *coup de main*'.[1]

The War Office confirmed this assessment in a situation report for the twenty-four hours ending at midday on 30 March. Despite the report that local Nazis in Danzig had been warned 'to hold themselves in readiness from March 28th onwards', there was 'no extensive reinforcement of East Prussia'. The main concentrations were still opposite the Posen district and Polish Silesia, and not even these formations were at full strength.[2] Cadogan minuted that 'this doesn't look to me very formidable as yet'.[3]

The Foreign Policy Committee still had great expectations of Mussolini, hoping that he 'might be able to approach Herr Hitler direct and to exercise his personal influence with him'.[4] They agreed to another personal letter from Chamberlain warning the Duce about the latest departure in British policy. In the event Cadogan and Wilson drafted a telegram together instead.[5] It was decided that the German Government should not be forewarned, however.

As the Government's plans for the unconditional guarantee to Poland matured, so the Parliamentary Opposition's insistence on the inclusion of Russia increased, constantly spurred by the Soviet Ambassador, Ivan Maisky.[6] After the Cabinet meeting that morning, Chamberlain had told the Deputy Leader of the Labour Party, Arthur Greenwood, and the Leader of the Liberal Party, Sir Archibald Sinclair, that because of reports of an imminent German attack on

[1] FPC Minutes, 30 Mar. 1939, CAB 27/624.
[2] General Staff (War Office), Summary of Information no. 9 (New Series): for 24 hours ending 1200 hrs. 30 Mar. 1939, C4745/19/18 (FO 371/22996).
[3] Minute by Cadogan, 30 Mar. 1939, ibid.
[4] FPC Minutes, 30 Mar. 1939, CAB 27/624.
[5] Dilks, ed., *Cadogan Diaries*, 31 Mar. 1939, p. 167.
[6] See Sidney Aster, 'Ivan Maisky and Parliamentary Anti-Appeasement, 1938–1939', in *Lloyd George: Twelve Essays*, ed. A. J. P. Taylor (New York, 1971).

Poland the Government were considering whether or not to issue an immediate declaration of support for her.[1] He had tried to reassure them about Russia but they, briefed by Maisky, were not satisfied. At 9 p.m. that evening the Executive of the Parliamentary Labour Party met to consider how they could best persuade the Government not to leave Russia out. Hugh Dalton suggested seeing the Prime Minister without delay 'to get something put in about Russia'. According to Dalton,

> We saw Chamberlain at 10.15 p.m. in the Cabinet Room at No. 10. He was alone. We told him that he would never get away with it tomorrow unless he brought in the Russians. We emphasized the state of opinion in our own party and elsewhere, and also the crude importance of having the Russians on our side if trouble came. Chamberlain said that the Government were anxious to consult the Russians and to keep in touch with them, but he had been surprised at the strength of the objections taken by many countries to having any dealings with them at all. There were not only difficulties with Poland, he said, but he also referred to Portugal, Spain and Canada—Roman Catholics in Quebec, no doubt. We urged him, at this critical hour, not to be influenced by these objections.

Chamberlain said that Halifax was due to see Maisky next morning at 10.30, and Dalton suggested postponing the statement on Poland to the afternoon so as to take account of their talk. Chamberlain was receptive but feared that delay might result in a leak, 'as always', from Paris.[2]

According to Neville Chamberlain's slightly different account to the Foreign Policy Committee, meeting again next morning at 9.45 a.m. (31 March), the Labour leaders had said that

> they would be satisfied with some reference to Russia, however slight. He had replied that he could not be placed in the position of inserting a reference to Russia at this late stage and subsequently of being criticized by the Poles for not having warned them that this was the intention.[3]

Halifax strongly objected to the idea of mentioning Russia in the declaration. He wanted the Labour leaders to be 'further informed' of the reasons for this, and to be told that he had discussed the whole matter with Maisky. He did not want to jeopardize the statement by alienating the Polish Government, who might legitimately point out

---

[1] Cab. Minutes, 31 Mar. 1939, CAB 23/98. Cf. Dalton, *The Fateful Years*, p. 237.
[2] Dalton, *The Fateful Years*, p. 238.
[3] FPC Minutes, 31 Mar. 1939, CAB 27/624.

that since the British had not said anything about including Russia to them, they had been misled.¹

Maisky by this time was annoyed because Halifax kept postponing their interview, originally set for 30 March, rescheduled for 10.30 a.m. on 31 March, and finally fixed for 1 p.m. that day. When at last they met, Halifax read out the proposed declaration and asked Maisky,

having regard to the importance of avoiding [the] appearance of divisions between the Governments concerned . . . whether there was anything the Prime Minister could say on the lines of assuming that the Soviet Government would not disapprove or even would approve the general line we were taking.²

Maisky objected that he could not possibly say what his Government might think since he had not had time to consult them. In any case they 'had no desire to force themselves on anybody'. He did not object to the anodyne reference to Russia that Halifax suggested: that Britain supposed that Russia would agree with the declaration, in view of Stalin's proclaimed policy of 'assistance against aggression for those who fought for their independence'. In fact of course, as Maisky very well knew, the British Government merely wanted 'to prevent any quarrelling on the part of the Opposition'.³ Halifax's idea was to make no mention of Russia in the statement itself but to anticipate supplementary questions about her attitude. He was, after all, also concerned with the appearance of Parliamentary unity. But this was as far as he would go to meet opposition pressure.

At the Foreign Policy Committee meeting at 9.45 a.m. on 31 March, Chamberlain said that he wanted to make his statement in the afternoon, so as to give the Cabinet a chance to approve it, and also because he had promised the Labour leaders that Maisky's views would be taken into account.⁴ But the President of the Board of Trade, Oliver Stanley, objected that the delay might cause a heavy fall in prices on the Stock Exchange. It was therefore to reassure the City that the Prime Minister told the House of Commons at 11 a.m. that he would make a statement on the European situation that afternoon, but that there was no official confirmation of the current rumours. This was quite true. The military intelligence section of the

---

¹ FPC Minutes, 31 Mar. 1939, CAB 27/624.
² Halifax to Seeds, 31 Mar. 1939, *DBFP* iv, no. 589.
³ Quoted in Aster, *Lloyd George: Twelve Essays*, p. 343.
⁴ FPC Minutes, 31 Mar. 1939, CAB 27/624.

THE UNCONDITIONAL GUARANTEE 201

War Office concluded on 31 March that 'there is as yet no concrete evidence that Germany is determined to force an immediate solution of the Danzig problem'. On the other hand discussions were taking place between Poland and Germany, and while it was 'not clear who initiated these . . . they are clearly the result of the German threat'. They did not appear to cover the Polish Corridor. The Germans were forcing the pace for one of two reasons:

> Firstly she may intend to occupy Danzig in the first week of April as a result either of agreement, of an ultimatum, or of forcible seizure.
>
> Secondly Germany may wish to intimidate Poland at a time when there are many indications of her drawing closer to the western powers and possibly to Soviet Russia, and at the moment when her Minister for Foreign Affairs is visiting England. This is the more probable reason.

The War Office thought the Poles would 'accept any solution of the Danzig problem which bore the semblance of an agreed solution' but would fight if faced with an ultimatum or with a resort to force.[1]

The latest information, Chamberlain told his colleagues on the Committee, 'seemed to point to it being unlikely that the Germans were contemplating any immediate *coup de main*'.[2] This being the case, he thought it best not to use the rumours as a pretext for making the declaration. But it was objected that if Chamberlain did not refer to the rumours, then 'critics would ask why it was considered necessary to make this unilateral declaration in favour of Poland and so give away a trump card on the eve of Colonel Beck's visit to London'. This was a very good question in any case, given the reassuring information at hand. The answer was that first of all the Government could not be *absolutely* sure that Hitler would not act over the weekend, traditionally his favourite time. The second and certainly more important reason, was that the Government feared that the Poles might give way to German pressure in the negotiations and slip from the British net.

The Foreign Policy Committee had a further item of business before them that morning. They considered a suggestion by Sir

---

[1] War Office (M.I.2) Memorandum: 'Poland and Danzig', 31 Mar. 1939, PREM 1/133A. For additional minutes on this memorandum and for a summary of the information on which it was based see C4622/54/18 (FO 371/23016). R. L. Speaight minuted on 4 April: 'This note was prepared without the knowledge of our statement about Poland, which can be presumed to have stiffened the Polish attitude. In any case it looks as if German action against the Corridor and/or Danzig has been postponed for the time being' (ibid.).

[2] FPC Minutes, 31 Mar. 1939, CAB 27/624.

Howard Kennard that the guarantee should be limited to cases of 'unprovoked' aggression against Poland. They rejected it, because 'the German technique of aggression is so varied and so insidious that . . . Poland might in certain circumstances be driven in self-defence to commit a technical act of provocation'.[1] Instead they agreed to instruct Kennard to warn the Poles that two conditions attached to the guarantee: '(i) that Poland would resist a threat to her independence, and (ii) that she would not indulge in provocative behaviour or stupid obstinacy either generally or in particular as regards Danzig'.[2] Halifax added a further reservation: Kennard was to call Beck's attention to the fact that the declaration was an 'interim measure designed to meet what is apprehended to be a possible danger pending the conclusion of the consultations [on the conditional guarantee project] which are now in progress with Poland and Roumania'. The continuance of the unilateral guarantee would depend 'on whether this scheme can in due course be put into operation'.[3] The telegram to Kennard was not dispatched, however, until 5 p.m. that afternoon, twenty-four hours after Beck had agreed to the Prime Minister's statement and two hours after that statement was made.

At midday the Cabinet met to consider the declaration. Its terms had been altered slightly since the previous day, to relate more directly to the interim period: 'This made the statement rather less final and weighty, and left us rather more leverage to obtain a reciprocal undertaking from Poland.'[4] Chamberlain outlined his interpretation of Britain's new obligation. First of all Polish independence must be clearly threatened, and 'it would, of course, be for us to determine what action threatened Polish independence'. A second condition was that Poland must resist such action with her national forces. 'This would prevent us becoming embroiled as the result of a mere frontier incident.' He thought 'the position was now safeguarded as far as was possible, consistently with the declaration attaining its object'. Lord Maugham made a last-ditch objection, that the Canadian public might be very surprised that Britain should enter 'into so binding a commitment' to Poland, about which they were very ignorant. The Cabinet agreed to it nevertheless.

[1] Halifax to Kennard, 31 Mar. 1939, *DBFP* iv, no. 584.
[2] FPC Minutes, 31 Mar. 1939, CAB 27/624.
[3] Halifax to Kennard, 31 Mar. 1939, *DBFP* iv, no. 584.
[4] Cab. Minutes, 31 Mar. 1939, CAB 23/98.

At 2.52 p.m. Chamberlain made his statement to a House of Commons packed and tense in anticipation.[1] He repeated that the rumours of a projected attack on Poland had not been officially confirmed, and said that there was no justification for substituting force or the threat of force for the method of negotiation. He continued:

> As the House is aware, certain consultations are proceeding with other Governments. In order to make perfectly clear the position of His Majesty's Government in the meantime before those consultations are concluded, I now have to inform the House that during that period, in the event of any action which clearly threatened Polish independence, and which the Polish Government accordingly considered it vital to resist with their national forces, His Majesty's Government would feel themselves bound at once to lend the Polish Government all support in their power. They have given the Polish Government an assurance to this effect.
>
> I may add that the French Government have authorized me to make it plain that they stand in the same position in this matter as do His Majesty's Government.[2]

Arthur Greenwood thought that Chamberlain's statement 'may prove to be in its consequences as momentous a statement as has been made in this House for a quarter of a century'. He then asked about Russia and what other powers would be asked to join the coalition. Chamberlain pointed out that this was an interim measure, and said that Halifax had seen Maisky for 'very full discussions'. The Prime Minister had 'no doubt that the principles upon which we are acting are fully understood and appreciated' by the Soviet Government. He assured the House that there were no ideological impediments in Anglo-Russian relations.[3]

The pressure of public opinion, morale in the Balkans, and developments in the Far East all contributed to the decision to convert the British scheme for a bilateral and conditional guarantee to Poland and Rumania into a unilateral, unconditional guarantee for

---

[1] The best description of the scene is in Harold Nicolson's Diary: 'Chamberlain arrives looking gaunt and ill. The skin above his high cheek bones is parchment yellow. He drops wearily into his place. David Margesson [the Chief Whip] proposes the Adjournment and the P.M. rises. . . . He reads his statement very slowly with a bent grey head. It is most impressive. The House does not cheer his explanatory part beyond a vague murmur of assent. But when he says he will support Poland, there are real live cheers from all parts of the House' (Nicolson Papers, Diary, 31 Mar. 1939).

[2] 345 HC Deb., 5 s., col. 2415.   [3] Ibid., cols. 2415–17.

Poland. A further, more important, reason was that the British were fearful of losing the potential of Polish resistance to Germany, not as a result of Germany's forcible subjugation of Poland, but as a result of a 'corrupt bargain': a Polish guarantee of neutrality in return for a compromise over Danzig. The British dilemma was that they could not prevent this without committing themselves to what they knew to be the most volatile area in Europe, Danzig. In this way they hastened the outbreak of war.

On the other hand, the springs of the British action are to be found not so much in fine calculations of strategic advantage or even vital interests, as in the psychology of British policy-makers humiliated by a long series of German successes and stung into action by the realization that Britain would no longer count in the world if she did nothing. To do nothing, as Halifax had pointed out to the Foreign Policy Committee on 27 March, would result in such a loss of sympathy and support in the world, particularly in the United States and the Balkans, and in such an increase in German power and influence, that he favoured the only possible alternative: 'our going to war'. Thus the guarantee was a deliberate challenge that would help recover British prestige, end the uncertainty, and allow the British to abandon at last the narrow dictates of state interest which had driven them to seek agreement with a Germany whose political system they loathed. As the Marquess of Zetland, the Secretary of State for India, wrote after the Cabinet had approved the guarantee:

> We separated with a feeling almost of relief with the knowledge that a definite decision had been taken, even though we realised that we were burning our boats and that we might be committed to war over a principle which we have all come to think transcends even the vital material interests of this country.[1]

[1] Quoted in Aster, *1939: The Making of the Second World War*, p. 107.

10

AFTERMATH

ALTHOUGH there was no immediate criticism, it was not long in coming. Lloyd George, the Liberal elder statesman, asked Chamberlain in a conversation following the announcement of the guarantee why Russia had not been included. The Prime Minister told him that Poland and Rumania objected. In that case why was Chamberlain now threatening to involve Britain in a war with Germany? Chamberlain replied that the German General Staff would never risk a war if they knew they would have to fight on two fronts simultaneously, namely in the west and in Poland.

Lloyd George burst into laughter and began to jibe Chamberlain, explaining that Poland had no air force to speak of, an inadequately mechanised army, worse than mediocre armaments, and that Poland was weak internally—economically and politically. Without active help from the U.S.S.R., therefore, no 'Eastern front's possible'. He told Chamberlain that in the absence of a firm agreement with Russia 'I consider your statement of today an irresponsible game of chance which can end up very badly'.[1]

The substance of Lloyd George's criticism was repeated, though in less extreme form, by much of informed opinion throughout the country. Viscount Cranborne, who had resigned as Parliamentary Under-Secretary for Foreign Affairs together with Eden in January 1938, anticipated that such criticism could divide the country and undermine the appearance abroad of British resolve. Having told the House of Commons that Chamberlain's statement had 'been received with great satisfaction in all parts of the House', he went on to propose that the foreign affairs debate arranged for the following Monday, 3 April 1939, should be postponed, since 'a debate in these delicate circumstances might land us in much more harm than good'.[2]

---

[1] Quoted in 'Soviet–British–French talks in Moscow, 1939' (A Documentary Survey), *International Affairs* (Moscow), July 1969, p. 80. Lloyd George had been briefed by Basil Liddell Hart, the military strategist (Liddell Hart, *Memoirs*, ii. 218).

[2] 345 HC Deb., 5 s., col. 2417.

Chamberlain was at first inclined to agree, but, as he explained when the debate took place as planned, he hoped that members would take the opportunity to show a united front.[1] With the exception of Lloyd George, the principal speakers acquiesced, but all agreed that the Polish guarantee was not enough. It was, in Hugh Dalton's words, only 'the first step in the right direction'.[2] The most important country to line up against Germany was Russia. However you assessed her military value, said Arthur Greenwood, she 'might well prove to be the final, decisive and smashing factor on the side of keeping the peace in the world'.[3] Sir Archibald Sinclair, the Liberal leader, agreed that 'Russia is obviously the key'.[4] He wanted Churchill and Eden in the Cabinet to replace men like Hoare and Simon (whom he called 'the evil genius of British foreign policy'), and called for further mobilization of Britain's industrial and manpower resources in preparation for war. Conspicuously absent from his or from any other speech, however, was the demand for conscription.

The most spectacular speech of the afternoon was delivered by Lloyd George, who stressed 'the tremendous importance . . . of securing the pledged support of the greatest military power on this earth', Soviet Russia. He said that it was not only important to demonstrate to Germany the determination to resist her. It was even more important to demonstrate the capacity to do so. Clearly neither Britain nor France could send 'a single battalion' to help Poland. The Polish army, brave though it may be, was no match for the Germans either in size or in weaponry. The Government's answer was that Germany must face a two-front war. But France might have to fight on three fronts, against Germany, Italy, and Spain. Furthermore the British fleet no longer held a monopoly of the Mediterranean. And what was supposed to happen to Poland while Britain instituted the naval blockade against Germany? The Government's strategic assumption was that 'Russia will come in sooner or later' to help, but where was the assurance?

> If we are going in without the help of Russia we are walking into a trap. It is the only country whose armies can get there. . . . With Russia you have overwhelming forces which Germany with her inferior army cannot stand up against. I appeal to the Government with all the earnestness I can command to take steps immediately. If Russia has not been brought

[1] 345 HC Deb., 5 s., col. 2482. [2] Ibid., col. 2570.
[3] Ibid., col. 2480. [4] Ibid., col. 2493.

into this matter because of certain feelings the Poles have that they do not want the Russians there, it is for us to declare the conditions, and unless the Poles are prepared to accept the only conditions with which we can successfully help them, the responsibility must be theirs.[1]

At least one member thought that this was treason, and even Harold Nicolson called it 'rather unfortunate', noting that 'the round, brown head of Maisky, the Soviet Ambassador, can be observed grinning like a little gnome above the clock'.[2]

Churchill and Eden took pains to stress their support for the Government, conscious and hoping, no doubt, that their own hour was fast approaching. Churchill did warn, with his incomparable command of military metaphor, that 'to stop here with a guarantee to Poland would be to halt in No-Man's Land under fire of both trench lines and without the shelter of either'.[3] On the other hand he characterized Britain's policy towards Russia as 'well-conceived':

The Government have been wise in not forcing matters. Rumania, Poland and the Baltic States all feel easier because this great mass of Russia is friendly behind them, and lies there in broad support. But we must be largely guided at this juncture by the feelings of those States. Upon the whole I think we may trust to the natural forces which are at work. It seems to me highly probable that that dominating identity of interest will prevail, and that without undue delay. I therefore accept the declaration of the Government upon this point as satisfactory for the time being.[4]

Churchill called for defensive readiness, but was prepared to leave conscription until 'the day that war breaks out'.[5]

Eden recognized the importance of Russia but also defended the Government's decision to put Poland first. With Poland as an ally on the eastern front the German army would be divided approximately into two, which would reduce the chance of an attack on the West or on the East. He noted that the new policy 'has united the nation in support of the Government in foreign affairs and that this is of immense value to anyone negotiating with foreign Powers'.[6] He offered to withdraw the motion he had sponsored on 28 March, and later did so.[7]

Chamberlain responded to the demand for further adherents to the

---

[1] Ibid., cols. 2509–10.
[2] Nicolson Papers, Diary, 3 Apr. 1939.
[3] 345 HC Deb., 5 s., cols. 2500–1.
[4] Ibid., col. 2502.
[5] Ibid., col. 2504.
[6] Ibid., col. 2515.
[7] See above, p. 176.

coalition with the assurance that discussions were still proceeding. With specific reference to Russia he contradicted his statement of 31 March by saying that ideological differences continued to exist. However, 'they do not really count in a question of this kind. . . . Therefore, we welcome the co-operation of any country, whatever may be its internal system of government, not in aggression, but in resistance to aggression.'[1]

If Chamberlain did not get quite the show of unity that he had called for, the House of Commons was at least united in its condemnation of *The Times*. On 1 April there had appeared in the paper a leading article entitled 'A Stand for Ordered Diplomacy' which contained an unfortunate passage:

> The historic importance of the British Government's guarantee is that it commits them to stand for fair and free negotiation. The new obligation which this country yesterday assumed does not bind Great Britain to defend every inch of the present frontiers of Poland. The key word in the declaration is not integrity but 'independence'. The independence of every negotiating State is what matters.[2]

Hugh Dalton demanded an explanation of this and of similar interpretations emanating from the Beaverbrook Press[3] and from Reuter's News Agency. He recalled the infamous *Times* leader of 7 September 1938 which had advocated the cession of the Sudetenland in advance of the Government's own proposal, and which was widely suspected of having been planted by the Government as a *ballon d'essai*:

> Now we have the same thing again—a similar article with a similar tendency; another Slav victim to be sacrificed on the altar of Printing House Square: the Poles today, the Czechs yesterday. These traitors of Printing House Square, this residue of the Cliveden set—[interruption]— I was going to use a Spanish metaphor; I was going to say, 'Hitler's fifth column in London'.[4]

Chamberlain and Simon both dissociated the Government from these interpretations, as the Foreign Office had already done, saying that they were the responsibility of the newspapers and the agency alone.

---

[1] 345 HC Deb., 5 s., col. 2486.   [2] *The Times*, 1 Apr. 1939, p. 15.
[3] The *Daily Express* and the *Evening Standard*.
[4] 345 HC Deb., 5 s., cols. 2577–8. Feeling against *The Times* ran very high. To make the point, Robert Boothby, the Conservative M.P., wrote a private letter to the editor, Geoffrey Dawson, saying: 'I trust that after today's debate you will not only resign the editorship of the "Times" but leave the country' (Nicolson Papers, Diary, 3 Apr. 1939).

In fact *The Times*'s leader had been wrong only in its timing. Before long other newspapers were arguing that the guarantee did not preclude negotiations under the right conditions.[1] Halifax and Chamberlain, according to the diary of the editor of *The Times*, Geoffrey Dawson, thought the leader 'just right on first reading'.[2] Chamberlain had indeed been preoccupied with its main point. But such thinking jarred in the euphoria of anti-German feeling then prevalent in London.[3]

Complaints were not restricted to the House of Commons. In the very early hours of 1 April Colonel Beck lodged a protest about the Reuter message, which had suggested that British officials believed a German-Polish settlement possible on the basis of Poland's ceding Danzig and a corridor across the Corridor. Sir Reginald Leeper instructed his staff in the Foreign Office News Department to 'wash Reuter's head', and the agency message was cancelled.[4]

At 4.20 p.m. on 3 April Colonel Beck arrived in London for his long-awaited visit.[5] He held discussions with Halifax and Chamberlain during the next three days. The British hoped for five things: (1) a reciprocal assurance of Polish assistance to Britain in case of a German attack, that is, direct reciprocity; (2) a Polish pledge to assist Britain and France 'if they became involved in war with Germany arising out of a German attack upon Holland, Belgium, Switzerland, Denmark or even Yugoslavia',[6] that is, indirect reciprocity; (3) a Polish pledge to assist Rumania in case of a German attack; (4) Polish acceptance of some arrangement for material assistance from the Soviet Union; (5) more information about German-Polish relations and in particular about Danzig.

Beck offered the first British *desideratum* of his own accord: it was clear, he said, that the engagement must be reciprocal, adding that 'this was the only basis that any self-respecting country could accept'.[7]

---

[1] Franklin Reid Gannon, *The British Press and Germany 1936–1939* (Oxford, 1971), p. 265.   [2] Quoted ibid., p. 264.

[3] James Maxton, the Independent Labour Party M.P., imagined the House to be 'very much in the mood that [it] must have been in during the days preceding August, 1914' (345 HC Deb., 5 s., col. 2516).

[4] Kennard to Halifax, 1 Apr. 1939, and minute by J. E. Coulson (News Department), C4531/54/18 (FO 371/23015).

[5] Beck was greeted on his way through Berlin by an official of the Foreign Ministry Protocol Department, von Halem, but the interview was so frosty that the latter had to leave the train 'as soon as was compatible with the requirements of courtesy' (Memorandum by von Halem, 3 Apr. 1939, *DGFP* vi, no. 148).

[6] Record of Anglo-Polish Conversations, 4 Apr. 1939, *DBFP* v, no. 1.

[7] Ibid.

The second question was more difficult. Beck refused to consider the case of Yugoslavia, which 'belonged to quite a different region', and could only agree to discuss the other countries at some future date. He would want to know, for instance, what obligations Britain herself had towards them. Halifax replied that Britain had treaty obligations towards Belgium, though none towards Holland or Denmark. Britain had, however, decided to treat a German attack on Holland as a *casus belli*, and he anticipated that the Government would take the same line about Denmark. An attack on Switzerland was to be treated in the same way, and Britain and France were in any case bound by the Treaty of Vienna of 1815, 'though it was not quite clear what this obligation amounted to'. Beck explained that he was reluctant to undertake new commitments. He did, however, agree that 'if Great Britain and Poland reached a permanent binding agreement, the Polish Government would not exclude friendly discussion on these points'.[1] Chamberlain replied that the principle of a permanent binding agreement was acceptable, but later attempted to turn the tables on Beck by pointing out that 'when it came to drafting the permanent agreement, the point about Belgium and Holland, etc., would be a vital one'.[2] Beck agreed that in his own personal opinion the final agreement would have to safeguard the point, but said that he had no authority to commit the Polish Government.

The third question was equally difficult. Beck insisted that he must consult the Rumanian Foreign Ministry about a Polish commitment to Rumania, but thought that any such commitment would throw Hungary into the arms of Germany. That was a contingency he had struggled to avoid in trying to improve relations between Bucharest and Budapest. He did not want to see 'too rigid a system' established in eastern Europe as this would preclude Hungarian co-operation. The British objected that it was surely important to know what the Poles would do in case of a German attack on Rumania, but Beck refused to be drawn. Privately, the British suspected that Beck 'would prefer that Roumania rather than Poland should be over-run by Germany'.[3] They also re-examined the assumption that they had always held about Hungary, that she was too far under German influence to be of any use in a coalition. The furthest they would go to woo her, however, was to agree to propaganda measures.[4]

[1] Record of Anglo-Polish Conversations, 4 Apr. 1939, *DBFP* v, no. 2.
[2] Record of Anglo-Polish Conversations, 5 Apr. 1939, ibid., no. 10.
[3] Cab. Minutes, 5 Apr. 1939, CAB 23/98. [4] Ibid.

The question of Russian assistance also proved intractable. Halifax defined the problem as one of 'how to get a maximum degree of collaboration from Soviet Russia without entailing dangerous consequences'. Beck stressed the latter. Germany might react violently to a fixed Polish-Russian alignment. He deprecated the value of Russian assistance, as Halifax did also, thus destroying his own argument.[1] The British were especially worried that Poland might issue a declaration dissociating herself from any agreement which drew Britain and France into a closer relationship with Russia: 'the result would be that we should either lose Polish support altogether or at least weaken the common front'.[2] Halifax was 'surprised at the vigour and persistence of Colonel Beck's reactions to the Russian problem'.

Beck was misleading, though not actually mendacious, on the subject of German-Polish relations. He said that 'no written demands had been presented to the Polish Government', a statement which was no doubt strictly true. But Halifax's interpretation in Cabinet next day was that 'no formal demands had been made'. Beck implied that the Danzig question had not been the object of negotiations, although 'conversations . . . had been going on for some time'. He informed the British that although his Government hoped for an agreement on Polish terms, they would fight if the Germans presented them with a *fait accompli*. Chamberlain thought that Beck was optimistic in his hope for an agreement.[3]

The British were pleased with the results of Beck's visit, which shows how little they had really expected of Poland in the first place. Although they secured only one of their requirements, they considered it the most important. It guaranteed that if Britain or France were attacked by Germany, Poland would be engaged on the eastern front. Polish resistance was assured. Halifax wrote to Sir Eric Phipps in Paris on 6 April that 'our conversations with Beck have been going pretty well. He has been very frank with us and quite definite in maintaining that Poland would defend herself and would accept a reciprocal guarantee between our two countries.'[4]

On the other hand British policy was not turning out quite as

[1] Record of Anglo-Polish Conversations, 4 Apr. 1939, *DBFP* v, no. 1.
[2] Cab. Minutes, 5 Apr. 1939, CAB 23/98. The Poles had done this once before —in the wake of the Franco-Soviet Pact of 1935.
[3] Record of Anglo-Polish Conversations, 4 Apr. 1939, *DBFP* v, no. 2. Cab. Minutes, 5 Apr. 1939, CAB 23/98.
[4] Halifax to Phipps, 6 Apr. 1939, H/XXVII/12 (FO 800/321).

Chamberlain had expected. As he told the Cabinet on 5 April, the Liberal and Labour Opposition were thinking in terms of a 'Grand Alliance' against Germany. He himself, at the beginning, had hoped for an understanding with Poland, Russia, Rumania, and later on with Turkey and Greece. Now the prospects had been reduced to an Anglo-Polish Pact. For if, as Beck maintained, the inclusion of Russia 'would be likely to cause an explosion', any arrangement with her 'was obviously one which required a great deal of consideration'. Chamberlain went on to say that

> he was by no means indisposed to negotiate a Two-Power Pact with Poland. After all, Poland was the key to the situation, and an alliance with Poland would ensure that Germany would be engaged in a war on two fronts. At the same time, it would be necessary to take the utmost care as to the presentation of this arrangement if the Government were to avoid a considerable outcry and criticism.

Halifax noted that 'it might be desirable for him to see the Russian Ambassador somewhat more frequently than in the past so as to avoid any suspicion that we were cold-shouldering Russia'.[1] This was an inauspicious beginning to a season of Anglo-Russian negotiations.

On 6 April the Polish and British delegates agreed on the terms of what amounted to a mutual assistance pact. The British did not want to conclude a formal alliance until the Poles agreed to help Britain and France in resisting German aggression against Holland, Belgium, Switzerland, or Denmark. Such an alliance was not made contingent on a Polish commitment to Rumania, however. In fact the danger to Rumania seemed at last to have assumed realistic proportions. As Chamberlain told the Cabinet on 5 April, 'it would be difficult for Germany to tackle Roumania directly. He thought that if Herr Hitler had designs on Roumania he would be likely to work through Hungary.'[1]

Nor was the Anglo-Polish agreement made contingent on Polish willingness to accept help from Russia. The terms of the final agreement were as follows:

> (a) If Germany attacks Poland His Majesty's Government in the United Kingdom will at once come to the help of Poland.
> (b) If Germany attempts to undermine the independence of Poland by

[1] Cab. Minutes, 5 Apr. 1939, CAB 23/98.

processes of economic penetration or in any other way, His Majesty's Government in the United Kingdom will support Poland in resistance to such attempts. If Germany then attacks Poland, the provisions of paragraph (a) above will apply. In the event of other action by Germany which clearly threatened Polish independence, and was of such a nature that the Polish Government considered it vital to resist it with their national forces, His Majesty's Government would at once come to the help of Poland.

(c) Reciprocally, Poland gives corresponding assurances to the United Kingdom.

(d) It is understood that the Polish Government and His Majesty's Government in the United Kingdom will keep each other fully and promptly informed of any developments threatening the independence of either country.[1]

There was no express mention of Danzig. As Roger Makins, of the Foreign Office Central Department, recognized,

Danzig may become a test case in resistance to German expansion. We are encouraging Poland to resist German demands, and in view of the importance to Poland, as much psychological as material, of the international status of the Free City, we may be forced to support Polish rights in Danzig.[2]

This was a further criticism that was soon voiced: that the British guarantee allowed Colonel Beck to adopt a 'non-possumus' attitude in the negotiations with Germany. The criticism became particularly acute when on 28 April Hitler for the first time published the terms on which he was prepared to come to an agreement with Poland.[3] They were widely recognized as mild, partly because he did not announce that they included Polish accession to the Anti-Comintern Pact, although of course the British Government were aware of this fact.

Sir Nevile Henderson, the British Ambassador in Berlin, was thoroughly upset. He wrote to Chamberlain's 'Chief Industrial' Adviser, Sir Horace Wilson:

I would have been far more uneasy over the March 31st guarantee to Poland had I been aware at the time of the Beck–Hitler negotiations. I

---

[1] Record of Anglo-Polish Conversations, Summary of Conclusions, 6 Apr. 1939, *DBFP* v, no. 16.

[2] Minute by Makins, 30 Mar. 1939, C4860/54/18 (FO 371/23016).

[3] Norman H. Baynes, ed., *The Speeches of Adolf Hitler, April 1922–August 1939* (London, 1942), ii. 1631.

fully appreciated the absolute necessity of letting Germany know quite clearly that we would not again sit by with folded hands and let her swallow up one country after another. It is true that I did not envisage the mention of specific countries, but at least the Polish guarantee seemed to afford Poland a chance of negotiating as equals a fair settlement of the Danzig case with Germany. I must equally admit that I regard Hitler's proposals as a fair basis of negotiation and in my innermost heart I regard the Poles as exceedingly unwise to make enemies of Germany and as dangerous allies for us. The Prague coup has affected our whole outlook towards Hitler but it has not altered the merits of the Danzig-Corridor case in themselves. I may be wrong but I am personally convinced that there can be no permanent peace in Europe until Danzig has reverted to Germany. The Poles cannot be master of the 400,000 Germans in Danzig—ergo Germany must be. I am sorry that I feel that way, but I fear that we are again on a bad wicket as we were over the Sudeten.

By all means be firm and say 'No' to the Dictators: I am all for that on two conditions (a) that we have the force to back up our 'No' if need be, and (b) that we supplement it by the fair and just solution. Granted that the first condition is fulfilled, are we going to see or be able to insist that the second is?

It is my doubt as to the answer to the second which makes me pessimistic.[1]

Wilson, while pointing out that Britain was trying to pursue a balanced policy, assured Henderson that it was 'inevitable that we should have "firmed up" during the last two or three months and all my information goes to show that it has proved wise to have done so'. Chamberlain was being 'quite flat-footed about the Polish situation'.[2]

Unfortunately, so was Hitler. On 3 April, having denounced the British policy of encirclement, he ordered the armed forces to be ready to attack Poland 'at any time as from September 1, 1939'.[3] Hitler naturally expected continued intransigence on the part of the Poles, and whereas before he had insisted on the strategy of steady pressure and attrition, he now seriously and for the first time contemplated the military option. This was an entirely foreseeable result. The Chiefs of Staff certainly foresaw it, and the South Africans, who were thought to understand the German psyche rather

[1] Henderson to Wilson, 24 May 1939, PREM 1/331A.
[2] Wilson to Henderson, 12 May 1939, ibid.
[3] Directive by Keitel, Chief of Army High Command, 3 Apr. 1939, *DGFP* vi, no. 149.

AFTERMATH 215

well, had warned Britain on 23 March that a policy of anti-German coalition-building

will and can have no other result but that of war, not because Germany necessarily wants war, but because such [a] policy of encirclement cannot be taken by her as meaning anything else than a declaration of hostilities differing but little, if at all, from a declaration of war.

That Germany would be entitled to so interpret such a policy I do not think anybody will doubt, and initiation of any such policy by Great Britain and her friends would be sufficient to throw upon themselves the responsibility for any war that may ensue, while it is sure to alienate from them a great deal of sympathy which has been aroused by Hitler's treatment of Czechoslovakia.[1]

It has been argued that a further result of the guarantee to Poland was that it deprived Britain of any leverage in further negotiations with Russia, 'whose territory was effectively screened by Poland against any attack by Germany'.[2] But if this was true, and if it was considered as an implication at all, it certainly caused the British no concern. On 14 April Britain asked Russia to announce her intention of helping, 'in such a manner as would be found most convenient', any of her European neighbours who were prepared to resist. But the motive was not serious. Cadogan noted that it was 'to placate our left wing in England, rather than to obtain any solid military advantage'.[3]

On 18 April the Russians proposed a mutual assistance pact under the terms of which Britain, France, and Russia would be bound not only to help each other but also to help Russia's neighbours from the Baltic to the Black Sea. Such an agreement was not in Britain's interest, since she would be obliged to help Russia in case of a Russo-German conflict over Latvia, for example, whereas Russia would not be bound to help Britain in case of a German attack on Holland or Belgium.[4]

But this was not the decisive objection. 'What it really comes down to', wrote Cadogan on 19 April, 'is that we have to balance

---

[1] Message from General Hertzog, Prime Minister of South Africa, to the British Government, 23 Mar. 1939, C4496/15/18 (FO 371/22968).

[2] E. H. Carr, *Britain. A Study of Foreign Policy from the Versailles Treaty to the Outbreak of War* (London, 1939), p. 186.

[3] Minute by Cadogan, 19 Apr. 1939, C5460/15/18 (FO 371/22969).

[4] For a good discussion of Soviet motives at this time see Adam B. Ulam, *Expansion and Coexistence. The History of Soviet Foreign Policy 1917-67* (New York, 1968), pp. 261 ff.

the advantage of a paper commitment by Russia to join in a war on our side against the disadvantage of associating ourselves openly with Russia.' He concluded that since Britain was trying to build a 'peace front' in Europe, 'it seems, on balance, better to refuse an offer that may alienate our friends and reinforce the propaganda of our enemies without bringing in exchange any real material contribution to the strength of our Front'.[1] Nor did he seem unduly worried about the possibility of a Russo-German *rapprochement*. He accepted the risk but dismissed it as a 'very remote' possibility. Once again Chamberlain and Halifax accepted these arguments. They concluded that Britain's best tack would be to 'play for time'.[2] This was to become the keynote of the summer.

[1] Minute by Cadogan, 19 Apr. 1939, C5460/15/18 (FO 371/22969).
[2] FPC Minutes, 25 Apr. 1939, CAB 27/624.

11

CONCLUSION

As early as February 1934 the British Government recognized that in future Germany must be seen as the major long-term threat to Britain. Almost every year thereafter the Joint Planning Committee of the Committee of Imperial Defence produced a new edition of their *magnum opus*, 'Planning for War with Germany'.[1] Ever conscious of their weakness, the British attempted during the 1930s to negotiate an agreement with Germany that would restrict her expansion in Europe, but they found themselves constantly outmanœuvred by Hitler in his quest for the restoration of Germany's Great Power status. Thus it was that in October 1938 Sir Alexander Cadogan came to ask himself: 'Can we take the initiative? Can we make the Germans guess, and so reverse the process, under which we have suffered for years, of the Germans "keeping us guessing"?'[2] This pathetic plea had little to do with Britain's favourite policy of holding her cards close to her chest, but was a manifestation of the profound shock that Hitler had administered to British morale, confidence, and capacity for action.

Long used to the almost effortless exercise of power and influence, the British had forgotten how to husband their now dwindling resources, to supplement them with imagination and cunning in the face of increasing pressure not only from Germany but also from Japan, Italy, and even the United States. They never formulated a vigorous line of policy to cope with this situation. 'Appeasement', for example, in the pejorative sense of attempting to buy off a potential enemy, was never seriously tried. How, therefore, can it be argued that it never worked? Such a policy would have involved,

---

[1] Note by Sir Maurice Hankey, 26 Mar. 1938, DP(P)23, CAB 16/138A. A. J. P. Taylor has written that 'if therefore we were (wrongly) to judge political intentions from military plans, the British government would appear set on war with Germany, not the other way round. But of course we apply to the behaviour of our own governments a generosity of interpretation which we do not extend to others' (Taylor, *The Origins of the Second World War*, p. 13).

[2] Minute by Cadogan, 14 Oct. 1938, C14471/41/18 (FO 371/21659).

essentially, giving Japan a free hand in North China, Italy a free hand in Abyssinia, or Germany a free hand in Eastern Europe. The British tried for too long to hold on to a position they could no longer maintain, in the Far East in particular because they recognized the vital importance of keeping on the right side of the United States in case of trouble with Germany. At the same time Britain's vulnerability overseas increased the importance of friendship with Germany. But she was not prepared to pay the price.

Instead the British tried to tie Germany down to an agreement on their own terms that would guarantee their security and the European *status quo*. If Chamberlain held on for slightly longer than his advisers to the illusion that a *rapprochement* was possible on Britain's terms, it was because he was more obsessed by the economic benefits to be derived from European co-operation and by the consequences of failure. Meanwhile he accepted the Foreign Office policy of resisting German expansion in central and south-eastern Europe by economic means, a policy vigorously promoted by Halifax although regarded with scepticism by those inclined to accept the inevitability of German supremacy in the area.

The significance of these efforts, unsuccessful though they were, is that even the 'appeasers' were anxious to maintain the balance of power in Europe in 1938–9. The reasons given were traditional: as the Foreign Office reminded the Cabinet in May 1938 when proposing their policy of economic pressure, 'it has always been the traditional policy of His Majesty's Government to prevent one Power attaining a predominant position on the Continent'.[1] German predominance could affect Britain's interest in maintaining the independence of the Low Countries, and threaten her control of the Eastern Mediterranean, essential to the security of her Middle Eastern line of communications. It could also negate the effects of Britain's main strategic weapon, the economic blockade, which aimed to deny Germany access to essential imports.

The Government's failure to contain Germany by peaceful means resulted in the commitment to go to war to prevent her from reaching full strength. It was the natural corollary of previous British policy, and by March 1939 the only real alternative to Britain's relegation to second class status. As Halifax described this dilemma to the Foreign Policy Committee, the choice was between 'doing

[1] Memorandum by Halifax, 'British Influence in Central and South-Eastern Europe', 24 May 1938, CP 127(38), CAB 24/277.

CONCLUSION 219

nothing', which would mean 'a great accession to Germany's strength and a great loss to ourselves of sympathy and support', and 'entering into a devastating war'. He preferred the latter course.[1] Thus the guarantee to Poland was never really thought of in terms of deterrence; it was regarded as a deliberate challenge. That it would be provocative to Germany and cause Polish intransigence on the questions at issue between the two countries, thereby increasing the probability of war, was expected. As Halifax had written in November 1938 when considering the means available to prevent Germany from realizing her ambitions in central and south-eastern Europe, 'power politics, i.e., alliances, military conventions, close understandings etc. ... is a possible policy but it almost certainly leads directly to war'.[2]

As we have seen, what finally convinced the British Government that this policy had to be adopted was the fear that Poland might give in to pressure from Germany to remain neutral in return for some acceptable solution of the Danzig problem. The British had to prevent this eventuality because they considered that it would be detrimental to their interests; so detrimental, in fact, that they were prepared to risk a war to prevent it. Such an agreement, coming in the wake of a long string of German successes culminating in the occupation of Prague, the annexation of Memel, and treaties with Slovakia and Rumania, would represent a further blow to Britain's prestige and influence and seriously undermine her power to organize resistance against Germany in the future. Furthermore, it would mean the loss of the eastern front which strategically was essential in a war with Germany. These were the options which the Foreign Office had all along been trying to keep open. Rather than accept their foreclosure, the British preferred to go to war.

Of course it was recognized that the ideal 'long and durable' eastern front was a combination of Poland and the Soviet Union. But the Russians were considered unreliable allies. Unless directly threatened

[1] See above, pp. 152–3.
[2] Memorandum by Halifax, 'Central and South-Eastern Europe', 10 Nov. 1938, CP 257(38), CAB 24/280. Cf. Robert Skidelsky: 'It is easy to read back the idea of deterrence into a pre-nuclear age. Few people at the time thought that such a 'Balance-of-Power policy' was a peace policy. How could they? It had always led to war in the past. The central fact which emerges from four hundred years of European history is that there was no system of deterrence capable of stopping a hegemonic bid by a determined power. No Grand Alliances had ever been formed in advance of such a bid: they only crystallised after the bid had started. Nor did Churchill ever really think that his policy would stop war' (Skidelsky, *Encounter*, 39, no. 1, p. 64).

they would never attack Germany, and they were obviously hoping that she would destroy herself in battle with the West. Furthermore, there was plenty of evidence that even if she wanted to, Russia would find it hard to bring forceful pressure to bear on Germany. But above all, the assistance of the Soviet Union entailed the westward spread of her power, which the British no less than other European Governments were reluctant to sanction. The Eastern Europeans in particular showed a distinct preference for German tutelage when faced with the prospect of Russian troops venturing beyond their own borders. The fear that a British association with Russia might be widely used as a pretext for abandoning Britain and France to face Germany alone was more than enough to sway the British decision in favour of Poland. At any rate it was a gamble which they felt had to be taken. The demonstration that Poland could be won for Britain might arrest the slide towards Germany that was gathering such rapid momentum. At the time, not even Churchill quarrelled with this appreciation.

What was the alternative? To insist on Russian participation at the outset, it was feared, might throw Poland into Germany's arms, thereby creating a buffer state between Germany and Russia—a zone of benevolent neutrality as wide as Germany herself—with no hope of a Russian challenge in the future and ensuring freedom of action for Hitler in the West. But the position of German hegemony that this implied was precisely what the British 'peace front' was supposed to prevent. Furthermore this extension of German power would once again have been accomplished overnight and without a struggle—another 'bloodless victory', as Halifax might have put it. On the other hand a Polish commitment against Germany would almost certainly result in open conflict between the two countries, leaving Germany victorious and Russia threatened, while reducing the pressure on the West and creating the prospect of a more viable eastern front. The problem was that the Poles would never commit themselves against Germany without a commitment from Britain. It was ironic that this meant a promise to uphold the *status quo* in Danzig, the most volatile spot in Europe. For the British had always considered it to represent one of the strongest cases for revision in favour of Germany.

It seems reasonable to argue that in choosing the path that they did in March 1939, the British Government took upon themselves a certain measure of responsibility for the conflict that ensued. They were fully aware of the probable consequences of their decision. The guarantee reduced the likelihood of a settlement between Germany and Poland and increased the probability of a clash between them. It is hardly acceptable to argue that Beck would have been intransigent anyway, even admitting that his attitude towards Hitler's hitherto rather polite initiatives had been firm all along. For we simply cannot predict how Polish policy would have evolved without the guarantee. What we do know is that there was no agreement over Danzig and that the issue resulted in war.

Nor does it seem valid to object that Britain was merely defending her independence against the German threat, and that the idea of 'responsibility' is best reserved for those who threaten the independence of states rather than for those who defend it. In the first place, it may be misguided even to attempt to make a distinction between wars of 'aggression' and wars of 'defence'. Indeed, if we accept that political adjustment to take account of changing power relationships is both necessary and desirable, then, as E. H. Carr has argued, 'the use or threatened use of force to maintain the *status quo* may be morally more culpable than the use or threatened use of force to alter it'.[1]

In the second place, even if we accept that the distinction between 'aggressive' and 'defensive' wars should be made, it is seldom possible in practice to do so with clear-cut precision. It is certainly arguable, for instance, that German hegemony in central and south-eastern Europe did not represent a threat to Britain's independence. Halifax had to counter such thinking in the Cabinet, and Cadogan always had his doubts.[2] In any case, even on the worst interpretation, the threat was only a contingent one and did not arise mechanically or necessarily from the mere fact of a shift in the European balance.

This brings us back to the question, on which much work remains to be done, of Hitler's intentions towards Britain. It is clear that the Foreign Office assessment changed radically during 1938–9 from willingness to believe in Hitler's peaceful assurances to the belief that 'what he would like best, if he could do it, would be to smash the British Empire'.[3] This was certainly a misinterpretation of Hitler's ideal, and reflected the failure of British policy-makers to stand up to the 'war of nerves' of January and February. It is true that the tone of Hitler's policy had become increasingly anti-British, but he

[1] E. H. Carr, *The Twenty Years' Crisis, 1919–1939* (London, 1939), pp. 264–5.
[2] See above, pp. 43 and 149. [3] See above, p. 85.

had not yet adopted a position of outright hostility—nor did he do so until well after the war had begun. What Hitler wanted was an alliance with Britain on his own terms, which would enable him to pursue his Eastern European plans without interference.[1] If the British would not agree, then they would have to be held 'politically and militarily in check' by the demonstration of Germany's military might and political determination.[2] There is too little certainty about Hitler's long-term intentions, which were in any case visionary, ill-defined, and inconsistent, to say conclusively whether the period of overseas expansion envisaged as the next stage of his programme was to be carried out in alliance with Britain or in opposition to her. That would no doubt depend on Britain herself. As we have seen, however, opposition even to Hitler's short-term aims was one of the principal characteristics of British foreign policy in the 1930s, including the years of 'appeasement'.

[1] Bullock, *Hitler*, pp. 307–8; cf. Klaus Hildebrand, *The Foreign Policy of the Third Reich*, trans. Anthony Fothergill (London, 1973), p. 52.
[2] Ibid.

APPENDIX

THE DOUBLING OF THE TERRITORIAL ARMY ON 29 MARCH 1939

IF the guarantee of Poland was not a last-minute improvization, the proposal to double the Territorial Army certainly was. It provides an interesting case study of how important decisions could be made in this hectic period without proper consideration of their implications. It also gives us a glimpse into the workings of the Prime Minister's Office and in particular into the role of Chamberlain's closest personal adviser, Sir Horace Wilson.

In a speech on 25 March 1939 the Director-General of the Territorial Army, General Sir Walter Kirke, referred to the 'spring tide' of new recruits. Yet there were reports that in some areas recruits were being turned away because complements were already full. Neville Chamberlain, who was due to address the Conservative 1922 Committee dinner at the House of Commons on 28 March, was forewarned that 'many of those present will wish him to say something about the greater use of the Territorial movement and especially to say what it is proposed to do to take advantage of the recent flow of Territorial recruits'.[1] That day Sir Horace Wilson suggested the possibility of forming new or 'Voluntary Training Corps' units, and asked Leslie Hore-Belisha, Secretary of State for War, to give Chamberlain his comments 'as early as possible this afternoon, so that he may consider what line to take this evening'.[1]

At lunch with Wilson that day, Hore-Belisha suggested some form of conscription as an alternative, but Wilson objected that the Trade Unions would oppose it. Chamberlain raised the same objection when Hore-Belisha saw him at the House of Commons in the early afternoon. On the other hand

> Halifax was insistent that some forthright action should be taken as immediate evidence that we meant business in resisting aggression. An

---

[1] Wilson to Hore-Belisha, 28 Mar. 1939, in Minney, ed., *The Private Papers of Hore-Belisha*, p. 186.

announcement of a bigger military effort on our part would be the most convincing gesture we could make in the present international tension.[1]

Chamberlain advised Hore-Belisha to stick to the Territorials. Hore-Belisha suggested the simple expedient of doubling their size by over-recruiting in every unit and then splitting each unit in two. Chamberlain 'liked the idea', but it was a step that required Cabinet and Treasury approval.

Hore-Belisha wanted the Treasury's approval quickly so as to be able to announce the proposal after the Cabinet meeting the next day, 29 March. Wilson promised him that 'if he would send across a note of his proposals I would get into touch with the Treasury'.[2] Wilson asked the Permanent Under-Secretary, Sir Richard Hopkins, to talk to Sir John Simon, the Chancellor of the Exchequer. Chamberlain authorized Wilson to represent him at this Treasury conclave.

The Treasury disliked the idea. It involved finding 170,000 men in addition to the 250,000 already required to fill existing shortages in all branches of the Services. There was little prospect of finding them quickly, and the increased deficiency on paper would provide an additional argument for conscription.[3] As Hore-Belisha himself had said, a 'real recruiting campaign' would be needed.[4] Secondly, 'the effect of throwing this enormous burden upon industry . . . must be to retard production. It can hardly be done without interfering with export trade.'[5] Thirdly, the effect on Hitler would be doubtful: 'Must he not realise that its immediate military value is nil, and that it can have no effective value for at least a year or 18 months?' The Treasury summed up their objections:

> This plan has been invented in the space of a few hours. It cannot be related to anything in particular, and must, prima facie, be full of flaws which will reveal themselves in the course of time.
>
> Heretofore the emphasis has been laid on the Air Force as the deterrent to aggression. This new proposal in which neither Navy nor Air [Force] appears is an important new step towards a commitment to fight the next war, like the last, in the trenches of France.

[1] Diary, 28 Mar. 1939, Minney, ed., *The Private Papers of Hore-Belisha*, p. 187.
[2] Memorandum by Wilson, 29 Mar. 1939, PREM 1/296.
[3] Unsigned memorandum, 'Proposal to double the Territorial Field Army', n.d.: in an accompanying memorandum, Wilson refers to this as a Treasury memorandum written on 28 Mar. 1939 (ibid.).
[4] Hore-Belisha to Wilson, 28 Mar. 1939, ibid.
[5] Treasury memorandum, n.d.

DOUBLING OF THE TERRITORIAL ARMY 225

Not for the first time the need for some plan which will augment the immediate strength of the country is lacking, and its place is taken by something which may become effective in a distant future.

The most serious question seems to be whether this vast number of new men can be obtained or whether the plan will merely prove a trap making conscription the less avoidable later on.

Although in the main the money cannot be spent at once, it will be a very formidable addition to the burden on our resources in subsequent years.

Sir John Simon agreed to the proposal, however, saying that the question 'must necessarily be looked at from a wider point of view than that of the Exchequer'.[1] Chamberlain revealed to the Cabinet on 29 March that he personally favoured compulsory national service, but was afraid to 'negate all the advances he had already made in respect of Labour's help in production increases'. Halifax thought the proposal utterly insufficient.[2] Chamberlain's apprehension was justified. When the announcement was made that day in the House of Commons, Labour wanted an assurance, which was given, that the Government intended 'to uphold the voluntary system as against conscription'.[3]

The Treasury was right. There was no inherent rhyme or reason in the doubling of the Territorial Army, and there is no evidence that it impressed anybody. It threw the plans for the existing army expeditionary force out of balance. It reduced the ratio of armoured to infantry divisions and diverted essential supplies. The most urgent need was the 'quick completion of the existing programme'.[4] But the decision to double the Territorial Army reveals Sir Horace Wilson in his true light: the ultimate civil servant, with long experience as such, able to establish immediate and sympathetic contact with his friends in the Departments of Whitehall. He had become 'an institution, for good or evil', wrote Cadogan in later years, 'but there he was, like the wind and the rain, and I came to the conclusion that we must make the best of him. . . . I did not, and do not, regret my attempt at co-operation with him.'[5]

[1] Memorandum by Wilson, 29 Mar. 1939.
[2] Cab. Minutes, 29 Mar. 1939, CAB 23/98.
[3] 345 HC Deb., 5 s., col. 2049.
[4] Liddell Hart, *Memoirs*, ii. 229.
[5] Cadogan to Templewood, 26 Oct. 1951, Templewood Papers, XIX (C): 12.

BIBLIOGRAPHY

I. PRIMARY SOURCES

1. UNPUBLISHED MATERIAL

British Government Archives (Public Record Office, London).
Hickleton Papers (Garrowby, Yorkshire; Public Record Office, London).
Inskip Papers (Churchill College, Cambridge).
Margesson Papers (Churchill College, Cambridge).
Nicolson Papers (Balliol College, Oxford).
Templewood Papers (Cambridge University Library).
Vansittart Papers (Churchill College, Cambridge).

2. PUBLISHED MATERIAL

(a) *Documents*

France: Ministère des Affaires étrangères, *The French Yellow Book; Diplomatic Documents 1938–1939* (Reynal & Hitchcock, New York, 1940).

Germany: Auswärtiges Amt, *The German White Paper; Full Text of the Polish Documents Issued by the Berlin Foreign Office* (Howell, Soskin, & Co., New York, 1940).

—— *Documents on German Foreign Policy 1918–1945*, Series D (Government Printing Office, Washington, 1949–54), especially vols. 4, 5, and 6.

Great Britain: Foreign Office, *British and Foreign State Papers* (London, 1841–).

—— *Documents on British Foreign Policy 1919–1939*, Third Series, ed. E. L. Woodward, and Rohan Butler (H.M.S.O., London, 1949–55), especially vols. 2, 3, 4, 5, and 8.

Republic of Poland: Ministry for Foreign Affairs, *Official Documents Concerning Polish-German and Polish-Soviet Relations 1933–1939. The Polish White Book* (Hutchinson, London, 1940).

U.S.S.R.: Ministry of Foreign Affairs, *Documents and Materials Relating to the Eve of the Second World War*, i, *November 1937–1938*; ii, *The Dirksen Papers 1938–1939* (Foreign Languages Publishing House, Moscow, 1948).

United States: Department of State, *Foreign Relations of the United States, Diplomatic Papers, 1939*, vol. i (Government Printing Office, Washington, 1956).

BIBLIOGRAPHY

(b) *Newspapers and Periodicals*

The Times; *Manchester Guardian Weekly*; *Daily Mail*; *Observer*; *Spectator*; *New York Times*.

(c) *Parliamentary Debates*

Hansard

II. SECONDARY SOURCES

I. BOOKS

ALDCROFT, D. H., *The Inter-war Economy. Britain* (Columbia University Press, New York, 1970).

AMERY, LEO S., *My Political Life*, iii, *The Unforgiving Years, 1929–1940* (Hutchinson, London, 1955).

Anon. [Stanley Morison], *The History of The Times* (Printing House Square, London, 1952), iv.

ASHTON-GWATKIN, F. T. A., *The British Foreign Office* (Syracuse University Press, Syracuse, 1949).

ASTER, SIDNEY, *1939—The Making of the Second World War* (Deutsch, London, 1973).

ATTLEE, CLEMENT R., *As it Happened* (Heinemann, London, 1954).

AVON, LORD, *The Eden Memoirs*, i, *Facing the Dictators* (Cassell, London, 1962).

—— ii, *The Reckoning* (Cassell, London, 1965).

BARNETT, CORRELLI, *The Collapse of British Power* (William Morrow, New York, 1972).

BARRACLOUGH, GEOFFREY, *An Introduction to Contemporary History* (Penguin Books, Harmondsworth, 1967).

BASCH, ANTONIN, *The Danube Basin and the German Economic Sphere* (Columbia University Press, New York, 1943).

BAYNES, NORMAN H., ed., *The Speeches of Adolf Hitler, April 1922–August 1939* (Oxford University Press, London, 1942).

BECK, JOZEF, *Final Report* (Robert Speller, New York, 1957).

BELOFF, MAX, *Imperial Sunset*, i, *Britain's Liberal Empire, 1897–1921* (Methuen, London, 1969).

BENEŠ, EDUARD, *Memoirs; From Munich to New War and New Victory*, trans. Godfrey Lias (Allen and Unwin, London, 1954).

BENNETT, EDWARD W., *Germany and the Diplomacy of the Financial Crisis, 1931* (Harvard University Press, Cambridge, Mass., 1962).

BENOIST-MÉCHIN, BARON, *Histoire de l'armée allemande*, vi, *Le Défi, 1939* (A. Michel, Paris, 1968).

BIRKENHEAD, LORD, *Halifax: The Life of Lord Halifax* (Hamish Hamilton, London, 1965).

BISHOP, DONALD G., *The Administration of British Foreign Relations* (Syracuse University Press, Syracuse, 1962).

BOND, BRIAN, ed., *Chief of Staff: The Diaries of Major-General Sir Henry Pownall* (Archon, Hamden, Conn., 1973).

BONNET, GEORGES, *De Munich à la guerre, défense de la paix*, 2nd edn. (Plon, Paris, 1967).

BOOTHBY, ROBERT, *I Fight to Live* (Gollancz, London, 1947).

BUDUROWYCZ, BOHDAN B., *Polish-Soviet Relations 1932–1939* (Columbia University Press, New York, 1963).

BULLOCK, A., *Hitler: A Study in Tyranny* (Odhams, London, 1952).

BURCKHARDT, CARL J., *Meine Danziger Mission 1937–1939* (Fretz & Wesmuth Verlag, Zürich, 1960).

BUTLER, EWAN, *Mason-Mac. The Life of Lieutenant-General Sir Noel Mason MacFarlane* (Macmillan, London, 1972).

BUTLER, LORD, *The Art of the Possible* (Hamish Hamilton, London, 1971).

CARR, E. H., *Britain. A Study of Foreign Policy from the Versailles Treaty to the Outbreak of War* (Longmans, Green, London, 1939).

—— *The Twenty Years' Crisis, 1919–1939* (Macmillan, London, 1939).

CHAMBERLAIN, NEVILLE, *In Search of Peace* (Putnam's Sons, New York, 1939).

CHATFIELD, LORD, *It Might Happen Again*, ii, *The Navy and Defence* (Heinemann, London, 1947).

CHESTER, D. N., and WILLSON, F. M. G., *The Organization of British Central Government, 1914–1956* (Allen & Unwin, London, 1957).

CHILD, F. C., *The Theory and Practice of Exchange Control in Germany; a Study of Monopolistic Exploitation in International Markets* (M. Nijhoff, The Hague, 1958).

CHURCHILL, WINSTON, *The Second World War*, i, *The Gathering Storm* (Cassell, London, 1948).

CIENCIALA, ANNA M., *Poland and the Western Powers 1938–1939, A Study in the Interdependence of Eastern and Western Europe* (Routledge & Kegan Paul, London, 1968).

COLLIER, BASIL, *The Defence of the United Kingdom* (H.M.S.O., London, 1957).

COLVIN, IAN, *Vansittart in Office. An Historical Survey of the Origins of the Second World War Based on the Papers of Sir Robert Vansittart* (Gollancz, London, 1965).

—— *The Chamberlain Cabinet* (Taplinger Publishing Co., New York, 1971).

BIBLIOGRAPHY

CONNELL, JOHN (pseud. Robertson, John Henry), *The 'Office': A Study of British Foreign Policy and its Makers 1919–1951* (Allan Wingate, London, 1958).

COOPER, A. DUFF, *Old Men Forget: The Autobiography of Duff Cooper (Viscount Norwich)* (Rupert Hart-Davis, London, 1954).

COOTE, COLIN, *A Companion of Honour* (Collins, London, 1965).

CRAIG, GORDON A., and GILBERT, FELIX, eds., *The Diplomats 1919–1939* (Princeton University Press, Princeton, 1953).

DALTON, HUGH, *The Fateful Years. Memoirs 1931–1945* (Frederick Muller, London, 1957).

DENNIS, PETER J., *Decision by Default. Peacetime Conscription and British Defence 1919–39* (Duke University Press, Durham, N.C., 1972).

DILKS, DAVID, ed., *The Diaries of Sir Alexander Cadogan, O.M. 1938–1945* (Cassell, London, 1971).

DIRKSEN, HERBERT VON, *Moscow, Tokyo, London; Twenty Years of German Foreign Policy* (University of Oklahoma Press, Norman, 1952).

EINZIG, PAUL, *Exchange Control* (Macmillan, London, 1934).

—— *The Exchange Clearing System* (Macmillan, London, 1935).

—— *Bloodless Invasion: German Economic Penetration into the Danubian States and the Balkans*, 2nd edn. (Duckworth, London, 1939).

—— *Appeasement Before, During and After the War* (Macmillan, London, 1942).

ELLIS, H. S., *Exchange Control in Central Europe* (Harvard University Press, Cambridge, Mass., 1941).

EUBANK, KEITH, *Munich* (University of Oklahoma Press, Norman, 1963).

FEILING, KEITH, *The Life of Neville Chamberlain* (Macmillan, London, 1946).

GAFENCU, GRIGORE, *Last Days of Europe, a Diplomatic Journey in 1939*, trans. E. Fletcher-Allen (Yale University Press, New Haven, Conn., 1948).

GANNON, FRANKLIN REID, *The British Press and Germany 1936–1939* (Clarendon Press, Oxford, 1971).

GEORGE, MARGARET, *The Warped Vision: British Foreign Policy 1933–1939* (University of Pittsburgh Press, Pittsburgh, 1965).

GIBSON, H., ed., *The Ciano Diaries, 1939–1943* (Doubleday & Co., Garden City, N.Y., 1946).

GILBERT, MARTIN, *The Roots of Appeasement* (Weidenfeld & Nicolson, London, 1967).

—— and GOTT, R., *The Appeasers* (Weidenfeld & Nicolson, London, 1963).

BIBLIOGRAPHY

GLADWYN, LORD, *The Memoirs of Lord Gladwyn* (Weidenfeld & Nicolson, London, 1972).

GLASER, KURT, *Der zweite Weltkrieg und die Kriegsschuldfrage: die Hoggan-Kontroverse* (Marienburg-Verlag, Würzburg, 1965).

GRAML, H., et al., *The German Resistance to Hitler* (University of California Press, Berkeley, 1970).

Great Britain, Public Record Office, *The Records of the Foreign Office 1782–1939* (H.M.S.O., London, 1969).

HALIFAX, LORD, *Speeches on Foreign Policy*, ed. H. H. E. Craster (Oxford University Press, London, 1940).

—— *Fullness of Days* (Dodd, Mead, & Co., New York, 1957).

HANCOCK, W. K., and GOWING, M. M., *British War Economy* (H.M.S.O., London, 1949).

HARVEY, JOHN, ed., *The Diplomatic Diaries of Oliver Harvey, 1937–40* (Collins, London, 1970).

HENDERSON, SIR NEVILE, *Failure of a Mission* (Hodder & Stoughton, London, 1940).

HEUSTON, R. F. V., *Lives of the Lord Chancellors 1885–1940* (Clarendon Press, Oxford, 1964).

HILDEBRAND, KLAUS, *Vom Reich zum Weltreich. Hitler, NSDAP und Kolonial Frage 1919–1945* (Wilhelm Fink Verlag, Munich, 1969).

—— *The Foreign Policy of the Third Reich*, trans. Anthony Fothergill (B. T. Batsford, Ltd., London, 1973).

HILLGRUBER, ANDREAS, *Hitler, König Carol und Marschall Antonescu. Die deutsch-rumänischen Beziehungen 1938–44* (Franz Steiner Verlag, Wiesbaden, 1954).

HOENSCH, J. K., *Die Slowakei und Hitlers Ostpolitik* (Böhlau Verlag, Köln, 1965).

HOFER, WALTHER, *War Premeditated*, trans. Stanley Godman (Thames & Hudson, London, 1955).

HOGGAN, DAVID L., *Der erzwungene Krieg; Die Ursachen und Urheber des 2. Weltkriegs* (Verlag der Deutschen Hochschullehrer-Zeitung, Tübingen, 1964).

HOWARD, MICHAEL, *The Continental Commitment. The Dilemma of British Defence Policy in the Era of the Two World Wars* (Temple Smith, London, 1972).

HULL, CORDELL, *The Memoirs of Cordell Hull* (Macmillan, New York, 1948).

IRVING, DAVID, ed., *Breach of Security. The German Secret Intelligence File on Events Leading to the Second World War* (William Kimber, London, 1968).

BIBLIOGRAPHY

JAMES, ROBERT RHODES, ed., *Chips. The Diaries of Sir Henry Channon* (Weidenfeld & Nicolson, London, 1967).

—— *Churchill: A Study in Failure, 1900–1939* (Weidenfeld & Nicolson, London, 1970).

JEDRZEJEWICZ, WACLAW, ed., *Diplomat in Berlin 1933–1939. Papers and Memoirs of Jozef Lipski, Ambassador of Poland.* (Columbia University Press, New York, 1968).

——*Diplomat in Paris 1936–1939. Papers and Memoirs of Juliusz Lukasiewicz, Ambassador of Poland.* (Columbia University Press, New York, 1970).

JOHNSON, ALAN CAMPBELL, *Viscount Halifax* (Ives Washburn, New York, 1941).

JOHNSON, F. A., *Defence by Committee: The British Committee of Imperial Defence* (Oxford University Press, London, 1960).

JONES, THOMAS, *A Diary with Letters, 1931–1950* (Oxford University Press, London, 1954).

JORDAN, W. M., *Great Britain, France and the German Problem* (Oxford University Press, London, 1943).

KENNEDY, JOHN F., *Why England Slept* (Wilfred Funk, New York, 1940).

KENNEDY, M. D., *The Estrangement of Great Britain and Japan 1917–35* (University of California Press, Berkeley, 1969).

KIRKPATRICK, IVONE, *The Inner Circle. Memoirs* (Macmillan, London, 1959).

KLEIN, BURTON, *Germany's Economic Preparations for War* (Harvard University Press, Cambridge, Mass., 1959).

KORDT, ERICH, *Wahn und Wirklichkeit. Die Aussenpolitik des Dritten Reiches. Versuch einer Darstellung* (Union Deutsche Verlagsgesellschaft, Stuttgart, 1948).

—— *Nicht aus den Akten. Die Wilhelmstrasse in Frieden und Krieg. Erlebnisse, Begegnungen und Eindrücke 1928–1945* (Union Deutsche Verlagsgesellschaft, Stuttgart, 1950).

LANGER, W. L., and GLEASON, S. E., *The Challenge to Isolation 1937–40* (Harper for the Council on Foreign Relations, New York, 1952).

League of Nations, *Enquiry into Clearing Agreements* (Geneva, 1935).

—— *Report on Exchange Control* (Geneva, 1938).

—— *Commercial Policies in the Inter-war Period* (Geneva, 1942).

LEE, BRADFORD A., *Britain and the Sino-Japanese War, 1937–1939: A Study in the Dilemmas of British Decline* (Stanford University Press, Stanford, 1973).

LEITH-ROSS, SIR FREDERICK, *Money Talks: Fifty Years of International*

BIBLIOGRAPHY

Finance: The Autobiography of Sir Frederick Leith-Ross (Hutchinson, London, 1968).
LEWIS, W. ARTHUR, *Economic Survey 1919–1939* (Allen & Unwin, London, 1949).
LIDDELL HART, B. H., *The Defence of Britain* (Faber & Faber, London, 1939).
—— *Memoirs*, 2 vols. (Cassell, London, 1965–6).
—— *History of the Second World War* (Putnam, New York, 1971).
LOUIS, W. ROGER, *British Strategy in the Far East 1919–1939* (Clarendon Press, Oxford, 1971).
—— ed., *The Origins of the Second World War: A. J. P. Taylor and his Critics* (John Wiley, New York, 1972).
LUKACS, J. A., *The Great Powers and Eastern Europe* (American Book Co., New York, 1953).
LUZA, RADOMIR, *The Transfer of the Sudeten Germans: a Study of Czech-German Relations 1933–1962* (New York University Press, New York, 1964).
MACARTNEY, C. A., and PALMER, A. W., *Independent Eastern Europe* (Macmillan, London, 1962).
McKENZIE, V., *Here Lies Goebbels* (Michael Joseph, London, 1940).
McLACHLAN, DONALD H., *Room 39* (Athenaeum, New York, 1968).
—— *In the Chair. Barrington-Ward of The Times 1927–1948* (Weidenfeld & Nicolson, London, 1970).
MACLEOD, IAN, *Neville Chamberlain* (Muller, London, 1961).
MACLEOD, RODERICK, and KELLY, DENIS, eds., *Time Unguarded: The Ironside Diaries 1937–1940* (McKay, New York, 1962).
MACMILLAN, HAROLD, *Winds of Change, 1914–1939* (Macmillan, London, 1966).
MAISKY, IVAN, *Who Helped Hitler?*, trans. Andrew Rothstein (Hutchinson, London, 1964).
MANSERGH, NICHOLAS, *Survey of British Commonwealth Affairs, Problems of External Policy, 1931–1939* (Oxford University Press, London, 1952).
MASTNY, VOJTECH, *The Czechs under Nazi Rule. The Failure of National Resistance, 1939–1942* (Columbia University Press, New York, 1971).
MAUGHAM, VISCOUNT, *At the End of the Day* (Heinemann, London, 1954).
MEDLICOTT, W. N., *The Economic Blockade*, 2 vols. (H.M.S.O., London, 1952).
—— *The Coming of War in 1939* (Routledge & Kegan Paul, London, 1963).
—— *Contemporary England* (McKay, New York, 1967).
—— *British Foreign Policy Since Versailles, 1919–1963*, 2nd rev. edn. (Methuen, London, 1968).

MEDLICOTT, W. N., *Britain and Germany: The Search for Agreement 1930–1937* (Athlone Press, London, 1969).

MIDDLEMAS, KEITH, *Diplomacy of Illusion. The British Government and Germany, 1937–39* (Weidenfeld & Nicolson, London, 1972).

—— and BARNES, A. J. L., *Baldwin* (Macmillan, London, 1969).

MINNEY, R. J., ed., *The Private Papers of Hore-Belisha* (Collins, London, 1960).

MOSLEY, LEONARD, *On Borrowed Time* (Random House, New York, 1969).

MOWAT, CHARLES LOCH, *Britain Between the Wars 1918–1940* (Methuen, London, 1955).

NAMIER, SIR LEWIS, *Diplomatic Prelude 1938–1939* (Macmillan, London, 1948).

—— *Europe in Decay 1936–1940* (Macmillan, London, 1950).

NEUMANN, FRANZ L., *Behemoth. The Structure and Practice of National Socialism* (Harper & Row, New York, 1966).

NICOLL, PETER H., *Britain's Blunder* (privately printed, London?, 1953).

—— *Englands Krieg Gegen Deutschland. Die Ursachen, Methoden und Folgen des zweiten Weltkriegs* (Verlag der Deutschen Hochschullehrer-Zeitung, Tübingen, 1963).

NICOLSON, NIGEL, ed., *Harold Nicolson. Diaries and Letters 1930–1939* (Collins, London, 1966).

NISH, IAN H., *Alliance in Decline. A Study of Anglo-Japanese Relations 1908–23* (Athlone Press, London, 1972).

NOËL, LÉON, *L'Agression allemande contre la Pologne* (Flammarion, Paris, 1946).

NORTHEDGE, F. S., *The Troubled Giant: Britain Among the Great Powers, 1916–1939* (Bell, London, 1966).

O'NEILL, ROBERT J., *The German Army and the Nazi Party, 1933–1939* (Cassell, London, 1966).

PETRIE, SIR CHARLES, *The Chamberlain Tradition* (Dickson, London, 1938).

Political and Economic Planning, *Economic Development in S.E. Europe* (P.E.P., London, 1945).

POSTAN, M. M., *British War Production* (H.M.S.O., London, 1952).

RACZYNSKI, COUNT EDWARD, *The British-Polish Alliance. Its Origin and Meaning* (General Sikorski Historical Institute, London, 1948).

—— *In Allied London* (Weidenfeld & Nicolson, London, 1962).

RAUSCHNING, HERMANN, *The Revolution of Nihilism; Warning to the West*, trans. E. W. Dickes (Longmans, Green, London, 1939).

REYNOLDS, P. A., *British Foreign Policy in the Inter-War Years* (Longmans, Green, London, 1954).

RIBBENTROP, JOACHIM VON, *The Ribbentrop Memoirs*, trans. Oliver Watson (Weidenfeld & Nicolson, London, 1954).

RICHARDSON, H. W., *Economic Recovery in Britain, 1932–9* (Weidenfeld & Nicolson, London, 1967).

RITTER, GERHARD, *The German Resistance, Carl Goerderler's Struggle Against Tyranny*, abridged and trans. by R. T. Clark (Allen & Unwin, London, 1958).

ROBBINS, KEITH, *Munich 1938* (Cassell, London, 1968).

ROBERTSON, E. M., *Hitler's Pre-War Policy and Military Plans 1933–1939* (Longmans, Green, London, 1963).

—— ed., *The Origins of the Second World War* (Macmillan, London, 1971).

ROCK, WILLIAM R., *Appeasement on Trial: British Foreign Policy and its Critics, 1938–1939* (Archon Books, Hamden, Conn., 1966).

—— *Neville Chamberlain* (Twayne, New York, 1969).

ROSKILL, S. W., *Naval Policy Between the Wars* (Collins, London, 1968).

ROWSE, A. L., *All Souls and Appeasement: A Contribution to Contemporary History* (Macmillan, London, 1961).

Royal Institute of International Affairs, *Political and Strategic Interests of the United Kingdom. An Outline* (Oxford University Press, London, 1939).

—— *South-Eastern Europe. A Political and Economic Survey* (Oxford University Press, London, 1939).

—— *Survey of International Affairs*, 1938, ed. A. J. Toynbee, i (Oxford University Press, London, 1941).

SALTER, ARTHUR, *Personality in Politics: Studies of Contemporary Statesmen* (Faber & Faber, London, 1947).

SCHACHT, HJALMAR, *Account Settled*, trans. Edward Fitzgerald (Weidenfeld & Nicolson, London, 1949).

SCHMIDT, P., *Hitler's Interpreter*, trans. R. H. C. Steed (Macmillan, New York, 1951).

SEABURY, PAUL, *The Wilhelmstrasse: A Study of German Diplomats under the Nazi Regime* (University of California Press, Berkeley, 1954).

SELBY, SIR WALFORD, *Diplomatic Twilight 1930–1940* (John Murray, London, 1953).

SETON-WATSON, R. W., *From Munich to Danzig* (Methuen, London, 1939).

SIMON, LORD, *Retrospect: The Memoirs of the Rt. Hon. Viscount Simon, GCSI, GCVO* (Hutchinson, London, 1952).

SLESSOR, JOHN, *The Central Blue: The Autobiography of Sir John Slessor, Marshal of the RAF* (Cassell, London, 1956).

SPEER, ALBERT, *Inside the Third Reich* (Macmillan, New York, 1970).

SPIER, EUGEN, *Focus: A Footnote to the History of the Thirties* (Oswald Wolff, London, 1963).

STRANG, LORD, *The Foreign Office* (Allen & Unwin, London, 1955).

—— *Home and Abroad* (Deutsch, London, 1956).

—— *Britain in World Affairs: A Survey of the Fluctuations in British Power and Influence, Henry VIII to Elizabeth II* (Deutsch & Faber, London, 1961).

—— *The Diplomatic Career* (Deutsch, London, 1962).

STRONG, SIR K., *Men of Intelligence: a Study of the Roles and Decisions of Chiefs of Intelligence from World War I to the Present Day* (Cassell, London, 1970).

SUCHENWIRTH, RICHARD, *The Development of the German Air Force, 1919–1939*, ed. by Harry R. Fletcher, U.S.A.F. Historical Studies: no. 160 (Arno Press, New York, 1970).

SZEMBEK, COMTE JEAN, *Journal 1933–1939*, trans. J. Rzewuska and T. Zaleski (Plon, Paris, 1952).

TAYLOR, A. J. P., *The Origins of the Second World War*, 2nd edn. (Penguin Books, Harmondsworth, 1963).

—— *English History 1914–1945* (Clarendon Press, Oxford, 1965).

—— *Beaverbrook* (Hamish Hamilton, London, 1972).

—— ed., *Lloyd George: Twelve Essays* (Athenaeum, New York, 1971).

TEMPLEWOOD, VISCOUNT, *Nine Troubled Years* (Collins, London, 1954).

THOMPSON, NEVILLE, *The Anti-Appeasers. Conservative Opposition to Appeasement in the 1930s* (Clarendon Press, Oxford, 1971).

THORNE, CHRISTOPHER, *The Approach of War, 1938–1939* (Macmillan, London, 1967).

TOSCANO, MARIO, *The Origins of the Pact of Steel*, 2nd edn., rev. (The Johns Hopkins Press, Baltimore, 1967).

TOYNBEE, A. J., and ASHTON-GWATKIN, F. T. A., eds., *The World in March 1939* (Oxford University Press, London, 1952).

TOYNBEE, A. and V., eds., *The Eve of War, 1939* (Oxford University Press, London, 1958).

ULAM, ADAM B., *Expansion and Coexistence. The History of Soviet Foreign Policy 1917–67* (Praeger, New York, 1968).

VANSITTART, LORD, *The Mist Procession* (Hutchinson, London, 1958).

VITAL, DAVID, *The Making of British Foreign Policy* (Allen & Unwin, London, 1968).

WATT, D. C., *Personalities and Policies: Studies in the Formulation of British Foreign Policy in the Twentieth Century* (Longmans, Green, London, 1965).

WEBSTER, C. K., and FRANKLAND, N., *The Strategic Air Offensive Against Germany*, 4 vols. (H.M.S.O., London, 1961).

WEIZSÄCKER, ERNST VON, *Memoirs*, trans. John Andrews (H. Regnery Co., Chicago, 1951).

WENDT, BERND JÜRGEN, *Economic Appeasement. Handel und Finanz in der britischen Deutschland-Politik 1933–1939* (Bertelsmann Universitätsverlag, Düsseldorf, 1971).

WHEELER-BENNETT, JOHN W., *Munich, Prologue to Tragedy* (Macmillan, London, 1948).

—— *The Nemesis of Power: the German Army in Politics 1918–45* (Macmillan, London, 1953).

WILLIAMS, FRANCIS, *A Pattern of Rulers* (Longmans, Green, London, 1965).

WOLFERS, ARNOLD, *Britain and France between Two Wars* (Harcourt Brace & Co., New York, 1940).

ZETLAND, MARQUIS OF, *Essayez; Memoirs* (John Murray, London, 1956).

2. ARTICLES AND ESSAYS

CARR, E. H., *Britain as a Mediterranean Power* (The Gust Lecture), University College, Nottingham, 1937.

COGHLAN, F., 'Armaments, Economic Policy and Appeasement', *History*, lvii, no. 190 (June 1972), 205–16.

DILKS, DAVID, 'Appeasement Revisited', *University of Leeds Review*, no. 1 (May 1972), 28–56.

EATWELL, ROGER, 'Munich, Public Opinion, and Popular Front', *Journal of Contemporary History*, no. 4 (1971), 122–39.

EUBANK, KEITH, 'The British Pledge to Poland: Prelude to War', *Southwestern Social Science Quarterly*, 45, no. 4 (March 1965), 340–8.

FISHER, A. G. B., 'The German Trade Drive in South-Eastern Europe', *International Affairs*, 18, no. 2 (March–April 1939), 143–70.

GIBBS, NORMAN, 'British Strategic Doctrine, 1918–1939', in Michael Howard, ed., *The Theory and Practice of War: Essays presented to Captain B. H. Liddell Hart on his seventieth birthday* (Cassell, London, 1965).

HILL, LEONIDAS, 'Three Crises, 1938–39', *Journal of Contemporary History*, 3, no. 1 (1968), 113–42.

LAMMERS, DAVID, 'Fascism, Communism, and the Foreign Office, 1937–39', *Journal of Contemporary History*, 6, no. 3 (1971), 66–86.

MACDONALD, C. A., 'Britain, France and the April Crisis of 1939', *European Studies Review*, 2, no. 2 (April 1972), 151–69.

—— 'Economic Appeasement and the German "Moderates" 1937–1939. An Introductory Essay', *Past and Present*, 56 (August 1972), 105–35.

BIBLIOGRAPHY 237

MANNE, ROBERT, 'The British Decision for Alliance with Russia, May 1939', *Journal of Contemporary History*, 9, no. 3 (1974), 3–26.

MITNITZKY, MARK, 'Germany's Trade Monopoly in Eastern Europe', *Social Research*, 6, no. 1 (February 1939), 22–39.

ROBERTSON, JAMES C., 'The Origins of British Opposition to Mussolini over Ethiopia', *Journal of British Studies*, 9, no. 1 (November 1969), 122–42.

ROCK, WILLIAM R., 'The British Guarantee to Poland, March, 1939: A Problem in Diplomatic Decision-making', *South Atlantic Quarterly*, 65, no. 2 (Spring 1966), 229–40.

SIPOLS, V., and PANKRASHOVA, M., 'Preparation of the Munich Deal. Britain's Road to Munich', *International Affairs* (Moscow), no. 4, pp. 78–87; no. 6, pp. 81–8; no. 7, pp. 70–9.

SKIDELSKY, ROBERT, 'Guessing Games', *Spectator*, 25 July 1970, p. 75.

—— 'Going to War with Germany. Between Revisionism and Orthodoxy', *Encounter*, 39, no. 1 (July 1972), 56–65.

TEICHOVA, ALICE, 'Great Britain in European Affairs March 15–August 21, 1939', *Historica* (Prague), 3 (1961).

WATT, D. C., 'Appeasement. The Rise of a Revisionist School?', *Political Quarterly*, 36, no. 2 (April–June 1965), 191–213.

WILLIAMS, T. DESMOND, 'Negotiations leading to the Anglo-Polish agreement of 31 March 1939', *Irish Historical Studies*, 10, no. 37 (March 1956), 59–93; no. 38 (September 1956), 156–92.

WOODWARD, SIR LLEWELLYN, 'The Origins of the Second World War', *Listener*, 72 (3 Sept. 1964), 327–31.

3. UNPUBLISHED ACADEMIC THESES

ADAMTHWAITE, A. P., 'French Foreign Policy, April 1938–September 1939, With Special Reference to the Policy of M. Georges Bonnet', Ph.D. thesis, Leeds University, 1966.

MYERS, KENDALL, 'A Rationale for Appeasement. A Study of British Efforts to Conciliate Germany in the 1930's', Ph.D. thesis, The Johns Hopkins University School of Advanced International Studies, 1972.

OVENDALE, R., 'The Influence of United States and Dominion Opinion on the Formation of British Foreign Policy, 1937–39', D.Phil. thesis, Oxford University, 1971.

RICHARDS, R. J., 'British Policy in Europe from the Munich Agreement to the Polish Guarantee, September 29, 1938 to March 31, 1939', M.A. thesis, Durham University, 1967.

INDEX

Abyssinia, Italian conquest of, 15, 26–7, 73, 136
Afghanistan, 42, 50 n.
Air Ministry, 11–13, 59–60
Air Parity Sub-Committee of the Committee of Imperial Defence, 14
Albania, 67 n., 112, 125
Amery, L. S., 101 n., 176
Anglo-American Trade Agreement (1938), 49, 108
Anglo-German Declaration (30 Sept. 1938), 4, 54, 63, 72
Anglo-German Naval Agreement (1935), 14–15, 26, 70, 74
Anglo-German Payments Agreement (1934), 82–4
Anglo-German Society, 84
Anglo-Italian Agreement (16 Apr. 1938), 4, 65, 73
Anglo-Japanese Alliance (1902), 21–2
Anschluss, *see* Austria
Anti-Comintern Pact, 75 n., 147; and Japan, 15, 179; and Poland, 158, 160, 167, 170, 172, 213; and Hungary, 167; and Italy, 179
'Appeasement', 63, 101; historiography of, 1–3, 5–6; dictionary definition misleading, 5; dictated by Britain's overextension, 3–4, 8, 30–2; Chamberlain's conception of, 29, 55, 87; economic, 48, 84; Soviet interpretation of, 130 n.; Halifax and, 186; never seriously tried, 217–18, 222
Arciszewski, Miroslaw, 132, 169, 171–2
Arita, Hachiro, 180
Arms limitation, *see* Disarmament
Ashton-Gwatkin, Frank, 37, 57, 62, 80, 81, 189
Atholl, Duchess of, 72
Attlee, Clement, 50
Auşnit, Max, 117 n.
Australia, 22, 126, 127–8
Austria, German *Anschluss* with, 1, 4, 18, 30, 33, 54, 115, 116, 122, and German influence in central and south-eastern Europe, 39, 42, 46–7,
and Anglo-German Payments Agreement, 82

Bad Godesberg, 68, 157–8
Balance of payments (British), 48 and n.
Balance of power, 6, 42–3, 64–5, 108, 134, 136, 148, 181, 187, 218, 219, 221
Baldwin, Stanley, 9, 11–13
Balfour Declaration, 42
Balkan Entente (1934), 110 and n.
Balkan States, German influence in, 4, 36–53 *passim*, 56–7, 64, 65, 107, 120; morale in, 141, 153, 177–8, 203, 204; *see also* Central and south-eastern Europe and individual countries
Baltic States, 25, 131 n., 207, 215
Barnett, Correlli, 27
Barraclough, Professor G., 143 n.
Barthou, Louis, 131 n.
Beck, Colonel Jozef, thought to be pro-German, 121, 133, 168, 172 and n., 173, 197, and anti-Russian, 164, 211; policy of equilibrium, 132–3, 157, 168; and Four-Power Declaration, 132–3; and Danzig, 134, 153, 159–60, 161, 162, 165, 169, 170, 202, 213, 221; proposes secret Anglo-Polish agreement, 145–6; visit to London, 152, 166, 167, 168, 172 n., 174, 186, 201, 209–13; Hitler–Ribbentrop talks (Jan. 1939), 159–60, 166–7, 171; seeks closer relations with West, 160, 163, 166, 168, 169; defines Poland's vital interests, 161; evasiveness, 166, 167, 171, 172, 211; 'corrupt bargain', 172–3, 196; 'required' by Hitler, 185; reciprocal commitment from, 192, 195, 201, 202, 209; and unconditional guarantee, 202; complains about Reuter's, 209; discussions with Chamberlain and Halifax, 209–13

INDEX

Belgium, 65, 98, 130 n., 156, 209, 210, 212, 215
Bibesco, Princess Marthe, 110
Biddle, A. J. D., 185, 192
Birmingham, Chamberlain's speech at, 104–5
Blockade, 118, 149, 151, 187, 188, 197, 206, 218
Blomberg, Field-Marshal von, 189 n.
Board of Trade, 40, 57–8, 79, 80, 84
Boetticher, Dr., 114
Bohemia and Moravia, German occupation of, 1, 81, 86, 88–92 *passim*, 96–8, 107, 108, 109, 110, 128, 149, 160, 169, 177, 179, 180, 181, 191
Bonnet, Georges, Anglo-French talks (Nov. 1938), 72–3, 94, (Mar. 1939), 134–8, 174; statement of Anglo-French solidarity, 77; and guarantee for Czechoslovakia, 92–4
Boothby, Robert, 208 n.
Borneo, 179
Bower, Commander R., 101 n.
Böttcher, Viktor, 162
Brauchitsch, General von, 162
Brazil, 141
Bressy, Pierre, 137 n.
Briand, Aristide, 7
British army, 106; continental expeditionary force, 10–11, 15, 17, 59, 73, 225; doctrine of 'limited liability', 11, 13, 17, 61, abandoned, 78; revised role of, 17, 78; Territorial Army doubled, 223–5; see also War Office
British Council, 117
Brown, F., 116
Brüning Government, 35
Bujoiu, Ion, 113
Bulgaria, 42, 45, 49, 52, 110, 111, 151
Bullitt, William, 152
Bullock, Alan, 59 n.
Burckhardt, Carl, 158
Butler, R. A. (Lord), 104, 105, 150 n., 151 n., 152 n., 186, 192
By-elections, 72

Cabinet, 54, 58, 59, 104, 110, 177, 187, 218; approves political credits for Turkey, 42; amends Export Guarantees Act, 50; favours heavy bomber policy, 60; approves naval expansion, 61; abandons doctrine of 'limited liability', 61, 78; discusses German occupation of Bohemia and Moravia (15 Mar. 1939), 98–100, 102; discusses alleged threat to Rumania (18 Mar. 1939), 118, 120–1; awareness of British weakness, 121, 125, 129; and Anglo-French guarantee for Poland and Rumania, 174; approves financial support for China, 180 and n.; and Colvin report, 182, 186, 192; and unconditional guarantee to Poland, 192–7, 202, 204, 212; and Territorial Army proposals, 224, 225
Cabinet Committee on Defence Policy and Requirements, 14
Cabinet Committee on Foreign Policy, 94, 204, 218; and resistance to Germany by economic means, 40–1, 49, 51–2; discusses Hitler's intentions (Nov. 1938), 69–71; endorses Chamberlain's visit to Rome, 73; and possible German attack on Holland, 75–7; and Anglo-French guarantee for Rumania and Poland, 151–4, 174; and unconditional guarantee to Poland, 197–8, 200–2, and Russia, 199–200
Cabinet Committee on Preparations for the Disarmament Conference, 10
Cadogan, Sir Alexander, 24 n., 62, 75 n., 112, 116, 137 n., 142, 144, 146, 150 n., 151 n., 171; and Sudeten crisis, 33, 68; on German expansion in central and south-eastern Europe, 43, 149, 221; on need for rearmament, 58; on policy after Munich, 66; on effects of Jewish persecution, 71; and Mussolini, 74, 125; on Hitler's intentions, 75–6, 85, 96, 97, 159 n., 185 n., 186; on secret intelligence reports, 77, 185 n.; advises against Anglo-German conversations, 86; and guarantee for Czechoslovakia, 92, 94, 95–6, 98, 99; and Chamberlain's speech in House of Commons (15 Mar. 1939), 100–1, at Birmingham, 104; confused, 105, 109, 134; interview with Tilea, 111, 113; on Germany 'keeping us guessing', 111,

INDEX

217; and Four-Power Declaration, 124, 132; on need for British commitment, 129; on need for a moral position, 134; and Anglo-French guarantee for Poland and Rumania, 149, 153, 154; on Mason-MacFarlane, 149, 188; on morale in the Balkans, 151; and unconditional guarantee to Poland, 152 n., 192, 197; and Colvin report, 183, 184, 186; on German opposition to Hitler, 190–1; on Vansittart, 191 n.; on German troop dispositions opposite Poland, 198; and association with Russia, 215–16; thinks Russo-German *rapprochement* unlikely, 216; on Sir Horace Wilson, 225

Calinescu, Armand, 110
Cambon, Roger, 131, 132
Campbell, Sir Ronald, 44
Canada, and Anglo-Japanese alliance, 21; isolationist, 127, 202; dislike of Russia, 141, 199
Canaris, Admiral, 182 n.
Canning, George, 58
Carol II, King of Rumania, in London, 49, 108; and Tilea 'ultimatum', 114, 117–18
Carr, E. H., 221
Cartland, Ronald, 101 n.
Central and south-eastern Europe, British policy of resistance to German expansion in, 3–6 *passim*, 31, 33–4, 37–53 *passim*, 55, 56–7, 64, 107–8, 118, 120, 125, 128, 149, 150, 218, 219; Hitler's intentions in, 70; *see also* Balkan States and individual countries
Chamberlain, Neville, and 'appeasement', 1–7 *passim*, 8, 29, 30–2, 55, 87, 101, 130 n., 217–18, 222, economic, 48, 84; and resistance to German expansion in eastern, central, and south-eastern Europe, 1–7 *passim*, 31, 40–3, 45, 49, 50, 52, 55, 56, 102, 120, 150, 218; and search for agreement with Germany, 4–7 *passim*, 29–30, 45, 54–6, 58–9, 63, 71–2, 74–5 and n., 78–9, 84–6, 87, 97, 102–3, 128, 150, 218; on war with Germany, 4, 19, 33, 120, 124, 149; and Italy, 4, 27, 71, 73–4, 75, 94, 123, 125–6, 145, 198; and Japan, 4, 11, 23, 31; and rearmament, 10–11, 15–17, 20, 58, 59, 60, 61, 75; 'limited liability' doctrine, 11, 13, 17, 61; Czechoslovak policy (1938), 19, 33–4, 54, 68, 92–3, 100, 105, 183; and Abyssinian crisis, 27; and colonial concessions to Germany, 28–9, 30, 54, 55, 58–9, 64, 85, 87, 130 n.; and Foreign Office, 41, 50, 61–3, 66, 98, 125–6, 150–1, 218; and Hitler's intentions, 54, 66, 71, 78, 79–80, 87, 104, 105, 128; and Anglo-French conversations, 65, (Nov. 1938), 72–3, 94, (Mar. 1939), 134, 137–8; and Halifax, 68–9, 85–6, 95, 104, 150–1, 176; and Jewish persecution, 71; and public opinion, 72, 101–5 *passim*, 175–6; statement of Anglo-French solidarity, 78; and guarantee for Czechoslovakia, 92–6, 98–9, 100; reaction to Prague coup, 98–106 *passim*; control over Cabinet, 99, 102, 120, 193; Parliamentary statements (15 Mar. 1939), 100–3, 104, (23 Mar. 1939), 103 n., (31 Mar. 1939), 200, 203; and Labour Opposition, 103 n., 143–5, 175 n., 176, 198–9, 200, 206, 225; Birmingham speech (17 Mar. 1939), 104–5, 112, Cadogan on, 134, approved by Dominions, 127 and n.; unwilling to enter new commitments, 105, 120, 122, 123, 132; on German threat to Rumania, 120, 143 n., 212; and Four-Power Declaration, 120–5, 131–2, 150; believes Poland the 'key', 121, 144; and Russia, 121, 122, 138–9, 144, 208, 212, 216; and fleet for Singapore, 126; and Anglo-French guarantee for Poland and Rumania, 138, 144–5, 150, 151–2, 155, 174; and unconditional guarantee to Poland, 152, 157, 182, 184, 193–4, 195, 196, 198, 200–3; and Colvin report, 182, 183–4; on German opposition to Hitler, 184, 190; fears Polish collapse under German pressure, 194, 195; interview with Lloyd George, 205; and foreign affairs debate (3 Apr. 1939), 206–9; discussions with Beck, 209–13; 'flat-footed' about Poland, 214;

Chamberlain, Neville (*cont.*):
and doubling of Territorial Army, 223–5; favours conscription, 225
Channon, 'Chips', 105
Chatfield, Lord, 118, 151 n.; on Kennedy, 126; on German–Rumanian Trade Treaty, 143 n.; and guarantee to Poland, 193, 194–5
Chiefs of Staff, 120, 121; warnings on Britain's overextension, 8, 10, 21, 30, 119; on rearmament constraints, 18; assessment of Czechoslovakia, 1938, 19; and Italy, 26, 178; on reoccupation of Rhineland, 28; regard Holland as vital interest, 76; endorse expanded continental expeditionary force, 78; on prospects of successful war with Germany over Rumania, 118–19, 129, 193; recommend alliance with Poland and Russia, 119, 138; estimate of Russian army strength, 139 n.; on military implications of Anglo-French guarantee for Poland and Rumania, 154–6, 196, 214; on Polish capacity for resistance, 155–6, 197; assessment of Greece and Turkey, 177–9; and unconditional guarantee to Poland, 193, 194, 195, 196; on German troop dispositions opposite Poland, 195, 198
Child, F. C., 36
China, Japanese expansion in, 3, 23–4, 180 n.; British interests in, 23–4, 180 n.; British financial support for, 50 n., 180 and n.
Churchill, Winston, 19, 101, 176 and n., 206; criticizes air force rearmament, 12; 'Grand Alliance', 66, 219 n.; on guarantee to Poland, 207, 220
Chvalkovský, František, 89, 90
Ciano, Galeazzo, 89, 125–6
Ciechanowski, Jan, 180–2
Cliveden set, 208
Clodius, Carl, 44
Coal trade, Anglo-German negotiations, 51, 57, 79
Codreanu, Corneliu, 117
Collier, Laurence, 62, 66; on value of Russian assistance, 143, on Ukraine, 159 n.
Colonial Office, 79

Colonies, concessions to Germany, 6, 27, 28–9, 30, 38–9, 54, 55, 58–9, 64, 65, 66, 70, 79, 85, 87, 130 n., 190 n.
Colvin, Ian, 182–4, 186–7, 192
Comintern, 76 n.
Committee of Imperial Defence (C.I.D.), 4, 10, 73, 83; Air Parity Sub-Committee of, 14; Defence Requirements Sub-Committee (D.R.C.) of, 10, 14, 23; and naval expansion, 61; Joint Planning Committee of, 217
Communist Party Congress, Moscow (1939), 130 and n.
Conscription, 59, 103, 106, 176, 206, 207, 223–5
Conservative Party, Opposition, 59, 101–2, 175–6; 1922 Committee, 223; *see also* Eden, Anthony
Cooper, Duff, 134 n., 176
Corbin, Charles, 106, 124, 137 n., 171
Corsica, 73
Craigie, Sir Robert, 24, 180
Cranborne, Lord, 101 n., 205
Crossley, Anthony, 101 n.
Czechoslovakia, British policy in 1938–9, 19, 33–4, 54, 62, 63, 68, 76, 92–101, 105, 136, 189; and France, 25, 29, 33, 93, 131, 164; German policy after Munich, 88–92, 96–8; German conquest of, 86, 106 n., 108, 109, 117, 185, 215; and Hungary, 89, 91; and Vienna Award, 89, 93, 110; and Poland, 91, 93, 121, 157, 158–9, 163 and n.; guarantee for, 92–100 *passim*; and Russia, 93, 154 n.; German press and, 186; *see also* Bohemia and Moravia, Ruthenia, Slovakia, Sudetenland

Daily Express, 208 n.
Daily Telegraph, 144
Daladier, Édouard, Anglo-French talks (Nov. 1938), 61, 72–3, 94; and guarantee for Czechoslovakia, 92–4; wants Polish guarantee for Rumania, 134, 169; on British commitment, 135
Dalton, Hugh, 144, 199, 206, 208
Danube, 39
Danzig, 63, 123; British support for

INDEX 243

Polish rights in, 1, 132, 153, 169–70, 172–3, 194, 196, 202, 204, 213, 220, questioned, 209, 214; Foreign Office decision not to fight for, 98, 169; rumours of German seizure, 112, 169–70, 174–5, 193–4, 198, 201; Poland seeks western support for, 134, 145–6, 169, might precipitate European war, 155; German–Polish negotiations, 157–73 *passim*, 186, 201, 204, 209, 211, 213, 214, 219, 221; Polish troop movements, 161–2, 170; Versailles settlement, 164–5; disturbances in, 168 n., 169

Dawes loan, 82
Dawson, Geoffrey, 208 n., 209
De Chair, S., 101 n.
Decision-making, as an analytical framework, vii–viii; Chamberlain's style of, 99, 102, 120; in March 1939, 136, 150–1, 154
Defence Policy and Requirements Committee of the Cabinet, 14
Defence Requirements Sub-Committee (D.R.C.) of C.I.D., 14; first report (1934), 10, 23
De la Warr, Lord, 136
Denmark, 209, 210, 212
Department of Overseas Trade, 40
Dienststelle Ribbentrop, 59
Dirksen, Herbert von, 55, 59, 74; on Chamberlain's position after Munich, 71, 72; complains about British press, 182 n.
Disarmament, League of Nations Conference, 9, 12; Washington Naval Treaty, 14, 22; London Naval Treaty, 14; British desire for agreement with Germany on, 55, 58–9, 64, 65, 66, 82, 84–5, 87, 102
Djibouti, 73
Dominions, 78; isolationist attitude of, 2, 127–8; and British policy in Far East, 21–2, 23, 126–7; and unconditional guarantee to Poland, 192; *see also* individual countries
Donner, P. W., 101 n.
Drummond-Wolff, Henry, 75 n.
Duggan, H. J., 101 n.
Dulverton, Lord, 49
Dunglass, Lord, 184
Ďurčanský, Ferdinand, 88, 90

East Fulham by-election (1933), 10
'Eastern Locarno', 25, 131 and n.
Economic Advisory Council, 20
Economic 'appeasement', 47–8, 84
Eden, Anthony, 13, 25, 62 n., 103, 206; on relations with Italy, 27; proposals for agreement with Germany, 28; Chamberlain's view of, 29, 176 n.; 'Eden Group', 101–2, 175–6; calls for all-party government, 101, 175–6; policy of 'keeping Germany guessing', 123; and Halifax, 175–6; resignation of, 205; on unconditional guarantee to Poland, 207
Egypt, 50 n.
Elliott, Walter, 177, 194
Emrys-Evans, Paul, 101 n.
'Encirclement', of Germany, 55, 65, 214–15
Evening Standard, 208 n.
Exchange control (German), 34–7, 47–8, 107, 190 n.
Export Credits Guarantee Department, 40, 41, 46
Export Guarantees Act (1937), 50 and n.

Far East, 21–5, 42, 85, 126, 179–80, 190 n., 203, 218
Fascism, in Rumania, 117; in Europe, 143 n.
Federation of British Industries, 58, 79, 80, 103
Finland, 131 n., 140, 143
Firebrace, Colonel, 139
Foreign Office, and resistance to German expansion in central and south-eastern Europe by economic means, 3, 34, 37–53 *passim*, 56–7, 150, 218, 219; and resistance to Japanese expansion in China by economic means, 3, 180 and n.; and agreement with Germany, 27–8, 30, 61–2, 79, 81; and Sudeten crisis, 33; and Chamberlain, 41, 50, 61–3, 66, 98, 125–6, 150–1, 218; and Italy, 48–9, 64, 65, 73–4, 125–6, 178; policy review after Munich, 63–6; and rumours, 77 and n., 184 n., 185 n.; and German intentions towards Britain, 69–70, 85, Holland, 75–7, Czechoslovakia, 95–8, Hungary and Rumania, 110–11, Poland,

INDEX

Foreign Office (*cont.*):
184–6, 194, Ukraine, 159 n.; and Anglo-German economic relations, 79–84 *passim*, 103; and guarantee for Czechoslovakia, 94–6, 98; confusion after Prague coup, 105–6, 109, 134; and Tilea report, 107, 109–13, 114–16, 118 and n.; sounds out 'threatened states', 112, replies, 122; and Four-Power Declaration, 124; anti-German group in, 114–15; and Mason-MacFarlane's views, 149, 187–8; and Anglo-French guarantee for Poland and Rumania, 138, 145, 146–54; assessment of Russia, 138–43; and German–Rumanian Trade Treaty, 143 n.; appears resigned to war, 149; takes the initiative in policy-making, 150–1; and German-Polish negotiations, 163–73 *passim*, 213; worried about Greece and Turkey, 177–8; on Japanese co-operation with Germany and Italy, 179–80 and n.; and Colvin report, 182 and n., 184; and unconditional guarantee to Poland, 152 n., 197; suspicious of Beck, 197; and press reactions to guarantee statement, 208–9

Foreign Policy Committee, *see* Cabinet Committee on Foreign Policy

Four-Power Declaration, 120–5, 130–3, 145; Russian attitude to, 130–1; Polish attitude to, 131, 132–3, 137, 138, 147; French views of, 131, 135; abandoned, 138, 147, 177

Four-Power Pact (1933), 7

France, 6, 66, 130 n., 177, 178, 224; and Locarno Treaties, 7; and 'limited liability' doctrine, 17 and n., 73; and 'Eastern Locarno', 25, 131 and n.; and Russia, 26, 44, 64, 65, 143, 148 and n., 150, 153, 154 n., 177, 211, 215; and Abyssinian crisis, 26, 27; and Italy, 26, 27, 73–4, 76, 85, 112, 125–6, 192; and reoccupation of Rhineland, 28; and Czechoslovakia, 29, 33, 92–4, 97, 164; Franco-Polish Alliance (1921), 44, 63, 64, 121, 135 n., 137, 159 n., 164; Anglo-French talks, 65, (Nov. 1938), 72–3, 94, (Mar. 1939), 134–8; Franco-German Declaration (6 Dec. 1938), 72–3; Anglo-French Staff talks, 73, 78; rearmament, 73, 156; Chamberlain's statement of support for, 78, 125; Hitler plans for war against, 88; trade talks with Rumania, 108; Chiefs of Staff recommend alliance with, 119; and 'peace' front, 110, 112, 120, 122, 188; and Four-Power Declaration, 122, 124, 130, 131, 132, 133, 135; Anglo-French guarantee for Poland and Rumania, 134–8, 144–5, 147–8, 151–7 *passim*, 174, 192, 197; suspicious of Poland, 172 and n.; and guarantee to Poland, 181, 195, 196, 197, 198, 203, 206, 209, 212

Franco, General, 85

Franco-Czechoslovak Treaty (1925), 29, 33, 93

Franco-German Declaration (6 Dec. 1938), 94

Franco-Italian Agreement (1935), 26

Franco-Polish Alliance (1921), 44, 63, 64, 121, 135 n., 137, 159 n., 164

Franco-Soviet Mutual Assistance Pact (1935), 26, 44, 64, 65, 148 and n., 150, 154 n., 177, 211 n.

Fraser, Colonel, 154 n., 163 n.

Fritsch, General von, 189 and n.

Funk, Dr. Walther, 80–1, 44–5, 56 n.

Gafencu, Grigore, 108, 112–13, 114, 117, 118, 173

German air force, 13, 19 n., 25, 60 n., 119

German army, 25, 96, 106; General Staff, 70, 97, 111, 163 n., 205; and Czechoslovakia, 88, 149; and Poland, 119, 160, 162, 183, 195, 198, 206; probable deployment in European war, 155–6, 207; strength assessed, 188; opposition to Hitler, 189–91, 192

German Foreign Ministry, 59 n., 88–9, 162, 163, 209 n.

German navy, 14–15, 26, 70, 74

German–Polish Declaration of Non-Aggression (1934), 63, 121, 131, 157, 158, 160

German resistance, 76 n., 182, 183, 184, 188–91

INDEX

German–Rumanian Trade Treaty (23 Mar. 1939), 109, 111, 143 and n., 146, 177, 181, 219
Germany, reoccupation of Rhineland, 1, 15, 28, 31; Anschluss with Austria, 1, 4, 18, 30, 33, 54, 115, 116, 122; and Sudetenland, 1, 33-4, 47, 63, 163, 183; occupation of Bohemia and Moravia, 1, 81, 86, 88-92 passim, 96-8, 107, 108, 109, 110, 128, 149, 160, 169, 177, 179, 180, 181, 191; British policy options towards, 3, 29, 32, 33, 63-6; expansion in central and south-eastern Europe, 3-6 passim, 31, 33-53 passim, 55, 56-7, 64, 65, 70, 107-8, 118, 120, 125, 128, 149, 150, 218, 219; British search for agreement with, 4-7 passim, 25-6, 27-30, 45, 54-6, 58-9, 61-2, 63, 71-2, 74-5 and n., 78-9, 81, 84-6, 87, 97, 102-3, 128, 150, 218; threat to Britain, 4-5, 10, 25, 32, 39, 69-70, 74, 85, 148, 217; Anglo-German economic relations, 4-5, 7, 48, 51 and n., 55-8, 79-84, 98, 103 and n., 108; British prospects for war with, 8, 19, 21, 118-19, 155-6; withdraws from League, 9; rearmament, 13, 19 n., 25, 60 n., 70, 74, 82-3, 188; and Japan, 15, 141, 179-80; and Italy, 15, 48-9, 71, 74, 79, 89, 93, 94, 98, 110, 178, 179; and 'Eastern Locarno', 25, 131 n.; exchange control system, 34-7, 47-8, 107, 190 n.; and Rumania, 44, 107-25 passim, 128, 134-5, 137, 147, 151, 185, 210; and Memel, 63, 112, 123, 160, 161, 170, 181, 185, 219; and France, 72-3; possible attack on the West, 75-7, 164, 167; and Vienna Award, 89, 93, 110; and Czechoslovakia after Munich, 88-101 passim; and Slovakia, 88-101 passim, 143, 160, 181, 219; and two-front war, 119, 136, 144, 147, 155-6, 167, 187-8, 191, 192, 195, 205, 206, 207; and Poland, negotiations in 1938-9, 121, 153, 157-73 passim, 186, 192-7 passim, 201-4 passim, 209, 211, 213-14, 221, threat to, 151, 155-6, 174-6, 181-6 passim, 192-8 passim, 200-4 passim; military-strategic assessment of, 148-9, 155-6, 187-8; and Ukraine, 159 and n.; pressure on Turkey, 177-8; British press and, 182 n.; political opposition in, 188-91; possible rapprochement with Russia, 216
Gladwyn, Lord, see Jebb, Gladwyn
Goebbels, Dr. Joseph, 15, 76 n., 189
Goerderler, Carl, 189, 190 and n.
Gold standard, 9
Göring, Hermann, 65, 68, 81, 90, 189 and n.
Great Britain, see under individual countries and topics
Greece, and British policy of economic assistance, 42, 49, 50 n., 51-2, 64, 66; strategic assessment of, 52, 177-9; asks for alliance with Britain, 53; and 'peace' front, 110, 112, 120, 148, 187, 212; morale weakening in, 151, 177-8
Greenwood, Arthur, 198, 203, 206
Greiser, Arthur, 162
Grenfell, David, 144
Grynszpan, Herschel, 71
Gunston, Sir D., 101 n.
Gunther, 114

Hácha, Emil, 91
Halem, von, 209 n.
Halford, A. S., 140
Halifax, Lord, 75, 77 n., 81, 112, 185 n., 220; and Anglo-American co-operation, 24, 126-7; visit to Hitler (1937), 29-30; and policy of resistance to German expansion in central and south-eastern Europe by economic means, 39-53 passim, 218; on strategic importance of Greece and Turkey, 42, 52, 178; and possible Polish alignment with Germany, 43-4, 136, 164, 167, 171, 195-6; on Italy, 48; and rearmament, 59, 70-1, 196; and Anglo-French talks, 65, (Nov. 1938), 72-3, 94, (Mar. 1939), 134-8; view of Hitler's intentions, 66, 67, 69, 77 n., 96, 192; character of, 67-9, 175 and n.; wishes destruction of Nazism, 68; relationship with Chamberlain, 68-9, 85-6, 95, 104, 150-1, 176; on Anglo-German relations after Munich, 69, 85-6; affected by

INDEX

Halifax, Lord (*cont.*):
religious and racial persecution, 69, 71; on French view of 'limited liability' doctrine, 73; visit to Rome, 94; and guarantee for Czechoslovakia, 94–5, 99; and Prague coup, 98, 100; and Danzig, 98, 146, 165–6, 169–70, 195–6; possible Prime Minister, 103; and public opinion, 104, 175 and n.; contacts with Eden, 104, 175–6; House of Lords speech (20 Mar. 1939), 105, 144; wants rift between German army and Nazi party, 106; and Tilea, 110, 113, 116, 118; and Vansittart, 115, 191; and Four-Power Declaration, 120–5, 134; and Russia, 122, 138, 147, 153, 164, 199–200, 212, 216; and Dominions, 126–8; ready for war with Germany, 135–7, 152–3, 196, 204, 218–19; and Anglo-French guarantee for Poland and Rumania, 135–8, 146–8, 150, 151–4, 155, 174; and Polish secret agreement proposal, 145–6, 147; takes the initiative in policymaking, 150–1; and unconditional guarantee to Poland, 152–3, 174, 182, 184, 186, 192–3, 195–200 *passim*, 202, 204, 209; favours all-party government, 175; and Chinese currency stabilization, 180 and n.; and Ciechanowski memorandum, 180–2; sways the Cabinet, 182, 186, 193, 221; and Colvin report, 182–4, 186–7, 192; and German opposition to Hitler, 188, 191; interview with Maisky, 199–200; discussions with Beck, 209–13; and Territorial Army scheme, 223, 225

Hallawell, Wing Commander, 139

Harrison, H. D., 183 n.

Hart, Basil Liddell, 138, 205

Harvey, Oliver, 61, 98, 105, 110, 146; on Halifax, 69, 175, 176 n., 186; on Chamberlain, 75, 104; on Four-Power Declaration, 124; on need for a moral position, 134 n.; on German-Rumanian Trade Treaty, 144 n.; on need for all-party government, 175 n.; on Ciechanowski, 180–1

Henderson, Sir Nevile, 84–5, 96, 98, 99, 106, 183 n., 213–14

Herbert, Sidney, 101 n.

Hesse, Dr. Fritz, 58

Heydrich, Reinhard, 189 n.

Himmler, Heinrich, 189 and n.

Hitler, Adolf, 26, 35, 41, 43, 84, 144, 145, 198; intentions, 1, 7, 25–6, 28, 43, 54, 63, 66, 67, 69–70, 74, 75–6, 78–9, 85, 87, 88–91, 96–8, 99, 105, 106, 115 n., 156–63 *passim*, 166–7, 181, 185–6, 190, 192, 201, 214, 217, 221–2; responsibility for Second World War, 6; and rearmament, 13, 25, 60 n.; and 'Eastern pact', 25; reoccupies Rhineland, 28, 31; claims free hand in eastern Europe, 28, 130 n., 222; and Britain, 28, 69–71, 74, 78–9, 85, 87, 162, 221–2; Halifax visit, 29–30; talks with Chamberlain after Munich, 55–6; fears price and wage instability, 56; and Sudetenland, 63, 68; and Ribbentrop, 69, 70, 185, 189; anti-Jewish measures, 71; and Holland, 75–9; speeches, 75 n., 79, 160; German opposition to, 76 n., 182, 183, 184, 188–91, 192; and Czechoslovakia after Munich, 81, 88–92, 93, 96–8, 99; and Hungarian annexation of Ruthenia, 91; peaceful assurances broken, 102, 104, 105, 106, 128, 221; threat to Rumania, 115 n., 185; and Russia, 130 n., 138, 143; and Poland, 133, 150, 156, 157–73 *passim*, 181, 184, 185–6, 192, 193, 201, 213–14, 221; and Fascist Europe, 143 n.; extremist influence on, 189; and army scandal, 189 n.; quest for Great Power status, 217; unlikely to be impressed by Territorial Army scheme, 224

Hoare, Sir Reginald, 112, 114, 116, 117

Hoare, Sir Samuel, 122 n., 151 n., 206; and Abyssinian crisis, 27; hints at European defence pact against Russia, 55; 'golden age' speech, 86; on importance of Russian support, 153, 177

Hoare-Laval Pact (1935), 27

Hohenlohe, Prince Max von, 81

Holland, 56, 98, 130 n.; possible German attack on, 75–8, 156, 166–7,

209, 210, 212, 215; *see also* Low Countries
Hopkins, Sir Richard, 224
Hore-Belisha, Leslie, 78, 99, 100, 223–4
House of Commons, 12, 63, 93, 184, 223; Chamberlain's statements (15 Mar. 1939), 99, 100–3, 104, (23 Mar. 1939), 103 n., (31 Mar. 1939), 200, 203 and n.; anxious about Poland, 176; foreign affairs debate, 205–8, 209 n.; Territorial Army announcement, 225; *see also* Parliament
House of Lords, Halifax's speech (20 Mar. 1939), 105, 144
Howard, Michael, 17
Hudson, R. S., 50–1, 86 n., 99, 100, 102
Hull, Cordell, 49
Hungary, and German threat to Rumania, 42, 109, 147, 210, 212; and British commercial policy, 49, 52; and Vienna Award, 89, 93, 110; occupation of Ruthenia by, 91, 92, 99, 111, 158, 164, 169, 181; British assessment of, 110–11, 210; warns against British association with Russia, 140; and Anti-Comintern Pact, 167

Imperial Conference (1921), 21–2, (1937), 128
Imperial preference, 46, 108
Imperial Tobacco Company, 49
India, 42, 68
India Office, 134 n.
Indo-China, 179
Industrial Intelligence Centre, 77 n., 84
'Inner' Cabinet, 122 and n.
Inskip, Sir Thomas, 78, 151 n.; on defence expenditure, 16–17, 21; on possible German attack on Holland, 77 n.; moral obligation to Czechoslovakia, 93; sees Dominions High Commissioners, 127
Intelligence Services, British, 76 n., 77 n.
Inter-Departmental Committee on Central and South-Eastern Europe, 39, 40, 41, 56; 1st Interim Report (Oct. 1938), 45–6, 49; 2nd Interim Report (Jan. 1939), 51–2
Iran, 42
Iraq, 50 n.

Iriye, Akira, 179 n.
Iron Guard, 117
Italy, 2, 31, 38, 64, 119, 177, 206, 217; Anglo-Italian Agreement (1938), 4, 65, 73; and Abyssinia, 15, 26–7, 73, 136, 218; 'Axis' with Germany, 15, 79, 88, 178, 179, 180; and France, 26, 27, 73–4, 76, 85, 112, 125–6, 192; and German expansion in south-eastern Europe, 48–9; British hope to separate from Germany, 64, 71, 73–4, 94, 112, 123, 126, 145, 147, 198; and Albania, 67 n., 112, 125; troops in Spain, 73; and Vienna Award, 89, 93, 110; and guarantee for Czechoslovakia, 93–4, 98; British policy after Prague coup, 125–6; effect of Anglo-Russian association on, 140; and Mediterranean security, 178; and Anti-Comintern Pact, 179; no evidence of major move by, 195; 'appeasement' of, 217–18

James, Robert Rhodes, 106 n.
Japan, 2, 4, 31, 64, 76, 112, 119; and China, 3, 9, 22–3, 180 and n.; threat to British Empire, 10, 127, 217; and naval treaties, 14, 22; and Anti-Comintern Pact, 15, 179, 180; Anglo-Japanese Alliance, 21–2; withdraws from League, 23; effect of Anglo-Russian association on, 140–1, 147; possible German alliance with, 141, 179–80; British economic pressure on, 180 and n.; 'appeasement' of, 217–18
Jebb, Gladwyn (Lord Gladwyn), 62; prefers American to German domination, 24 n.; on Italy, 48–9; on policy after Munich, 64–6; on German intentions, 111; on German 'moderates' and 'extremists', 191
Jews, persecution of, 69, 71, 165; in Czechoslovakia, 89; in Poland, 168
Joel, Dudley, 101 n.
Johnson, Herschel, 185
Joint Planning Committee (Committee of Imperial Defence), 217

Kennard, Sir Howard, 165, 197; and Four-Power Declaration, 132, 133;

Kennard, Sir Howard (*cont*.): estimate of Polish resolve, 140; on Polish alignment in Sept. 1938, 163–4; on Beck's desire for co-operation with the West, 166, 167–8; on German desire for Polish neutrality, 167; reports anti-German mood in Poland, 168; reports German terms for agreement with Poland, 169, 170–1; on rumours of German attack on Danzig, 170; suggests amendment to unconditional guarantee statement, 201–2
Kennedy, Joseph, 126–7, 152
Keppler, Wilhelm, 91
King, Mackenzie, 127, 141
Kirke, General Sir Walter, 223
Kirkpatrick, Ivone, 140, 142; on Hitler's intentions, 74, 96–7, 106, 185–6; on Mason-MacFarlane, 187, 188
Knatchbull-Hugessen, Sir Hughe, 177–8
Knox, Sir George, 111
Kordt, Theodor, 24 n., 113

Labour Party, Opposition, 59, 102, 212; refuse to serve under Chamberlain, 103, 175 n., 176; ask for sanctions against German exports, 103 n.; interviews with Chamberlain (23 Mar. 1939), 143–5, (30 Mar. 1939), 199; and Russia, 148, 176, 198–200; and unconditional guarantee to Poland, 192, 203, 206; and conscription, 225
Lancaster, Colonel C. G., 101 n.
Lascelles, D. W., 142
Latvia, 215
Laval, Pierre, 27
Law, Richard, 101 n.
League of Nations, Disarmament Conference (1932–4), 9, 12; Germany and, 9, 30; and Manchurian crisis, 22–3; Britain and, 9, 22, 26–7, 28, 31; and Abyssinian crisis, 26–7; Covenant (Art. 10) quoted, 123 and n.; New Zealand and, 127; and Danzig, 161, 164–5
Leeper, Sir Reginald, 62 and n., 66, 105, 183, 184, 209
Léger, Aléxis, 122, 134, 172 and n., 197

Leith-Ross, Sir Frederick, recommends support for China, 23; chairs Inter-Departmental Committee on Central and South-Eastern Europe, 41; 1st Interim Report, 45–6, 49; 2nd Interim Report, 51–2; European trade liberalization proposal, 56–7; on Anglo-German trade negotiations, 80; on Anglo-German Payments Agreement, 83
Liberal Party, 102, 103, 198, 212
'Limited liability' doctrine, 11, 13, 17, 61; French attitude to, 73; abandoned, 78
Lipski, Jozef, 158–62 *passim*, 171
Lithuania, 112, 123, 164, 181
Little Entente, 93
Litvinov, Maxim, 122, 131
Lloyd, Lord, 117–18
Lloyd George, David, 205, 206–7
Locarno Treaties (1925), 7, 8, 9, 28, 41
Locock, Guy, 80
London money market, 47, 48, 83
London Naval Treaty (1930), 14
Loraine, Sir Percy, 41–2
Low Countries, 11, 61; *see also* Holland
Luftwaffe, *see* German air force
Lukasiewicz, Juliusz, 133, 135, 152
Lyons, J. A., 126, 128

McCormick, Pat, 67 n.
MacDonald, Ramsay, 9
Machiavelli, 64
McKenzie, Vernon, 115–16
Macmillan, Harold, 67 n., 101 n., 176
Maginot Line, 156
Magowan, J. H., 82–4, 103
Maisky, Ivan, 170, 177 and n., 198–200, 203, 207
Makins, Roger, on Four-Power Declaration, 124; on Poland, 168; 172–3, 195, 213
Malkin, Sir William, 95, 98, 146
Manchester Guardian, 101
Manchuria, Japanese conquest of, 9, 22–3
Margesson, David, 72, 176, 203 n.
Mason-MacFarlane, Colonel F. N., urges strong line, 148–9; and Colvin, 182–4, 187; advocates preventive war, 187–8; on German opposition,

INDEX

188, 191; fears Polish collapse under German pressure, 194
Maugham, Lord, 193, 196, 202
Maxton, James, 209 n.
Medlicott, Professor W. N., 2, 29
'Mein Kampf', 69, 190
Memel, 63, 112, 123, 160, 161, 170, 181, 185, 219
Metaxas, General, 178
M.I.5, 77 n.
M.I.6, 77 n.; *see also* Secret Intelligence Service
Middlemas, Keith, 3
Milanović, Vladimir, 116
Ministry of Economic Warfare, 52
Ministry of Supply, 59
Moltke, Hans Adolf von, 162, 169, 170
Monteiro, Dr., 141
Morrison, W. S., 151 n.
Morton, Desmond, 84
Moscicki, Ignacy, 197 n.
Mosiuc, V., 113
Mounsey, Sir George, 62
Munich Agreement, 19, 33, 72, 85, 110, 138, 157, 158; Chamberlain's view of, 54, 55, 63, 100, 105; Halifax's view of, 68; Hitler's view of, 69; and guarantee for Czechoslovakia, 93, 97, 98
Mussolini, Benito, and Four-Power Pact (1933), 7; and Abyssinia, 26; and Albania, 67 n., 125; Chamberlain's hopes of, 71, 73-4, 75, 85, 125-6, 145, 198; troops in Spain, 73; Chamberlain and Halifax visit, 74, 94; and guarantee for Czechoslovakia, 93-5, 97; Foreign Office wish to warn, 125-6; maintains claims against France, 126; and Prague coup, 137, 145

Namier, Sir Lewis, 117
National Federation of Corn Trade Associations, 45 n.
National Register, 70
National Socialists, 59 n.; extremists, 66, 76, 78-9, 188, opposition to, 189-91; Halifax's view of, 68, 69, 106; in Danzig, 165, 198
'New Plan', 36-7
New Zealand, 22, 127
News Chronicle, 182 and n., 186
Nice, 73

Nicholson, G., 101 n.
Nicolson, Harold, on Chamberlain, 62, 101, 103, 203 n.; and 'Eden Group', 101 n., 175-6; and Tilea 'ultimatum', 117 n.; on rumours of German attack on Poland, 194; on Lloyd George speech, 207
Noël, Léon, 197

Observer, 174
Office of the Four-Year Plan, 107
Ogilvie-Forbes, Sir George, 182, 184 n.; on Hitler's intentions, 75, 82-3; confirms German-Polish negotiations in progress, 171; on Mason-MacFarlane's views, 187
Oliphant, Sir Lancelot, 61, 142, 178
Ottawa Agreement (1932), 46, 50 n., 108

Palestine, 15, 42, 66
Parliament, 50, 95; *see also* House of Commons, House of Lords
Patrick, Mark, 101 n.
'Peace Ballot', 26
Pearl Harbour, 126 n.
Perth, Lord, 73 n., 74, 140
Phipps, Sir Eric, 25, 43, 137 n., 164, 165, 211
Pilsudski, Marshal Jozef, 157, 160, 181
Pinsent, G. H. S., 56 n., 81
Poland, unconditional guarantee to, vii, 1-2, 5-6, 43, 52, 53, 119-20, 136, 137, 152-3, 157, 163, 170, 180-2, 185 n., 186, 191-204 *passim*, 215, 218-21, 223, statement of, 203, 204, parliamentary debate on, 205-9, *The Times* and, 208-9, Henderson's view of, 213-14; and 'Eastern Pact', 25, 131; possible alignment with Germany, 43-4, 63, 76, 156-73 *passim*, 184, 194-6, 201, 204, 219; and Czechoslovakia, 91, 93, 121, 157, 158, 163 and n.; treaty with Rumania (1931), 110, 135 n.; and 'peace' front, 110, 112, 120; Chiefs' of Staff advice on, 119-20, 154-6; military value of, 119, 136, 139-40, 155-6, 197, 205, 206; policy of balance between Russia and Germany, 121, 131, 132-3, 144, 157; negotiations with Germany, 121, 153, 157-73 *passim*, 186, 192, 194,

Poland (*cont.*):
195, 196, 201, 204, 209, 211, 213–14, 219, 221; and Four-Power Declaration, 122, 123, 125, 131, 132–3, 144–5; objects to association with Russia, 131, 132–3, 140, 141, 142, 145, 146, 161, 164, 207, 211, 212; and guarantee for Rumania, 134–5, 137–8, 169, 209, 210, 212; and Danzig, 134, 153, 157–73 *passim*, 201, 202, 204, 209, 211, 213, 219, 221; Anglo-French guarantee for Rumania and, 137–8, 144–5, 147–8, 150, 151–6, 157, 174, 175, 192, 197, 202, 203; Soviet assistance for, 138–9, 142, 145, 154, 156, 205, 207, 209, 211; proposes secret agreement with Britain, 145–6; and Polish Corridor, 150, 155, 157–73 *passim*, 183, 190 n., 195, 201 and n., 209; and common frontier with Hungary, 158, 164, 169 and n.; and Ukraine, 159 and n.; mobilization measures, 161–2; anti-German demonstrations in, 162, 168 n.; German press and, 162, 186; public opinion in, 164, 167–8, 194; possible German attack on, 176, 182, 184–5 and n., 186, 192, 193, 194, 195, 198, 201 and n., 203, 204; German troop dispositions opposite, 195, 198, 200–1; negotiations with Britain, 209–13; Anglo-Polish Pact, 212–13

Polish–Rumanian Treaty (1931), 110, 135 n.

Polish–Russian Treaty of Non-Aggression (1932), 131, 157

Portugal, 50 n., 65, 141, 147, 199

Potocki, Jozef, 146

Press, British, 27, 62, 86, 101, 103, 144, 174–5, 182 and n., 208–9; German, 114–15, 162, 186; Polish, 169 n.

Pružinský, Dr., 90

Public opinion, British, 2, 9, 10, and Abyssinia, 26–7, and Munich, 33, 72, and Prague coup, 105–6, 112, increasing pressure of, 134, 136, 143–4, 174–7, 203; Polish, 164, 167–8; German, 160

Punch, cartoon, 86

Raczynski, Count Edward, 145–6, 170
Radar, 61 n.

Rath, Ernst vom, 71
Rearmament, British, 9–21, 30, 58–61, 65, 73, 78, 119, 120, 156, 188, 196–7, 223–5; German, 13, 19 n., 25, 60 n., 70, 74, 82–3, 188; French, 73, 156
Red Army, 131, 139 and n., 142
Reichsbank, 34, 80, 189
Reichsgruppe Industrie, 58, 79, 103
Responsibility for the Second World War, 6, 155, 173, 196, 204, 214–15, 220–1
Reuter's News Agency, 183 n., 208–9
Rhineland, reoccupation of, 1, 15, 28, 31
Ribbentrop, Joachim von, 81; Dienststelle Ribbentrop, 59 n.; extremist influence of, 69, 70, 185, 189; wants free hand in the East, 78–9; and Vienna Award, 89; no guarantee for Czechoslovakia, 94; in negotiations with Poland, 158–62, 167; believed pressing for attack on Poland, 185; attitude towards Britain, 185
Riga, Treaty of (1921), 157
Roberts, Frank, on Slovak crisis, 97; on association with Russia, 140, 142; on French suspicions of Beck, 172 n.; on Colvin, 182
Roosevelt, Franklin Delano, 23, 126
Royal Air Force, rearmament, 10–15, 17–19, 59–61, 196; offensive bombing strategy, 11–13, 17, 18, 60; priority given to, 11, 224; intelligence, 13, 77 n.
Royal Navy, rearmament, 10–11, 14–15, 224; two-power standard, 14 n., 59, 61; fleet for Singapore, 126–7; co-operation with Polish navy proposed, 166; no longer monopolizes Mediterranean, 206
Rumania, economic relations with Germany, 36, 44, 107–18 *passim*, 143 and n.; German threat to, 42, 107–25 *passim*, 134–5, 137, 159 n., 185, 186, 210; and British commercial policy, 44–5, 49, 50 n., 51–2, 53, 108, 109; and Little Entente, 93; and 'peace' front, 99, 110, 112, 120, 122, 212; trade negotiations with France, 108; German–Rumanian Trade Treaty, 109, 111, 143 and n.; internal political situation, 117–18; and Russia, 131,

138-9, 141 and n., 142, 145, 154, 156, 205, 207; a French vital interest, 134; Polish guarantee for, 134-5, 137-8, 169, 209, 210, 212; Anglo-French-Polish guarantee for, 137-8, 144-5, 147-8, 150, 151-6, 157, 174, 192, 197, 202, 203; minorities in, 150; military-strategic assessment of, 154-6; and unconditional guarantee to Poland, 192, 195

Rumours, origins of, 62 n., 76 n., 77, 185 n., 195; of German attack on the West, 75-7, 195; of German attack on Czechoslovakia (May 1938), 76; British inability to assess, 77; of German ultimatum to Rumania, 107-18 *passim*; regarding German-Polish negotiations, 164; of German attack on Poland, 169-70, 175, 193-4, discounted, 195, 198, 200, 201, 203; Foreign Office encourage reporting of, 184 n.

Ruthenia (Sub-Carpathian Ukraine) 88, 89, 93; occupation by Hungary, 91, 92, 99, 111, 158, 164, 169, 181

St. Martin's-in-the-Fields, 67
Sandys, Duncan, 101
Saracoğlu, Şükrü, 177
Sargent, Sir Orme, 61, 83, 96, 97, 98, 105, 112, 131, 146, 185; on guarantee to Czechoslovakia, 95; interview with Tilea, 109; on importance of Poland in anti-German coalition, 142-3; wants guarantee of Greece and Turkey, 178; on German intentions regarding Poland, 186; on German 'moderates', 189
Saxe-Coburg, Duke of, 84
Schacht, Dr. Hjalmar, 36-7, 56 n., 80, 188-9
Schmidt, Gustav, 115-16
Second World War, responsibility for, 6, 155, 173, 196, 204, 214-15, 220-1
Secret Intelligence Service, 76 n., 77 n., 97, 111, 112, 115 n., 139, 184-5 and n.
Seeckt, General von, 191
Seeds, Sir William, 130, 131, 142
Shepherd, Gerald, 170
Sheppard, Dick, 67 n.

Shinwell, Emmanuel, 144
Sidor, Karol, 91
Simon, Sir John, 13, 16, 25, 78, 151 n., 206, 208; and Manchurian crisis, 22; and resistance to German expansion by economic means, 41, 42, 45, 52; and heavy bomber policy, 60; and guarantee to Czechoslovakia, 100; wants no extension of Britain's commitments, 102; and Four-Power Declaration, 120, 121, 123; and unconditional guarantee to Poland, 193; fears Polish surrender under German pressure, 194; and Territorial Army scheme, 224, 225
Sinclair, Admiral, 112, 139, 190
Sinclair, Sir Archibald, 198, 206
Singapore, 9, 126, 179
Sino-Japanese War, 23, 180 n.
Skidelsky, Robert, 3, 219 n.
Slovakia, 93; German policy after Munich, 88-92, 96-7; Hungarian claims on, 89, 110; German Treaty of Protection, 143, 160, 181, 219; and Poland, 169
Smigly-Rydz, Marshal, 197 n.
Smuts, General Jan, 23
Snow, T. M., 140
Somerville, A. A., 101
South Africa, 23; isolationist, 127; dislike of Russia, 141; warning against anti-German coalition, 214-15
Southby, Sir Archibald, 101 n.
Soviet Union, threat to Europe, 6, 55, 64; and France, 25, 26, 44, 64, 65, 143, 148 and n., 150, 153, 154 n., 177, 211, 215; alliance with Czechoslovakia, 93; and 'peace' front, 110, 112, 120, 122, 181, 187, 201, 211, 212; military-strategic assessment of, 119, 138-40, 142, 143, 153, 154 and n., 219-20; political assessment of, 120, 130-1, 140-3, 153, 154, 175, 219-20; fear of in eastern Europe, 121, 131, 132-3, 137, 140, 141 and n., 142, 145, 146, 147, 161, 164, 207, 211, 212; conference proposal, 122, 131, 144; and Four-Power Declaration, 122, 125, 130-3, 145, 147; and Polish-Rumanian Treaty, 135 n.; assistance for Poland

Soviet Union (*cont.*):
  and Rumania, 138–9, 142, 145, 154, 156, 205, 207, 209, 211; Red Army, 139 and n., 142; air force, 139; and Anglo-French guarantee for Poland and Rumania, 148, 150, 153–6; pressure for association with, 153, 176–7, 198–200, 203, 205–7, 212; claims on Poland, 157; and Ukraine, 159 and n.; and Japan, 179–80; and unconditional guarantee to Poland, 198–200, 203; proposes mutual assistance pact, 215; possible *rapprochement* with Germany, 216
Spain, 73, 84, 141, 147, 199, 206
Spanish Civil War, 15, 39, 74, 85
Speaight, R. L., on Hitler's intentions in Czechoslovakia, 97–8; on Polish policy, 166, 167, 168; suspicious of Beck, 171, 172; and unconditional guarantee to Poland, 201 n.
Spears, Sir Edward, 101 n.
Spectator, 103
Spratley Islands, 179
Stalin, Joseph, 130 and n., 200
Standstill Agreements, 35
Stanley, Oliver, 151 n.; opposes Rumanian wheat purchase scheme, 45; and Export Guarantees Act, 50; and proposed visit to Berlin, 81, 84, 86 n., 98, 99, 100, 102; and Four-Power Declaration, 121; on German–Rumanian Trade Treaty, 143 n.; fears Stock Exchange fall, 200
Steward, George, 58
Stock Exchange, 200
Strang, William, 62, 137 n., 146; memorandum on future policy, 63–4; on possible German attack on Holland, 76–7; on association with Russia, 141–2; on Beck–Hitler talks, 166–7; on political reporting, 184 n.
Stresa Front, 49
Sub-Carpathian Ukraine, *see* Ruthenia
Sudetenland, 1, 33–4, 47, 63, 68, 93, 163, 183, 208, 214
Swinton, Lord, 18
Switzerland, 76, 77, 98, 209, 210, 212
Sword, Colonel, 139

Syrový, General, 91
Szembek, Count Jean, 133 n., 146, 160

Taylor, A. J. P., 88, 217 n.
'Ten year rule', 8–9
Territorial Army, 15, 78, 223–5
Teschen, 121, 157, 163
The Times, 183 n., 208–9
Thomas, J. P. L., 101 n.
Thompson, Neville, 101
Tilea, Virgil, warns Foreign Office of threat to Rumania, 107, 109–10, 112; interview with Cadogan, 111, 113; explanations for his 'ultimatum' report, 113–18
Tiso, Jozef, 88, 91
Trade negotiations, Anglo-German, 5, 7, 57–8, 79–81, 98, 103, 108; German–Rumanian, 44, 107–9; Franco-Rumanian, 108
Trade Unions, 18, 223
Transylvania, 110
Treasury, 29; and Foreign Office use of economic weapon, 3, 40, 52, 180; and rearmament, 8, 9, 16, 59; and Anglo-German Payments Agreement, 82, 83–4; and Territorial Army scheme, 224–5
Tree, Ronald, 101 n.
Trianon, Treaty of (1920), 110
Tuka, Vojtech, 90
Tunis, 73, 98
Turkey, British assistance for, 41–2, 53, 64, 66, 177; German credit for, 45; and 'peace' front, 52, 99, 110, 112, 120, 187, 212; and Anglo-French guarantee for Rumania and Poland, 145, 148; morale weakening in, 151, 177–8; strategic assessment of, 177–8

Ukraine, 75, 159 and n.
United States of America, 2, 6, 76, 78, 104, 217; navy, 14 n., 126 and n.; and Washington Naval Treaty (1922), 14, 22; and British policy in the Far East, 10, 21–2, 23–5, 31, 126, 180 n., 218; Anglo-American Trade Agreement (1938), 49, 108; opinion in, 134 n., 137, 152, 153, 185, 204
United States Tariff Commission, 35

INDEX

Vansittart, Sir Robert, 29, 61, 62, 98, 143, 146; proposals for agreement with Germany, 27–8; on Hitler's intentions, 66, 96, 159 n., 191 n.; on Hungarian intentions, 111; and Tilea 'ultimatum', 114–15; and Beck, 133, 197; and French State visit, 134 n.; on necessity for British initiative, 136–7; information network, 182 and n., 185 n.; and German 'moderates', 191

Versailles, Treaty of (1919), 1, 28, 30; revision of, 63, 157; and Danzig, 164–5

Vienna Award (2 Nov. 1938), 89, 93, 110

Vienna, Treaty of (1815), 210

Völkischer Beobachter, 114

War Office, pressure for continental expeditionary force, 61, 78; on German–Japanese contacts, 179; on German troop dispositions opposite Poland, 195, 198, 200–1

War plans, British, 10, 128, 154–5, 'European Appreciation 1939–40', 177–9, 'Planning for War with Germany', 217 and n.; German, 88–90, 155–6, 180 and n., 214

Washington Naval Treaty (1922), 14, 22

Weber, Dr., 80

Weizsäcker, Ernst von, 59, 90, 162 and n., 183 n.

Wells, H. G., 182 n.

Williams, Professor T. Desmond, 62 n.

Wilson, Sir Horace, 55, 62, 144, 151 n., 198; correspondence with Henderson, 213–14; and Territorial Army, 223–5

Wilson, Woodrow, 67

Wohlthat, Helmuth, 107, 108

Wolmer, Lord, 101 n., 176

Wood, Sir Kingsley, 18, 59–60

Young loan, 82

Yugoslavia, 42, 45, 49, 52; and Little Entente, 93; and Balkan Entente, 110 n.; and 'peace' front, 110, 112, 120; dislike of Russia, 141; and Anglo-French guarantee for Rumania and Poland, 145, 148, 152, 174, 209, 210

Zeeland, Paul van, Report, 57

Zetland, Marquess of, 197, 204

Zilina Agreement (7 Oct. 1938), 88